Lands and Peoples

THE WORLD IN COLOR

Volume 1

BRITISH ISLES   WESTERN EUROPE

Grolier
INCORPORATED
New York

DISTRIBUTED IN THE UNITED STATES BY
THE GROLIER SOCIETY INC.

DISTRIBUTED IN CANADA BY
THE GROLIER SOCIETY OF CANADA LIMITED

International Studies, The Johns Hopkins University

INDIAN PENINSULA

JOHN USEEM, PH.D., Head, Department of Sociology and Anthropology, Michigan State University; author (with Ruth Useem) of *Western Educated Man in India*

SOUTHEAST ASIA

FRANK N. TRAGER, PH.D., Professor of International Affairs; Acting Director, Center for International Affairs and Development, New York University; specialist on southeastern Asia

EASTERN ASIA

JOHN H. THOMPSON, PH.D., Professor, Department of Geography, Syracuse University; specialist on eastern Asia

COMMUNIST CHINA

C. MARTIN WILBUR, PH.D., Professor of Chinese History; Director, East Asian Institute, Columbia University

AUSTRALASIA

LESLIE PETER HERDSMAN, past President, Royal Geographical Society of Australasia (Queensland)

SPECIAL CONTRIBUTORS

The body of the chapters listed below, discussing the basic features of a country or region, have been written by the contributors indicated. However, the material at the beginning of chapters, summarizing current conditions, is by the editors.

HARTNEY ARTHUR Australian journalist, with the Australian News & Information Bureau, N. Y. AUSTRALIA

ROBERT BARRAT French journalist, a frequent contributor to English-language periodicals such as *Commonweal* FRANCE

CHARLES BARRETT Australian writer and naturalist; editor, *Victoria Naturalist;* honorary co-editor, *Emu;* Corresponding Member, Zoological Society AUSTRALIA'S ABORIGINES

JOSEPH A. BARRY, A.C., A.B.L.S. Formerly Chief, Paris Bureau, Sunday *N. Y. Times;* author of *Left Bank, Right Bank;* contributor to many periodicals PARIS

CARLETON BEALS, M.A. Writer and lecturer, author of numerous books and articles on Latin America, including *Rio Grande to Cape Horn* and *The Long Land Chile* MEXICO

NEST BRADNEY, B.A. Welsh journalist, correspondent of the *N. Y. Times;* daughter of Gwili Jenkins, who was Archdruid of Wales WALES

MOSHE BRILLIANT Resident Israeli correspondent of the *N. Y. Times;* contributor to such magazines as *Harper's* ISRAEL

GEORGE BRYANT New Zealand Embassy THE MAORIS

G. M. CRAIG, PH.D. Professor of History, University of Toronto THE ATLANTIC PROVINCES

DOUGLAS M. DAVIS, M.A. LUXEMBOURG

R. B. DEGROSBOIS, B.J. Chief of Publicity, Canadian Government Travel Bureau CANADA'S PARKS

ANGEL DEL RIO, PH.D. Professor of Spanish, Director of the Hispanic Institute, Columbia University; author of *Historia de la literature española* and contributor to numerous periodicals SPAIN

WILLIAM H. DILLINGHAM, A.B. Civil engineer, with long experience in South America; contributor to *The Book of Knowledge, Encyclopedia Americana,* etc. HYDROELECTRIC PROJECTS

N. E. DONOVAN New Zealand Embassy NEW ZEALAND

JOHN ROBERT DUNKLE, B.A.E., PH.D. Instructor in Physical Sciences, University of Florida; contributor to *The Book of Knowledge*
UNITED STATES CITIES

GEORGE EDINGER, B.A. (Oxon.) Author of *Horatio Nelson, Prince Rupert of the Rhine, Gladstone;* contributor to numerous periodicals; newspaper correspondent
LONDON

E. S. FERGUSON, PH.B. Former Deputy Administrator-General of the finances of Iran; contributor, *The Book of Knowledge Annual*
JORDAN LEBANON SYRIA

ANNE FREMANTLE Associate Editor, *Commonweal;* assistant professor, Fordham University; editor in UN Secretariat
ENGLAND

THOMAS GLADWIN, PH.D. Lecturer in Anthropology, Georgetown University; co-author of *Truk, Man in Paradise*
THE PACIFIC ISLANDS

ROBERT M. HALLETT Latin American Editor, *Christian Science Monitor;* widely traveled in Latin America
BRAZIL

WILLIAM A. HANCE, PH.D. Assistant Professor of Economic Geography, Columbia University
EMERGING AFRICAN STATES

AGNES NEWTON KEITH, A.B. Lived in Borneo before World War II; author of *Land below the Wind* and *Three Came Home*
INDONESIA

GEORGE KISH, SC.D., PH.D. Professor of Geography, University of Michigan; author of *Introduction to World Geography* and numerous articles
PORTUGAL

MAURICE LEAHY, D.LITT. Irish-born writer and lecturer, contributor to *The Book of Knowledge*
IRELAND

GUNNAR LEISTIKOW Danish-born journalist; has lived in many European countries and is a contributor to English-language reference works such as the *Encyclopedia Americana*
DENMARK GERMANY

TRYGVE LIE Norwegian statesman, the first secretary-general of the United Nations
THE UNITED NATIONS

HENRY MICHAEL, PH.D. Instructor in Department of Geography, University of Pennsylvania; staff, University Museum
THE RACES OF MANKIND

JONATHAN A. MILLER, B.A. (Oxon.)
GREAT BRITAIN

ROBERTO MUJICA-LAINEZ Argentine journalist and diplomat; editor of *Hablemos,* Latin American weekly published in N. Y.
ARGENTINA PARAGUAY URUGUAY

RICHARD L. NEUBERGER, A.B. Late writer, economic analyst and U. S. Senator from Oregon
ALASKA AND HAWAII

SAMUEL M. OSGOOD, PH.D. Instructor in history, Clark University, Mass.
BELGIUM

LINDESAY PARROTT Former Tokyo chief, *N. Y. Times;* reported events in Asia for many years
JAPAN

RAHMAN PAZHWAK Director General, Political Department, Foreign Ministry, Government of Afghanistan
AFGHANISTAN

ORA BROOKS PEAKE, PH.D. Head, Department of History, Colorado State College of Education; author, *A History of the United States Indian Factory System, 1795–1882*
THE UNITED STATES

ANGELO M. PELLEGRINI Associate Professor of English, University of Washington, Seattle; author of *Immigrant's Return, We Who Escaped*
ITALY

W. P. PERCIVAL, PH.D. Director of Protestant Education, Department of Education, Province of Quebec
QUEBEC

BENJAMIN RIVLIN, PH.D. Associate Professor of Political Science, Brooklyn College; author of numerous articles on African affairs and of two studies, *The United Nations and the Italian Colonies* and *Self-Determination and Dependent Areas,* published by Carnegie Endowment for International Peace
MOROCCO

ROBERT BLACKWOOD ROBERTSON, M.D. Scottish physician and writer; in 1950 appointed senior medical officer on Antarctic whaling expedition; afterward wrote *Of Whales and Men* SCOTLAND

B. K. SANDWELL, LL.D., D.C.L., F.R.S.C. Editor Emeritus of *Saturday Night,* Toronto; 1942–45, rector of Queen's University, Kingston; contributor to *The Book of Knowledge Annual* CANADA

WILHELM SCHLAG, JUR.DR. Executive Secretary, Fulbright Commission in Austria 1950–55; Deputy Director, Austrian Institute, New York AUSTRIA

ABDELMONEM SHAKER Egyptian writer and lecturer on the Middle East EGYPT

R. D. HILTON SMITH, F.L.A. Former Deputy Chief Librarian, Toronto Public Libraries CANADIAN CITIES

WALTER SULLIVAN Foreign correspondent, the *N. Y. Times;* reported on events in Europe for some years and, more recently, on Antarctica BERLIN

PAULINUS TAMBIMUTTU Education Department, Government of Ceylon; author of numerous articles on Ceylonese history, art, anthropology; life member, Royal Asiatic Society CEYLON

SENIHA TASKIRANEL, A.M. Turkish journalist; Fulbright exchange scholar; in UN Radio Division ISTANBUL TURKEY

ARNE THORÉN United States correspondent for the *Stockholm* (Sweden) *Expressen* SWEDEN

JAMES RAMSEY ULLMAN, A.B. Explorer, novelist, playwright; author of *The White Tower, The Sands of Kara-*korum and (with Tenzing Norgay) *Tiger of the Snows* INTRODUCTION

RUTH M. UNDERHILL, PH.D. University of Denver; formerly with the Indian Service of the United States AMERICAN INDIANS

HENRIETTE VAN NIEROP Visual Aid Department, Netherlands Information Service THE NETHERLANDS

JOSEPH WECHSBERG Foreign correspondent, *The New Yorker;* contributor to *Atlantic Monthly, Holiday, Saturday Evening Post,* etc.; author of *Homecoming, The Self-Betrayed* CZECHOSLOVAKIA

PETER WELGOS American Field Service (international scholarships program); has lived in India and speaks Hindi INDIA

JOHN H. WUORINEN, PH.D. Chairman, Department of History, Columbia University; adviser to *Lands and Peoples* FINLAND

STEPHEN G. XYDIS Lecturer on modern Greek civilization, Columbia University; contributor of numerous articles to American, British and Greek periodicals on Greek affairs and Byzantine culture GREECE

GREGORIO F. ZAIDE, PH.D. Head of History Department, Far Eastern University, Manila; author, *Philippine Political and Cultural History,* other books and numerous articles PHILIPPINE ISLANDS

MORRIS ZASLOW, M.A. Department of History, University of Toronto; contributor to *The Book of Knowledge* THE YUKON AND NORTHWEST TERRITORIES

Facts and Figures sections prepared by Melvin Morris, M.I.A.

Volume 1

TABLE OF CONTENTS

The Country of the Kandemor

MANY years ago, when I was a boy, I had an atlas that contained a very special map. It was a map of Africa, and at first sight it seemed the same as any other map: blue and pink, green and yellow, with the countries and cities, coast lines and rivers all in their usual places. But then one day while studying it I found the thing that made it "special." Deep in the yellow Sahara, in a region that on other maps was labeled "desert" or "uninhabited," or simply left as a great blank, was written, in tiny letters, "The Country of the Kandemor."

I remember asking my teacher about it and that she shook her head in puzzlement. Everyone else I've ever asked has shaken his head. Never in any other atlas, in any geography, history or travel book, have I found mention of a place or a people called The Kandemor. What is it? Or what are they? I still don't know. And although I've tried hard to find out, I'm rather glad that I haven't been successful. In dreary fact The Country of the Kandemor might be only an empty waste or a heap of stones or, even worse, a map maker's mistake. I prefer to keep it what it was for me as a boy and what it has remained for me ever since—the country of my imagination—strange and distant, full of mystery and wonder.

We all have our Country of the Kandemor. Some men, in days gone by, called it El Dorado. For others it was Cathay or the Northwest Passage or the Spice Islands. It does not matter where, or even what, it is. What does matter is that our imaginations are stirred by the lure of far places; that the world, in spite of all that has happened to it, is still a wide and wonderful place.

Start at home. A boy (or why not a girl?) hears the whistle of a locomotive in the night. He watches a great ship move down a river to the sea, a plane become a silver speck in the blue vastness of the sky. And in his imaginings he goes with them. That is the beginning. He is already a traveler and explorer in his heart. His next day's journey, alas, may be only as far as school, or possibly to the dentist's, but the desire to go, to see, to know, is already deep within him.

Perhaps some of you have already read Joseph Conrad's wonderful story called *Youth*. It is told by an English seaman who has been almost everywhere and seen almost everything, and at the end of the story he thinks back to what he decides was the greatest of all his experiences. This had come when he was little more than a boy, on his very first voyage to the East. His ship had anchored at night off a great and mysterious city. Then the dawn came, a small boat was let down, and he and his shipmates rowed toward land. The sun came up. The palms and temples glittered. Bells rang, strange voices called out, strange faces looked out from the shore. And looking back at them, moving toward them, the young sailor was suddenly overcome with a feeling of wonder, mystery and excitement such as he was never to know again during the rest of his life. As Conrad makes clear, as much of the magic was in the boy's heart as in the city to which he came.

"But the world has become so small!" we hear people say. "There are no really strange or far places left in it." If it is a small world, it is also still a big world—big not only in mere miles but in its endless variety. Consider one city: Paris. Depending on what one is looking for, it can be called the city of art, the city of restaurants, the city of strikes, the city of dressmakers, the city of the guillotine. It is all of these. Plus three million people. Plus two thousand years of history.

Or take, not a city, but a region: the great basin of the Amazon in South America. What is it? To the traveler flying over it, merely a wilderness of jungles and rivers. But to the Indians dwelling there it is home. To the early Spanish and Portuguese explorers it was the promise of riches and empire. In the years since, men have searched there for gold, for rubber, for oil, for strange plants and animals, for lost tribes, for lost cities. The Amazon is not merely water, mud, trees, insects. It is what the imagination and will of men make of it.

For most of us, happily, there is more to living than mere existence, more to the world than the little part of it that has become familiar. Home is good, no doubt about it. But the rest is good, too; good in its broadness, its variety, its lure, its challenge. And we are not really strangers to that "rest"; we ourselves are part of it. Whatever our home address, we have another one besides—The World.

Small world—big world. A contradiction, but true. And you will see both its smallness and its bigness spread vividly before you as you read the stories and study the pictures in these books. Through most of human history it mattered little to people on one side of the globe what was happening on the other. The life of a person in America or England was scarcely touched by events in Russia, China, India or Africa. But that, as we know all too well, is no longer true. The earth has grown small. Nation jos-

tles against nation, race against race, culture against culture, until we are almost as closely involved with people ten thousand miles away as with our next-door neighbors. It is enormously important that we know these people as they really are—as they live their lives—as they think and work and play. And that is exactly what these seven books of *Lands and Peoples* can bring to us: an understanding of the world we live in.

But is understanding all of it? No, I don't think so. The other great and equally important thing that these books will do—and now we are back to the beginning—is to stir the imagination. There are dreary folk in the world who will tell you that living is a routine and dull business and that imagination is for poets and small children. Don't believe them for a minute. Instead, look through these books and then back into history at the men who opened up the world they describe. What was it but imagination that sent the old Phoenicians exploring in their galleys? That sent Columbus to the New World, Marco Polo to Cathay, Cartier to the St. Lawrence, Captain Cook to the Pacific, Livingstone to darkest Africa, Peary and Amundsen to the poles? What is it but imagination that drives men today to study the earth—to try to know it better, understand it better—and to try to make it a better place to live in?

In our complex and organized world a man is known by many labels. He is called a citizen, a subject, a producer, a consumer, a student, a worker, a provider. Let us remember that he is also, in his heart, an adventurer. Beyond the fact, the thing, the number lies the hope and the dream. Beyond the school and the library, the city and the farm lies the whole wide earth. Beyond the mountains and the deserts lies The Country of the Kandemor.

JAMES RAMSEY ULLMAN

9

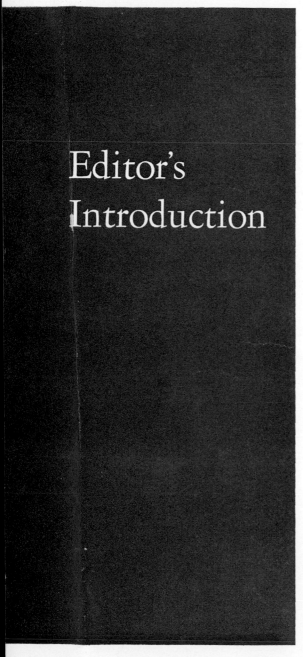

Editor's
Introduction

CHANGE is the only certainty. It is the law of growth, no less in the development of nations and civilizations than in nature. Stripped to their essentials, man's major problems have always hinged on the necessity of making adjustment to the irresistible force of change. Willingly or no, he has constantly been wrenched from the comfortably familiar and pushed into the new and strange. The success or failure of an individual or of a civilization is in large part a measure of adaptability to the flow of circumstance.

No single century before ours, however, has ever witnessed such speed of change and in so many fields at once. Also as never before, the changes are affecting the whole globe, not merely one country or region, and reaching directly into the life of every human being on earth. All this makes the latter half of the twentieth century one of the most exciting periods in history—and the most challenging. A new world is in the making. How well it is shaped to fulfill man's deepest aspirations depends in large part on our understanding of the molding forces.

One of the chief purposes of *Lands and Peoples* is to contribute to that understanding. The set deals primarily with geography, in the broad sense of meaning man's earthly environment and his relations with that environment. Geography is the sister of history, past and present, and of culture. Though man's mental powers win ever greater victories over nature, no people can be understood and appreciated unless we have some knowledge of the form, the climate, the resources of their land. Until quite recent times over large areas of the globe, it was the natural environment that decided how man's basic needs—for food and, outside of warm regions, clothing and shelter—

were satisfied. This in turn influenced the patterns of family and community life.

In the isolation of the past, widely different traditions, scales of value, attitudes toward life developed. The weighty heritage has not been lopped off. Rather, as modern communications and transportation have toppled the old isolating barriers of time and distance, the world's variety of cultures are being brought face to face. All the earth's peoples are now close neighbors. This new intimacy, in which disparate cultures are being jostled, underlies much of the friction and conflict of our time.

Not so long ago the globe and its peoples could be blocked out with some assumption of permanence. From 1815, when Napoleon's vaulting ambition to bring all of Europe under his sway met final defeat at Waterloo, Europe enjoyed a century of relative stability. Great Britain was mistress of the seas and as such balanced the power of the nations on the Continent. Though there were wars and revolutions in this period, in both Europe and the Americas, they were localized conflicts. Spain and Portugal were losing their overseas possessions but for most of the other western European nations the century was one of colonial expansion. They gained a firm grip on much of Africa and Asia.

Peace at home, national prestige, trading advantages—all were factors in the situation. But another support for the world leadership of western Europe was being forged, the industrial revolution. Beginning late in the 1700's it was a turn from hand craftsmanship to machine-made production in factories. It was a tremendous upheaval, affecting the lives of countless men, women and children. Nevertheless its influence was confined largely to western Europe. (It had a profound effect on the United States as well but that country was fairly isolated at this period, partly because of the width of the Atlantic and no little out of preference.)

Until the industrial revolution, certain features of society were generally accepted as foreordained: sharp division into classes; and poverty and want among the masses on the lowest rung of the ladder. Any easing of distress depended on private charity. This attitude did not change overnight with the introduction of the factory system and it accounts in part for the frightful conditions that prevailed in the first years of the industrial revolution. On the other hand, the increased production made possible by the factory system gave rise to the hope that industrialization would eventually end the worst extremes of poverty and raise the over-all standard of living. This did happen to some extent. Moreover, with the growth of industrialization, society became somewhat more mobile (above all, in the United States). The emerging middle class became ever more powerful, and the ideas of freedom sowed by the American and French political revolutions were gradually taking root. At the same time, steady progress was fostered because the balance of power, maintaining peace, allowed the nations of western Europe a relatively long period in which to make adjustment to the industrial revolution.

This era of peace and progress was shattered in 1914. World War I sucked in some part of every continent, the European balance of power was destroyed and the United States stepped onto the world stage. Though the United States did not join the League of Nations there were American delegates at most of the many international conferences during the 1920's and 1930's. Rumbles of discontent

11

could already be heard from the colonies in Africa and Asia. Also, the airplane came of age during the war, forerunner of a new revolution.

The new upheaval is termed the technological revolution. In essence it is a marriage of science and industry. Actually it began before World War I in theories, discoveries and inventions that at the time made only trifling impact on the world at large. The principles of electromagnetic waves and of radioactivity —from which radio, television and atomic energy were to develop—were all known before 1900. The internal-combustion engine—which was to provide power for automobiles and the first airplanes—was also invented before 1900. Celluloid, the granddaddy of a host of plastics, was patented as early as 1869. Not long after 1900 the importance of vitamins to health was established, eventually to be followed by an array of almost miraculous drugs, such as penicillin and the other antibiotics, and amazing new surgical devices and techniques.

Yet it was not until after World War I that the results of this surging scientific activity began to have a noticeable effect on everyday life. The activity itself has been self-multiplying. Each breakthrough in both pure and applied science has led to still others. And the pace was accelerated immeasurably by the demands of the second World War. Atomic energy is the first consequence that springs to mind but there have been many others. Automation is revolutionizing office and factory procedures. On commercial airlines, propeller planes are being superseded by jet planes, flying at almost the speed of sound. Chemistry has been applied so successfully to farming in the United States that although some 1,800,-000 farms have been abandoned since

1940, food production continues to mount. In 1850, four farmers could provide enough food for five persons; by 1940, one farmer could provide for ten; today one farmer can provide sufficient food and fiber for twenty-four persons.

It is not only the technological revolution itself but its social and economic repercussions that are reshaping the world. A *London Times* editorial sums up one aspect: "Instantaneous communication: this is the paramount contribution which electrical engineers are making to the world. Power is carried instantaneously from waterfalls to cities. Messages are carried from one continent to another. . . . Europeans have had little more than a century to adjust themselves to the shock of instantaneous communication and the shock is only now reaching millions in Africa and Asia, destroying centuries of tradition, driving society at a fresh pace. It is not sufficient to understand the technology which causes the shock: the shock itself must be understood too."

Lands and Peoples aims to show in some measure how that shock is affecting the various countries, how it defines their position today and is shaping their future. Even the most remote, poverty-stricken people are now aware that somewhere else whole nations are living in abundance. Radio, motion pictures carry the evidence around the globe of the material well-being that industry, technology and science can produce. From the same countries that have led the technological revolution and are benefiting most obviously the underdeveloped lands have also heard the clarion call of "Freedom!" Thus the shock has two main, complementary waves: economic-social and political.

On the economic and social side looms the vast discontent of the millions who have been living on a near-starvation level. They may be ignorant but having had a glimpse of the "promised land" they are determined to find a place in it for themselves—not a century or two from now but at least soon enough for their children to enjoy. Thus the "revolution of rising expectations" is one of the strongest forces at work today.

As this insistent demand presses on governments it cannot be divorced from the political side of the upheaval. The rising hopes of these people are intermeshed with the idea of freedom, however dimly understood. In Africa and Asia it has asserted itself as nationalism, the craving for national identity and the dignity of self-government, which has led to the rapid break-up of the old colonial empires. Essentially most of the new states are democratic in the sense that all the people share the same desires. Unfortunately, most of them as yet have only the shadow but not the substance of democracy. They are still some distance from freedom as Paul H. Nitze, widely known authority on international affairs, defines it: "The essence of freedom is the opportunity to choose—and the responsibility of freedom is the duty to decide one's choice wisely and well." Understanding of the obligations and the discipline required for truly democratic government can come only with education—and the vast majority of their peoples are illiterate. For the new states to become stable and healthy, schools and colleges are needed quite as much as factories. They will need help in any case, some probably for years to come.

The stakes in this new era being born are just as crucial, though in a different way, for the advanced nations. By their own inventive genius they have shrunk the globe and they could not if they would ignore the clamor of the "have-not" peoples at their gates. Even if their prosperity were not threatened as long as there is misery and suffering in other lands, the two world wars and events since 1945 have shown beyond doubt that all the world's peoples are really interdependent. The Marshall Plan, for example, was devised after World War II not only to help Western Europe recover but because its impoverishment would have pulled other areas down with it and left it open to communist inroads. Today there is a host of international co-operative organizations, some military but many others economic such as the Common Market (European Economic Community).

Along with this central fact of interdependence runs a deep fissure in the world body politic. Should human society be ordered on the democratic or the totalitarian model? Basically it is a question of freedom versus tyranny, though the tyranny is less obvious to peoples newcome to self-government. Considering that the leaders of the two camps, the United States and the Soviet Union, are the most powerful nations on earth, the conflict seems likely to last for many years. Thus the challenge: to stand up to a period of tension, neither peace nor war, and at the same time to strive to build a world in which freedom can prosper and grow. This is the only guarantee of our own freedom.

It is the hope of the editors of *Lands and Peoples* that these seven volumes will shed light on the problems that affect all of mankind so deeply and stimulate efforts to find solutions. As the new generation comes to maturity, we believe that it will find the courage, the patience, the intelligence and the emotional balance to carve a better world than the one that is passing.

HELEN HYNSON MERRICK

Great Britain ...*and the Commonwealth*

DURING World War II the United Kingdom was a major world power. Alone in 1940, beleaguered by submarines and pounded by bombers, it withstood the onslaught of Hitler's Germany. Its armies were in continental Europe, Africa, the Far East and the Middle East. Its fleets steamed from Hong Kong in China, Singapore in Malaya, Trincomalee in Ceylon, Simonstown in South Africa, Gibraltar in Spain, Malta in the Mediterranean, Bermuda in the West Indies and Alexandria in Egypt. The Empire, dominion and colony alike, rallied behind Britain, sustaining the equivalent of a hundred divisions in the field. It was the zenith of the British Empire, the greatest the world has seen.

Since then there has been a precipitate decline. Not only were British forces cut back with the end of the fighting but also British political control of vast areas began to wane. Australia, Canada, New Zealand—the mainly Anglo-Saxon countries—and the Union of South Africa had been granted independence as dominions long before. No longer held together by military needs they have been drifting away from England's orbit. Australia and New Zealand have been drawn toward the United States by their common interests in the Pacific area. Canada has also drawn close to the United States, led by economic interests. Newfoundland has followed suit as a province of Canada since 1949. South Africa, with its large Afrikaner element and its special ethnic

»

problems and policies, has had less and less in common with Britain.

Nearly all the important British possessions that remained in 1945 have been given their freedom. By 1980 Britain will have scarcely any dependencies left under direct rule. The Indian subcontinent was divided into the states of India and Pakistan and granted independence in 1947. Then came Burma, Ceylon, Republic of Ireland, Gold Coast and British Togoland—Ghana—Malaya, Singapore, Nigeria and Cyprus. Britain also ended its rule over certain territories entrusted to it by the League of Nations and the UN. It gave up control successively of Iraq, Jordan, Palestine, the Anglo-Egyptian Sudan and British Somaliland. Most

WHITEHALL, London, is more to a Briton than a street (the dark one running in from the right). It means authority. For on it are the Admiralty (center right edge), the War Office, the Air Ministry (white building), the Treasury (opposite it), Downing Street; and two blocks holding the Foreign Office, the Cabinet Office and many ministries. The monarch is seldom far from Buckingham Palace (top left), Westminster Abbey (center) or Parliament (on the river).

former colonies became "Members of the Commonwealth" as distinct from "countries within the Commonwealth." But former trusteeships have left the Commonwealth. Eire too broke its links with the Commonwealth but is not considered a foreign country by the British Government.

The Empire, then, has become the Commonwealth. Its members were described in 1926 as "autonomous communities. . . . equal in status, in no way subordinate to one another in their domestic or external affairs though united in common allegiance to the crown and freely associated as Members of the British Commonwealth of Nations." The Commonwealth is not a federation, nor are there any contractual obligations between Members. It does not even have a written constitution but adapts itself to the needs of the moment. Some Members no longer owe allegiance to the crown; they merely acknowledge the Queen as a symbol of their free association.

Yet despite the vagueness of its nature and despite the strained relations that exist between some Members (India and Pakistan, Malaya and South Africa), the Commonwealth is held together quite firmly. Most Members have governors general who represent the Queen and assent to legislation. English common law prevails in all of them except Ceylon and the Union of South Africa. They cooperate in defense matters. (A Commonwealth division fought in Korea.) They are united also in economic schemes like the Colombo Plan, which aids the underdeveloped countries.

Far more important than these formal links are the unofficial, informal ones. The British administrative background shared by all Commonwealth countries has created an influential network of per-

sonal contacts. The leaders of the emerging independent countries were educated in England: Tom Mboya of Kenya went to Oxford, Jawaharlal Nehru of India to Cambridge, Mohammed Ayub Khan of Pakistan to Sandhurst and Kwame Nkrumah of Ghana to the London School of Economics. These ties are reinforced by regular meetings of Commonwealth prime ministers which are kept on an informal basis. Membership in the Commonwealth carries an obligation to inform or consult all the other Members on any projected action that might affect their interests, especially in relation to foreign affairs. Every effort is made to keep political discussions on a frank and informal level, though technical questions are covered by a number of special organizations and institutions. All matters are co-ordinated by the Commonwealth Relations Office in London.

By 1960 there were ten Members of the Commonwealth and over thirty dependencies within it. These consist of colonies, outright possessions of the crown, like Hong Kong; protectorates, territories under the protection of Great Britain, like Uganda; protected states, sovereign states subject to Britain by treaty, like Brunei; and trust territories, former enemy territories administered under trusteeship agreement with the UN, like Tanganyika. Whatever their status at the moment they are all destined for self-government. As British Prime Minister Harold Macmillan has pointed out, imperialist Britain has given freedom to 500,000,000 people since 1945 while communist Russia has enslaved 100,000,000.

Not that the British record is spotless. Though in most cases it has been one of patient work in administration, medicine, education and economic development, there are some stains. Most terrible is the history of British rule in Ireland. Apart from that there are isolated instances of misrule in Canada, such as the expulsion of the Acadians; in India, with the Amritsar massacre; in Burma, with the Burmese wars; and elsewhere. But these examples are the exceptions.

There have also been colonial emergencies, which can be described as wars of independence, terrorism, communist agitation or nationalist revolts according to one's political view. In every case issues have been tangled and there has been the unhappy story of brutality inevitable in any appeal to arms. The Malayan Chinese rebelled with communist aid bringing terror to the white settlers and native Malays. The Kikuyu tribesmen of Kenya produced the Mau Mau organization. Though associated with legitimate African nationalist organizations the Mau Mau carried on a campaign of barbarous ferocity against the British and the tribesmen loyal to them. The Greeks in Cyprus who wanted union with mainland Greece supported the EOKA organization which fought the British troops garrisoned on the island. The Jews in Palestine fought against the British in the first stages of their struggle to create the state of Israel. Though these struggles have been of great political importance, the casualties have been relatively low on all sides. None of them has been on the same scale as the French troubles in Algeria and former Indochina.

Wholly disproportionate in extent to Great Britain itself, the dependencies have never profited the Government. Except for a few contributions to defense, they have paid no taxes or tribute of any kind to London. They are free to trade with

Independent members of the Commonwealth

United Kingdom
Australia
Canada
Ceylon
Republic of Cyprus
Republic of Ghana
Republic of India
Federation of Malaya
New Zealand
Federation of Nigeria
Pakistan
State of Singapore
Union of South Africa

Semi-independent members of the Commonwealth

Federation of Rhodesia and Nyasaland
Federation of the West Indies (Barbados, Jamaica, Leeward Islands, Trinidad and Tobago, Windward Islands)

other countries and by 1956 over 50 per cent of their export trade and 51 per cent of their import trade was with countries outside the Commonwealth. For the most part the non-self-governing possessions are underdeveloped and unattractive to private investment. The burden of development has fallen on the British taxpayer. The Colonial Developments and Welfare Acts provided over $600,000,000 in the decade 1945 to 1955 when Britain's own economy was not strong. With the European economic boom of the late 1950's aid has increased. The sum of $175,000,000 was devoted to colonial territories alone in the fiscal year 1959–60.

After independence, Commonwealth countries usually remain members of the sterling area and become a major field of British investment. Britain reaps some commercial advantages from tariff preferences, but on balance the Commonwealth countries get a good bargain. For instance, Britain buys almost twice as much from the Federation of Rhodesia and Nyasaland as it sells to the Federation. Since the war, Britain has invested some $840,000,000 there. South Africa has received $1,400,000,000 in investment, and Australia $1,120,000,000.

Britain's choice

However, British resources are not sufficient either to build up the economies of its underdeveloped territories or to realize the full economic potential of the Members of the Commonwealth. In the world war against poverty which is just beginning, Britain can no longer stand alone. It must choose whether to join with Western Europe and co-operate with the Common Market, which contains the world's greatest industrial system, or to remain aloof and rely on the Commonwealth.

By and large Britain's task is done. It has given the world parliamentary institutions and a whole system of humane political and legal principles whose precepts are acknowledged if not practiced by all. It has helped to spread English as the world's most important language, a medium of communication among all nations. It has given freedom, faith and food to millions of people. But now it has been overshadowed and overtaken.

Economically it is dwarfed by the United States and Russia and it may soon be dwarfed by the Common Market countries. Politically it is less and less important in the world. The 1950's have seen the British facing this truth as it affects major political issues. Shall Britain have an independent nuclear deterrent? Shall Britain impose its will on the Middle East by force? Shall Britain join the European Common Market or the European Free Trade Association? Shall

---

Dependencies of the United Kingdom

AFRICA
Cameroons
Gambia
Kenya
Pemba
Sierra Leone
Tanganyika
Uganda
Zanzibar

High Commission Territories
Basutoland
Bechuanaland
Swaziland

MEDITERRANEAN
Gibraltar
Malta

MIDDLE EAST
Aden
Bahrein
Kuwait
Qatar

Trucial Oman

ASIA
Brunei
Hong Kong
North Borneo
Sarawak

THE AMERICAS
Bahamas
Bermuda
British Guiana
British Honduras
Cayman Islands
Turks and Caicos Islands
Virgin Islands

WESTERN PACIFIC
Gilbert and Ellice Islands
Pitcairn Island
British Solomon Islands
Tonga

ATLANTIC AND INDIAN OCEAN
Falkland Islands and Dependencies
Maldive Islands
Mauritius

St. Helena (with Ascension and Tristan da Cunha)
Seychelles

Commonwealth Dependencies

Australia: Ashmore and Cartier islands, Australian Antarctic Territory, Christmas Island, Cocos Island, Heard and Macdonald is'ands, Macquarie Islands, Nauru, Norfolk Island, Papua and (N.E.) New Guinea
India: Bhutan, Sikkim
New Zealand: Chatham Island, Cook Islands, Kermadec Islands, Niue Island, Ross Dependency, Tokelau or Union Islands, Western Samoa
South Africa: Prince Edward and Marion islands, South-West Africa (disputed)

Condominiums

Canton and Enderbury islands (*Britain and U.S.A.*), New Hebrides (*Britain and France*)

JORDAN

March 1946
340,000
*includes 5
independent members

PALESTINE
(ISRAEL)

May 1948
1,934,000

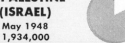

INDIA AND
PAKISTAN

August 1947
417,443,000

BURMA

January 1948
17,500,000

CEYLON

February 1948
6,633,000

SUDAN

January 1956
8,961,000

GOLD COAST
(GHANA)

March 1957
4,548,000

MALAYA

August 1957
6,250,000

SINGAPORE

June 1959
1,461,000

SOMALILAND
(SOMALIA)

June 1960
650,000

CYPRUS

August 1960
549,000

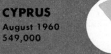

NIGERIA

October 1960
34,634,000

18

1938

11%
23%
36%

BRITAIN AND THE COMMON- WEALTH

«

FREEDOM ROLL CALL.
The map shows the amount
of the earth's surface that
has won independence from
Britain since 1945. The pie
charts (left) show the number of people that have won
freedom. In 1946 the white
slice stands for 100,000,000
who enjoyed independence
and the dark slice for the
500,000,000 who did not. By
1961 the dark shrank to a
mere 45,000,000 and the white
grew to 640,000,000. The colors (same as map key) of the
strips show whether or not
the new nations have stayed
in the Commonwealth.

»

OFFICIAL SOVEREIGNTY.
(red) and unofficial control
(pink) define the empire at
its zenith (1920) and today.

IMPERIAL
HIGH NOON

IMPERIAL
TWILIGHT

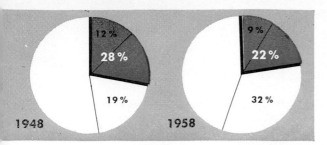

BRITISH AND STERLING AREA EXPORTS
are less important today in free-world trade than
in 1938. Their red segment in the pie charts has
grown less since 1948 than the white one (with
the percentage) representing Western European
exports, even though Britain was very well
placed at the end of World War II. Co-operation
with Europe, therefore, might well revive Britain's drooping commerce (the black figure in
the sterling area segment).

«

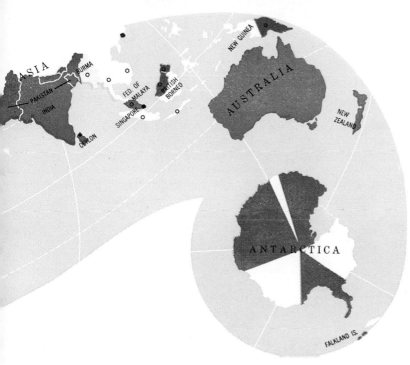

Dependencies under
direct rule of Britain or
other independent Members of
the Commonwealth.

Dependencies with some
internal self-government
(by traditional rulers or new
democratic institutions).

Independent Members of
the Commonwealth.

Independent countries
formerly in the Common-
wealth (or Empire) but now outside it.

O Foreign countries and
enemy held territories occupied or garrisoned by British
and Commonwealth forces during World War II.

■ Major British naval bases.

Britain insist on control of its own military bases? Shall Britain sacrifice any
control of its armed forces to NATO?
These are all reflections of one basic issue: is Britain a great power?

More and more the British are admit-
ting that it is not. But they maintain that
in association with the Continent, Britain
can be part of a new power in the world.
The break with the imperial past has not
been easy to make either in spirit or in
practice. Unable to join the European
Common Market at its formation because
of Commonwealth obligations, Britain
has had to forge new links piecemeal.
Since the end of World War II such
grand designs as the Western European
Union, the Council of Europe, the European Defence Community and the extension of NATO to politics have failed.
The best path today seems to lie through
less ambitious schemes: Euratom, to
which England could contribute enormously; the European Coal and Steel
Community, the biggest industrial unit in
the world; Anglo-French space projects,
to which Britain can bring the technical
knowledge and skill formerly used in developing the ICBM Blue Streak; and
even a Channel tunnel joining England
and France.

A strong Britain in a strong Europe
means not only the frustration of communist designs but also a mighty new
force, which could act through a remodeled Organization for European Economic
Cooperation against world poverty.

By Jonathan A. Miller

19

England

...crown and people

TRADITION soaks all the institutions of England: government, the armed forces, the universities, the law and the church. The jobs they do may be repetitive and humdrum, but nearly all the pageantry and color of English life are associated with them. Brilliant ceremonies, old-fashioned ways of speech, strict rules of procedure preserve the forms of an older world, peopled with princes and lords, comptrollers and lords commissioner, chamberlains and ushers. A Member of Parliament will refer to an opponent in heated debate as "the Honorable Member"; a lawyer will call his adversary "my Learned Friend"; the Queen will assent to legislation with the medieval Norman formula: *"la Reyne le veult"* (the Queen wishes it); the Chancellor of Oxford University will address its convocation in Latin.

But these are the forms not the substance of the past. They conceal the flexibility of the British system of government, based as it is on a few documents and many unwritten laws which change with the times. Even since World War II there have been major constitutional developments, associated with the welfare state and the growth of the Commonwealth.

Nominally the powers of the sovereign have not changed since the time of George III or even before. In practice the whole structure of government is totally different. The Queen must acknowledge the primacy of a cabinet that is almost entirely the product of the House of Commons. It is the prime minister who really rules England, wielding most of the powers formerly used by the crown. He and his cabinet are accountable to Parliament and take joint responsibility for all decisions. The prime minister works closely with the Opposition in promoting the most fruitful parliamentary debate. The Leader of the Opposition is a recognized office, bringing in more pay than an ordinary Member of Parliament receives.

Leader of the Opposition is a new office, being officially recognized only in 1937. This was, however, merely recognition of a political fact that had existed for perhaps half a century. On the other hand, new duties have been attached to old offices. The Lord President of the Council, who sounds as if he came from the court of Queen Elizabeth I, now finds himself supervising the Department of Scientific and Industrial Research. The Chancellor of the Duchy of Lancaster, whose office dates back to the fourteenth century, has recently become a sort of government public-relations man.

Whatever their titles, all ministers are political appointments, Members of Parliament and answerable to Parliament. The House of Commons can force them to resign though this has not happened very often. The heads of the armed forces, the First Lord of the Admiralty and the secretaries of state for the Army and the Air Force, are politicians too. Thus Sir Winston Churchill, when he took over Britain's war effort in 1940, had experience as First Lord in World War I behind him.

Parliament, which is the supreme authority in the country, consists of the House of Commons, the House of Lords and the monarch. Though the House of Commons is most important, all legislation passes through the Lords as well before receiving the royal assent. The Lords do a considerable amount of revision with special skill. Of course, it is undemocratic that this house is composed mainly of people who need no qualification but birth for the job. Reforms have been suggested but they have all threatened either to make the body ineffective or a rival to the Commons. At present only about one in eight of the hereditary peers attends regularly. Those that do are often of very high caliber and they are assisted by Lords who owe their position to special merit: the bishops, the life peers and peeresses (since 1958) and the judges. These last do a great deal of work, because the House of Lords is the highest

Court of Appeal in all of Great Britain.

Very little governing is left to the Queen by the Lords and Commons: she reigns but does not rule. She assents to legislation. She might have to choose a new prime minister from the majority party in the event of the death or resignation of the one in office. She might exert considerable personal influence in her regular meetings with the prime minister. But, first and foremost, she is a public servant, if an exalted one. She lives on money from Parliament in palaces run by the Ministry of Works. She is head of a Church whose bishops and archbishops are appointed by the prime minister, not her. She has the prerogative of mercy for condemned men, but only the Home Secretary can exercise it. At the Trooping of the Color she reviews a brigade from the Army which she does not control on a "birthday" not her own.

Nevertheless the crown stands at the head of a system that has been in a state of flux for a thousand years. It is inevitable that the past should survive in the memories and traditions of successive generations. There are dynasties like the Churchills and the Cecils whose members have always been public figures; there are families whose members have always been in the law, the Army, the colonial service, Parliament or even the sciences. Away from the center there are more ancient country families whose forefathers may always have been sailors, farmers, fishermen, tanners, smiths, builders. The ancient core of the population, guardians of an age-old unrecorded heritage, theirs is the most important history in England.

THE CHIEF YEOMAN WARDER of the Tower of London with a Scots Guards escort in the Ceremony of the Keys.

BLOODY TOWER

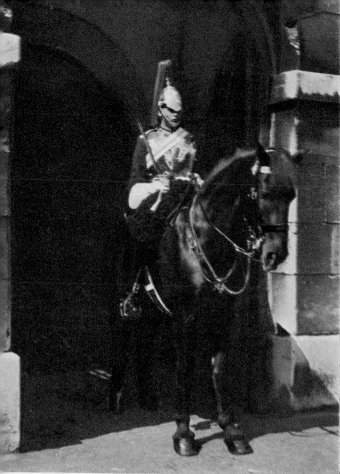

A HORSE GUARD, member of the colorful household troops that serve the royal family. A scarlet horsetail plume tops off his uniform.

GRENADIER GUARDS step out smartly in front of Buckingham Palace, London, to the tuneful blare of their regimental band.

CHOIR BOYS, in vivid robes, examine the tomb of Archbishop Chichele in Canterbury Cathedral. This Archbishop blessed Henry V on the way to the Battle of Agincourt in 1415.

Before the seventeenth century the population of England remained for hundreds of years at something between two and four millions, the chief variations being due to war and plagues. In the seventeenth century the population began to increase; in the eighteenth century it doubled; and in the nineteenth century it trebled. About 1820 the population of England and Wales was 12,000,000. Today about 45,000,000 people live in England and Wales, and most of them are town dwellers.

The Record of Human Habitation

The history of man's occupation of England is long, and many stocks have occupied the country in turn. Flint tools and weapons used by those who lived before the dawn of history have been found in many places. Most students think that the strange monuments at Stonehenge were built by these prehistoric people and not by the later Celts.

When Julius Caesar invaded Britain in 55 B.C. he found the country inhabited by Celts, who had probably arrived from Gaul (present-day France). They worked bronze and iron, had coins of gold and showed marked artistic ability. In 43 A.D. the Romans began the conquest of Britain in earnest, and soon overran part of Scotland as well. They were unable to hold all of this territory, however, and early in the third century retreated below the wall built by Emperor Hadrian some eighty-five years before.

In the south they built many walled towns and luxurious villas. Several modern cities, among them Colchester, Lincoln, Gloucester and St. Albans, stand on the sites of Roman settlements. London was a fortified town and the springs at present-day Bath were developed.

Germanic Tribes Arrive

Later emperors found it necessary to withdraw troops from Britain, and left the island to its fate. Barbarians swarmed in from every direction. Of these, three Germanic tribes, the Angles, the Saxons and the Jutes, were the most important. In the course of time they brought the whole country under their control. They built chiefly of wood, rather than of stone as the Romans had done, so there are fewer relics of Saxon than of Roman England. Some of the Saxon names still survive in English counties, such as Essex and Kent. The land was made up of small kingdoms but finally, about the year 827, the King of Wessex was recognized as overlord of the whole country. Soon, however, the Danes were invading it in force and much of the land was given up to them. The territory they captured was governed under the ancient Danelaw; and the Danegeld, a land tax, was imposed.

For a time we find the king of Denmark also the king of England. Then, in 1066, came the invasion of the Normans from France. These Northmen from Scandinavia had settled in France centuries before and had become more French than the French themselves. To England they brought a new language, new laws, new customs, new methods of building—in short, a higher degree of civilization. The Saxons were stubborn, however, and the newcomers were finally swallowed up in the mainstream of English life. The English language shows many words brought in by the Normans, the laws were affected, many Norman buildings still stand, and English architecture was permanently influenced by these Norman builders. The Normans also played an important part in establishing the feudal system in England.

London Recalls the Past

In modern England much of the past remains firmly embedded. Mighty London, for instance, in its broad expanse is, for the most part, a creation of the nineteenth century. Old market gardens are now asphalt streets. London mushroomed very much as Chicago and other large cities in North America grew during the same period. Nevertheless, it is amazing how much of old England may still be found even in London.

It is not merely that old churches, such as Westminster Abbey, still survive as they have been for centuries. Old streets, such as those that we find in the square mile known as the City, and old institutions, like the Inns of Court are relics. There are still to be seen bits of the old life going on unchanged. The royal procession at the opening of Parliament, the Lord Mayor's procession, and the procession of judges from Westminster Abbey to the House of Lords at the beginning of the legal year—all are pageants that have survived from the time when London was a small town.

The beefeaters at the Tower of London are veritable Yeomen of the Guard of the fifteenth century. The Life Guardsman who stands mounted on his black horse in Whitehall has come from the gay court of Charles II, the Merry Monarch.

Rural districts, of course, have changed less than the towns, and here the features of old England may be most clearly traced. First of all there are the men and women themselves. In remote places one may still recognize the original types from which the modern mixed English people have been made up. These differences show themselves in physical traits, such as size of head and color of hair and eyes, and also in variations of accent, dialect and custom. The tall, fair-haired, blue-eyed descendants of the Vikings may still be found north of the Humber River. Farther south, on the east and south coasts and in the midlands, are the descendants of Danes, Angles, Jutes and Saxons, golden-haired, more sturdily built and, as we approach the Saxons, more rugged in features. In the heart of England and toward the west we also find the ancient Britons, whom Caesar found in possession. Scattered throughout the country, but chiefly toward the west, in South Wales and in Cornwall, we find the dark hair and smaller stature of a still more ancient stock, which preceded the others and probably came originally from the shores of the Mediterranean Sea.

The workers on the land and the fisher

JUDGES LEAVING WESTMINSTER ABBEY FOR THE HOUSE OF LORDS

Lawyers divide the legal year into terms and vacations and consider that it properly begins on Michaelmas Day, September 29, when the judges attend services in Westminster Abbey. Afterward they walk, dressed in the same sort of wigs and robes that English judges have worn for hundreds of years, to breakfast in the House of Lords.

Historic Locations in Great Britain

Durham

Exeter

AS THE HOME of a people whose culture and language have spread to the far corners of the earth, Great Britain is rich in historical sites that are familiar even in distant lands. The maps below show where many of these sites are and in what period they made their mark. On the map at left, below the title, the line drawn from Exeter to Durham traces the division between lowlands and highlands. Many of the original inhabitants were pushed or fled into the high-

THE EARLIEST PERIOD in history—the written record—is a story of invasions and conquests: by the Romans, beginning in 54 B.C.; the Jutes, Angles, Saxons and eventually Danes, A.D. 300–1020; and the Normans (originally a Celtic people but speaking French) under William the Conqueror, 1066. The Romans affected chiefly the land, leaving cities, roads and walls. From a blending of the others came the English people and the English language.

PREHISTORIC MAN came to the island along the routes indicated by arrows.

New Stone age, around 3000 B.C.

Bronze age, lower left, 1900–1000 B.C.

Late Bronze, early Iron ages (Celts), upper right, 1000–450 B.C.

Belgae, other » northern tribes, 250 B.C.–A.D. 100.

Distribution by A.D. 486.

Angles, Saxons, Jutes

Britons

Picts

Scots

ANCIENT BRITAIN (to 1066)

Antonius' Wall

Hadrian's Wall

Jarrow

Whitby

York

Chester · · Maiden Castle

Ely Monastery

Cirencester (Silchester) Gloucester · Sutton Hoo (Woodbridge)

Camulodunum (Colchester)

Forest of Dean

Caerleon Verulamium Kent

Aquae Solis (Bath) Malmesbury London

Deorham Victory Canterbury

Glastonbury Abbey

Dover Strait

Mendip Hills Hastings

Isle of Wight Sussex Weald

Stonehenge Andresweald

Avebury Circles

Battle of Ethandune (Ashingdon)

lands, where ancient tongues survive to this day. The lowlands, on the east, were naturally more open to conquerors and settlers, and history was enacted there on a larger scale. Out of the variety of stocks who eventually settled in the lowlands was to be formed the English people and their language. The Romans had imposed an artificial unity but the acceptance of Christianity in the sixth century was a major step toward the real unity of the whole island. In medieval times other unifying forces besides the Church were stirring: demands for rights from the monarch, in the Magna Charta; the expansion of commerce, hence the importance of the privileged Cinque (Five) Ports. To these influences, after 1540, were added global exploration and discovery, the spread of knowledge by the printed word, and—after bitter civil war—the establishment of the British Constitution, thus a constitutional monarchy form of government.

TWO ELEMENTS dominated the monastic (late medieval) period: the expansion of religious institutions, including the building of magnificent cathedrals and, because the Church was the center of learning, the founding of such universities as Oxford and Cambridge; and the organization of British life into the feudal system, hence the many castles. There were also a century-long war with France and struggles at home over succession to the throne.

THE DISSOLUTION of the monasteries in 1540 by Henry VIII signaled the advent of the Protestant Reformation and the Renaissance in Britain. England was now firmly united under a single ruler, sounding the knell of feudalism. As industry and trade prospered so did the power of the growing middle class, finally curbing the monarch's authority and making Parliament the chief governing body. An overseas empire was gained—today's Commonwealth.

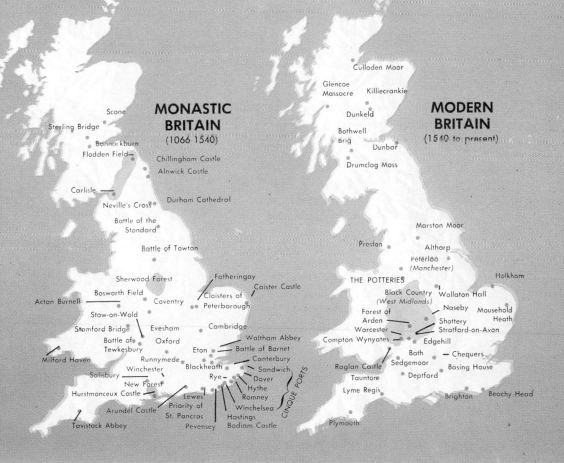

folk have changed least of all the peoples of England. Men who thus earn their daily bread are in direct contact with the elements. Their minds are stored with the lore of the weather and of the soil, of the ways of beasts and fishes. The machine hand of the towns seeks distractions in his hours of leisure from the monotony of his daily tasks. He is quick, volatile, changeable, restless. The country man and the fisher think long, slow thoughts and love the peace of nature.

Sheep must still be tended, and the shepherd is a lonely man by habit and inclination. He is no chatterbox, but he has a retentive memory, and he can tell you tales of adventure among men and beasts upon the moors and fells and hills, which have never been written down in books, but have been handed from generation to generation. There is no better guide and companion in the country than the shepherd, whether he be of the Salisbury Plain, the South Downs, the Yorkshire moors or the Cumberland fells.

England was once mainly covered with forests, in which the scattered little hamlets each had its own clearing for tillage and pasture. The forest yielded timber and firewood and game. A bold hunter might find a living there, as did Robin Hood and his merry men. The clearings yielded bread, milk, butter, cheese, wool, mutton and beef. The folk needed nothing from the outside world. They lived in the most complete isolation, one hamlet hardly knowing what happened in the next.

Today most of the forests are cleared and the land is under the plow. Only some remnants of the ancient forests remain. Of these the chief is New Forest. Epping Forest comes right up to the confines of London. Richmond Park, forest and meadow, is also near by. Then there are the famous Tintern Woods, in Monmouth, and various woods strewn up and down the country, representing what were once great forests, such as Arden and Sherwood.

Many of the folk dances, such as the Morris dance, which so many young peo-

PIX

THE SURVIVAL OF A MEDIEVAL FROLIC

The Play of the Mummers is eight hundred years old. Dressed in shaggy costumes made of paper strips, the players parade around the village led by the town crier with his bell. There are sham fights with sticks among the mummers, who represent such characters as Old Father Christmas, King William, Little John, the Doctor and Beelzebub the Devil.

PIX

AN ELIZABETHAN PAGEANT, THE HORN DANCE, HELD IN STAFFORDSHIRE

There are twelve dancers—the Jester, a lad riding a hobby horse (the two shown here), an archer representing Robin Hood, a man dressed as Maid Marian, two musicians playing a triangle and a melodeon, and six men bearing huge reindeer antlers—who perform set "figures." The dance began as a symbol of the villagers' right to hunt in Needwood Forest.

ple enjoy today, have come down to us from old England. As one old jingle goes:

> When Tom came home from labor,
> Or Ciss from milking rose,
> Then merrily went the tabor,
> And nimbly went their toes.

Children's games are often survivals of ancient popular ceremonies, dating from before the time of Queen Elizabeth. Punch and Judy has been traced back to an old mystery play about Pontius Pilate and Judas Iscariot. Mystery plays, on re-ligious subjects, were not "mysterious" but were given by a ministry, or mystery, the old name for a craft or guild.

Many of England's most famous food specialties also have a long history. The cheeses are as various as the dialects—Stilton, Cheshire, Cheddar. And when English fare is not restricted by rationing, there are the delicious Cornish pasties, Devonshire cream, Melton Mowbray pies, Bath buns, Yorkshire pudding. Worces-tershire sauce and English biscuits and marmalade are prized everywhere.

ELIZABETHAN CHARM is kept spruce in the twentieth century—rethatching an old cottage in Suffolk.

TURNED OUT IN "PINK." The term refers to formal attire for fox hunting and not to the crimson coat.

"OYEZ, OYEZ!" calls a town crier, in a pageant. His ancient role has been taken over by newspapers and radio.

A TITHE BARN built around 1400 near Banbury (of "Banbury Cross" fame). Once farmers brought produce here in payment of church tithes (a tenth part).

IN THE "HOP COUNTY" of Kent—stripping the catkins from hop vines. The catkins are dried in the pointed kilns and are then ready for use in brewing.

England ...*town and country*

THE kingdom of England occupies the southern half of the island of Britain. Scotland occupies the northern half and Wales takes up an outlying section of England's west coast. Both Scotland and Wales are mountainous, but England is low-lying. It is as if a colossus had put his weight onto the southeast corner of Britain, forcing it down till the water lapped over its edge and raised the north and west clear of the ocean.

The east and west coasts are deeply indented, the former by river and marsh and the latter by deep bays between rocky peninsulas. The south coast is fairly straight, a line of low cliffs backed by rolling downs.

These downs constitute South England, which is bounded to the north by the Thames and the Severn valleys, and to the west by the Exe River. The long tail of England, which lies on the other side of the Exe and trails off into the Atlantic is called the West Country. The Midlands, logically enough, cover the middle of England, up to the River Trent. North of them again is the North Country, a long upland strip that runs to the Scots border.

Before man arrived England was a dismal land of heath, swamp and forest. But generations of invaders have transformed it. Men of the Stone and Bronze ages marked it with tracks, earthworks and

temples. Then came the Romans who tamed the land.

By the third century A.D. they had broken the tyranny of natural communications by a network of roads that is still the basis of the English road system. The lowlands of the south and east were dotted with luxurious villas, thriving marts, like Silchester, imposing cities like London and St. Albans, and resorts, like Bath.

In the end, Roman Britain split apart and Teutonic invaders initiated a second transformation of England. They created thousands of villages, cleared the forests and cultivated the heavy earth of the broad river valleys.

The glory of medieval England was its churches. The cathedrals, some two dozen, were the brightest architectural stars in a firmament made up of monasteries, parish churches, chapels, shrines, priories and chantries. Most of the cathedrals were erected in the south, many of them on the sites of Roman towns. Every village had its parish church, here with the sturdiness and squat towers of the twelfth century, there with the airiness of the fourteenth century. All of them blazed with stained, or painted, glass.

A traveler in medieval England came upon many castles as well as churches. To the trained eye each told a story: a round-towered "concentric" castle in Wales, clearly the work of a thirteenth-century English king; a massive, square keep in Yorkshire, refuge of some twelfth-century border magnate; a small, round fortress on an artificial mound in Sussex, the hasty defense of some eleventh-century Norman knight; a trim, many-roomed, moated fortress in Kent, retreat of an overmighty subject; an imposing

A GARDENER plants spring flowers on a grave at Acton Burnell in Shropshire. The fortified manor house dates from 1283, the year that one of the earliest parliaments met there. Nearby are remains of the ancient Celts and Romans.

complex of donjons and bastions set about a central court, the lair of a great fourteenth-century lord on the Welsh Marches.

The age of faith and battle gave way to one of reason and leisure. For perhaps two centuries, England was a country of stately homes. Royalty lived in new palaces, like Greenwich and Hampton Court. The great aristocrats, who ruled the land, built their mansions, like Blenheim Palace and Chatsworth, on magnificent classical lines, creating around them artfully landscaped parks. In many places, castles were converted and old manor houses modernized.

Towns too were transformed. Narrow buildings, huddled under high gables and lofty steeples, gave way to noble terraces, squares, parks and crescents. A lighter, more domesticated church architecture, less awesome than the medieval, was developed by Sir Christopher Wren and his successors.

No sooner had this transformation been completed than the country was in the throes of the industrial revolution. The balance of wealth and population shifted from south to north, following the coal and iron deposits. First an extensive canal system was built, then a dense net of railways appeared, spanning valleys on massive brick viaducts, and rivers on huge iron and steel bridges. For freight there were also the narrow boats plying England's extensive canal system. Industry and a soaring population produced the great industrial towns of the north: Manchester, Stoke-on-Trent, Middlesbrough, Jarrow-on-Tyne, Barrow-in-Furness, Newcastle-upon-Tyne, Leeds, Sheffield and many more. The Midlands developed light industries, based on Birmingham, Coventry, Luton, Wolverhampton and elsewhere. A new landscape appeared, blackened by the soot of innumerable foundries and furnaces and dominated by factories and smokestacks.

The industrial revolution has been followed by the urban revolution. Since

1900 cities and towns have mushroomed, spurred by an expanding economy and by postwar reconstruction. Great, sprawling, loosely connected masses of suburb, industry, town, village and city emerged. The term "conurbation" has been coined to describe them. To limit conurbation many authorities have tried creating "Green Belts" round cities, building self-contained towns away from cities and encouraging the wholesale shift of population to towns in outlying rural areas. But imaginative though these schemes are, they cannot get around the fact that England is too small.

A population about a quarter of the size of the United States' is crammed into an area less than a seventieth the size. The kingdom is crowded with factories, villages, towns, cottages, millions of cars and over 42,000,000 people. It is crowded with the paraphernalia of modern industry, power lines and pylons, pipelines and power stations. For two thousand years man beautified the land. Now relentless economic progress is making it ugly. On balance man may have gained more than he has lost. But, hearing echoes of the past from every side, it is hard not to believe that the older England was a lovelier, more gracious land than the hectic modern one.

Dover, on the twenty-one-mile wide Strait of Dover, is the nearest point in England to the Continent. During World War II, shells from the French coast fell on the town day after day but the people refused to leave their town.

The port lies in a little valley, interrupting the line of the famous White Cliffs. A symbol of England, they are of gleaming chalk which rises straight up from the sea as much as four hundred feet. High on the cliffs to the east of Dover the Romans built a fort and a pharos, or lighthouse. Remains of the pharos still stand, though Dover Castle, largely a relic of Norman times, took the place of the fort. Beneath the castle one may wander through passages and casemates (chambers) hewed into the cliff.

In the Norman period, Dover joined in the formation of the Cinque (Five) Ports with Hastings, Sandwich, Romney and Hythe. These ports contributed to sea defense in return for special privileges.

Twenty miles northwest of Dover is Canterbury, dominated by its Cathedral. This, though it was begun under the Normans, is largely Gothic in design. Thomas à Becket was murdered in the cathedral in 1170 and when he was made a saint two years later it became a shrine for crowds of pilgrims. Chaucer wrote of such a band of pilgrims in *Canterbury Tales*.

Southwest of Dover is Romney Marsh, once the haunt of smugglers. Much of it is now a fertile meadow, and cattle and sheep are brought from other parts of the country to pasture there.

The "ancient towns" of Winchelsea and Rye, each of which is on a knoll, nestle close to each other farther along the coast. The sea has receded here, and though this ruined the towns commercially, it saved them artistically. The parish church of Winchelsea, built around 1300 in honor of Thomas à Becket, has some of the best modern stained glass in England. Winchelsea used to be walled and still has three of its old gates.

Hastings is near where William the Conqueror defeated King Harold in 1066. The old part of the town is a pretty fishing village, with boats drying on the sands.

In this vicinity are some enchanting medieval structures. Battle Abbey—a school today—was built on the very spot where Harold fell. Bodiam Castle is a bold fourteenth-century fortress complete with parapets, a portcullis and a moat where water lilies float.

Hurstmonceux Castle has two of its original great gateway towers. Today it is the home of the Royal (Greenwich) Observatory, moved here from Greenwich (London) in 1948–49. Standing among the Sussex oaks and bracken, in spring almost moated with wild hyacinths, Hurstmonceux is a thrilling example of what can be achieved in brick. Old buildings in the English countryside reflect the kind of soil they stand on. Where it is clay, cottages are of brick and roofed with thatch. In localities that were once largely forest, the houses are timbered. Wher-

THE UNITED KINGDOM—GREAT BRITAIN AND NORTHERN IRELAND

35

MARKET CROSS AND CATHEDRAL SPIRE IN CHICHESTER

The Market Cross stands where the town's two main streets meet. Such structures, usually cross-shaped, were erected in the center of many town market places in medieval times.

UNDER A LEAFY ARCH ON THE BRIDPORT ROAD NEAR DORCHESTER

The fine modern highway traces a military road constructed by the Romans. On most of the approaches to Dorchester there are avenues of trees, a plan begun early in the 1700's.

ever stone could be found, stone was used, even if it was only a tiny quarry.

At Bexhill-on-Sea, in contrast, there is a striking example of modern architecture, with much glass—the De La Warr Pavilion. Built in the middle 1930's, it was designed by Eric Mendelsohn and Serge Chermayeff, who were considered daring architects at the time.

At Beachy Head, a chalk headland almost six hundred feet high, the South Downs begin. The downs are treeless chalk hills that roll back from the coast. Those between London and Dover—in the counties of Surrey and Kent—are called the North Downs. The South Downs, largely in Sussex, are much nearer the coast. On their gentle slopes graze the famous Southdown sheep. At lambing time the hills are an entrancing sight, with thousands of little balls of wool frisking about on the springy turf.

In the South Downs at Wilmington, a strange figure—the Long Man—is cut out on the side of a hill. It is 240 feet high and carries a staff in each hand. The Celts are supposed to have gouged it out long, long ago and it may represent a god of journeys. There are other such figures wherever there are downs. Perhaps the best-known of all is the Giant of Cerne Abbas, in the Dorset Downs. This one is 180 feet long and carries a club.

Lewes, the charming seat of Sussex County, lies in the very heart of the South Downs. On a height in the center of the town is a Norman castle. Nearby are the ruins of the Priory of St. Pancras, founded by William the Conqueror's stepdaughter. On the downs above Lewes, Henry III was defeated by Simon de Montfort in 1264. Henry was taken prisoner, and Simon called a meeting of Parliament. From this meeting the House of Commons developed. Lewes is

THE PALACE PIER, Brighton, provides boat trips, tea rooms, dancing, a funfare and a place to relax in the sun.

a center for painters and has many art exhibitions. A few miles away is Glyndebourne, a beautiful estate, where opera festivals are held in the summer.

Brighton is the largest and best-known seaside resort in England. It is sometimes called "London by the Sea." The resort became fashionable in the late 1700's. Dr. Johnson and his circle came to stay; and the Prince of Wales (later George IV) built an imposing pavilion. Along the ocean front are piers for promenading, and dignified Georgian houses delight the eye along the streets.

The Tract Called the Weald

Just outside Brighton is the Devil's Dyke, a natural amphitheater. From above it, standing on the remains of a camp of the early Britons, you can see the whole Weald. This is the dale enclosed by the ranges of the North and South Downs. *Weald,* or *wold,* is an Anglo-Saxon word meaning a wood. Here and there in the tract charcoal burners still ply their ancient craft. Once upon a time there were iron-ore mines, as many of the lovely old iron gateways and lampposts still found in Sussex attest.

In this part of Sussex in the spring, there are fields of wild daffodils, of primroses, cowslips, orchis. In the woods bloom bluebells, windflowers, cuckoopint, or lords-and-ladies. Gardens display a wealth of wistaria, laburnum, magnolia and even camellias.

Around Arundel in May, the beechwoods are breath-taking. This quiet little town is in a gap cut through the downs by the River Arun, which moats Arundel on two sides. The town grew up in the shelter of Arundel Castle, the seat of the Dukes of Norfolk. Whoever becomes Duke of Norfolk also becomes the first peer and the Earl Marshal of England. One of his duties is to act as "stage manager" of coronation ceremonies.

Chichester, about ten miles from Arundel, is one of the oldest and most attractive of English cathedral towns. It was called Regnum by the Romans, and the Roman ground plan is followed by today's streets. The ancient town walls can still be traced. When the Saxons came, they bestowed the name of Cissa Ceaster on the village. In Chichester Cathedral are two well-preserved Saxon sculptures: the Raising of Lazarus, and Christ at the Gate of Bethany. They have influenced many modern sculptors. The Saxon works probably are from the earlier church built on the site of the cathedral. Largely Norman, it was begun in 1085.

Between Portsmouth and Southampton (in Hampshire), there is no real country. Both cities have the bustle and tang of shipping centers. Portsmouth is England's biggest naval base, and Southampton is the biggest port in England after London. Their harbors are admirably sheltered by the triangular Isle of Wight. The channel on the northwest is called the Solent; the northeast channel entrance is called Spithead. Southampton has double tides, which prolong high water. The first tide comes in through the Solent; two hours later the second rushes in through Spithead. It was at Southampton, perhaps, that King Canute rebuked his flattering courtiers, who thought that he could command the sea to roll back. From Southampton sailed some of the Crusaders; and here the Pilgrims hired the Mayflower for their great venture.

The Isle of Wight

The Isle of Wight is a beguiling mixture of rolling downs inland and sandy beaches and cliffs along the coast. Almost in the center of the island, on a hill with a commanding view, is Carisbrooke Castle. Here Charles I was imprisoned for a time before his trial and execution. The island abounds with stately Elizabethan manor houses. On the western side are the Needles, three pointed masses of white chalk, a hundred feet high. Cowes, on the Solent, is the yachting center of England. Thousands of sails gleam on the sparkling waters during the summer and autumn. During the first week in August—Cowes Week—the gayest regattas of all are held.

From Lymington, a yacht-building center on the mainland shore of the Solent, the New Forest extends to the northwest.

ARUNDEL CASTLE BATTLEMENTS, OVERLOOKING THE CASTLE PARK

Feudal times seem vivid on these ramparts. Archers drew their bows in the crenels (the open spaces) and knights paced the parapet. The ancient castle withstood siege twice in the 1100's.

REPAIRING SHIPS AT BRISTOL

Bristol has a large harbor on the Avon River a few miles inland from the Bristol Channel.

These 140 square miles of woodland and heath were named New Forest by William Rufus, William the Conqueror's surly son, who claimed the land as a royal hunting ground. Though it is hardly a real forest today, there are great oaks, beeches, yews and hollies.

The South Downs (also called the Dorset Downs here) meet the sea again at the so-called Isle of Purbeck. It is really a little peninsula. Purbeck marble (shelly limestone) and potter's clay are found. Studland, a headland that rises up out of the moors, is aflame all summer with nutty-smelling gorse. On the Dorset Downs pasture small, horned sheep that lamb twice a year.

Thomas Hardy called Dorsetshire "Wessex" in his novels. The county seat, Dorchester, is the setting for his *Mayor of Casterbridge*. South of the town are the Maumbury Rings, the most perfect

WHERE THE MEMORY OF ANNE HATHAWAY STAYS GREEN

The straw-thatched farmhouse with half-timbered walls was the home of William Shakespeare's wife. It is at Shottery, in Warwickshire, only about one mile from Stratford-on-Avon.

Roman amphitheater left in England. Nearby Abbotsbury is a long, meandering village with a ruined monastery and a famous swannery. About a thousand swans glide around the pond.

From Weymouth, on the coast, is the shortest passage to the Channel Islands—chiefly Jersey, Guernsey, Alderney and Sark. Though these are much closer to France than to England, they have been united with England for more than eight centuries. Their laws are somewhat different, however, and they have a large measure of self-government. Both French and English are official languages, and a Norman-French dialect is spoken by many of the people among themselves. The cattle bred in the islands are famous the world over.

As we said earlier, Devon and Cornwall are considered a region apart from the South Coast. In this extreme southwest-

HALL AT WADHAM COLLEGE, OXFORD

The dining hall is celebrated for its hammer-beam roof and Jacobean screen (at far end).

THE CATHEDRAL TOWN OF TRURO IN THE HILLS OF CORNWALL

Though the cathedral, in Early English Gothic style, looks very old, it was built between 1880 and 1910 on the site of an earlier church. The spires dominate a pleasant market town.

A QUIET VILLAGE AMONG THE FENS OF CAMBRIDGESHIRE

The low, marshy ground of the fens is a paradise for wild life. Near the village of Wicken Fen, the area is preserved as a sanctuary for birds and flowers—and for insects!

APPLEBY, ON THE EASTERN EDGE OF THE LAKE DISTRICT

The town is in the lovely Vale of Eden and is the county seat of Westmorland. Old whitewashed houses face the street and the gray-stone building at the end keeps a look of Norman days.

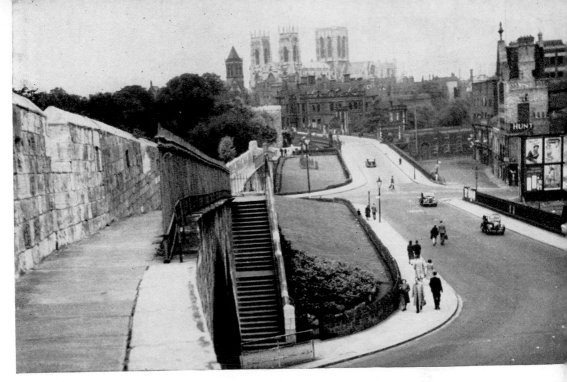

ANCIENT CITY WALLS PARALLEL A HILLY STREET IN YORK

William the Conqueror built a castle at York in 1068, and the old walls date in part from that time. Four bars, or gates, still remain. In the distance hover York Minster's towers.

ern peninsula of England, the land is hilly and in places wild. The cliffs on the coast are not chalk, but rock. In fact, Land's End—the tip that projects out into the Atlantic—is a mass of granite. So are the little Isles of Scilly, which lie about thirty miles southwest of Land's End. The climate is exceptionally mild, and semitropical plants flourish.

Exeter, the county seat of Devon, is one of the oldest towns in England. Here the Britons came out of hiding in Dartmoor and Cornwall after the Romans left. They lived peacefully side by side with the Saxons for several centuries until they were driven out again by King Athelstan early in the tenth century.

Exeter Cathedral is justly celebrated. Though most of it is Gothic, it has two massive Norman towers. Inside the cathedral is a plaque in memory of Richard Blackmore, author of *Lorna Doone*. Though his name is associated with Devon, the scene of his novel is Exmoor —which is mostly in Somerset, not far from the Bristol Channel. There is a real Doone Valley in Exmoor, though it is not

CATHEDRAL ON A SUMMIT

The great Norman bulk of Durham Cathedral looms over its city from the midst of woods.

43

DELICATE TINTS FOR FINE POTTERY
Flower designs are typical of Staffordshire
pottery. The best quality is hand-painted.

as rugged as Blackmore described it.

Dartmoor is a larger and really wilder
expanse of treeless plateau, to the west of
Exeter. Here masses of granite crop out
in what are known as "tors." Through
the moor race clear streams, which pause
now and then to form quiet pools where
wily trout lurk. But beware of bright
green grass on Dartmoor; the vivid color
indicates a swamp.

In the lovely valleys of Devon there are
unspoiled villages, dreamlike in the spring
when the fruit orchards around them are
in bloom. Devon cattle are a prized
breed; and the clotted cream of the shire
is an epicure's delight.

Plymouth, on the coast, was the starting point for many expeditions of the
Elizabethan sea rovers—Drake, Hum-
phrey, Hawkins—as well as the later
Captain Cook. It was on the Hoe—an
elevated esplanade—that Drake is supposed to have been bowling when the
Spanish Armada hove in sight. From the
quay called the Barbican, the Mayflower
set sail in 1620.

For many years Falmouth, on the Cornish coast, was a busy port, but since the
middle 1800's it has become more a resort.
One of its main attractions today is the
subtropical garden of Penjerrick.

From Falmouth it is only a few miles
to the peninsula called the Lizard. On its
breezy downs blooms the Cornish heath.
The cliffs here are particularly beautiful,
and there are secluded coves.

Cornwall has many remains of the ancient Britons and the Druids. Heaps of
stone still stand that were once baronial
castles, and many of the legends of King
Arthur are associated with Cornwall.
The eldest son of the English monarch
always bears the title Duke of Cornwall,
as Prince Charles does today. The Cornish language, a Celtic one, is no longer
spoken, though there are hints of it in the
present-day speech of Cornishmen and its
literature has been preserved.

No place in England is more than a
hundred miles from the sea, but the most
truly inland country lies among the Cots-
wold Hills. They form the watershed
between the Thames and Severn valleys.
Limestone ridges, their highest point is
Cleeve Hill, 1,031 feet, above Cheltenham.

The Cotswolds were once the center of
the wool trade, from around 1300 to
Henry VIII's time. England's wool
trade, then virtually a world monopoly,
made her people the richest in Europe.
English cottages were palaces as compared with the dwellings of workers in
any other part of the known world. Many
of these cottages, with modern improve-
ments, are lived in now.

By Cheltenham's Waters

Late in the 1700's the mineral waters
of Cheltenham transformed it into a fashionable spa. George III helped to make
it popular; and the graceful mansions that
make it so charming were erected during
his reign and in the Regency period that
followed. A profusion of lime and chestnut trees gives them a verdant frame.

On the Severn River is Gloucester, the
county seat of Gloucestershire and a cathedral city. It is also important commercially with a number of industries.
The cathedral, which is magnificent, was

built between 1097 and 1472. As one would expect from these dates, its core is Norman but its most noticeable features are Perpendicular Gothic.

Near Moreton-in-the-Marsh is Compton Wynyates, perhaps the most famous of English manor houses. Built of timber, brick and stone, its style is a bridge between Gothic and Renaissance.

Oxford University, Blenheim Palace (the Duke of Marlborough's vast mansion), Stratford-on-Avon and the Royal China Factory at Worcester are all on the edge of the Cotswolds.

The Lake District is not far inland from the Irish Sea. Though the tract—due east of the Isle of Man—is only thirty-five miles square, its mirror-like tarns and aloof mountains have an unexpected wildness. History has trod lightly here. It was not until the early 1800's that the Lake District was really appreciated. Then Wordsworth, Coleridge, Southey and their friends—the Lake school of poets—extolled the region's beauties.

The largest of the lakes, Windermere, is but ten miles long. Derwentwater is considered the most beautiful. Above it, to the north, rears Skiddaw, a peak 3,053 feet high.

In fact, the Cumbrian Mountains of this district are as celebrated as the lakes. Helvellyn, just over 3,000 feet, is one of the most perfect in shape. From the heights of Place Fell and St. Sunday Crag one can see the Scottish Border and the Irish Sea. Near Wastwater, the most savage of the lakes, Scafell Pike reaches 3,210 feet into the sky, the highest point in England. All are far more impressive than their rather low heights suggest; and they are so rugged that Alpine climbers practice on them.

The Scottish Border has a grandeur all its own—high, remote, almost grim, with yellow trefoil and heather on the slopes and verdant valleys through which brooks and waterfalls splash. It is romantic country; history or legend is associated with almost every spot. At Flodden Field

PHOTOS, BRITISH INFORMATION SERVICES

BUSY FACTORIES THAT HELP ENGLAND'S FOREIGN TRADE

On the left warp threads for wool fabrics are being spun. The operator is on the alert for any breaks. Right, motorcycles are given final adjustments as they move on the assembly line.

the "flowers of the forest" were mowed down in 1513, when the Scots met a disastrous defeat under James IV. Sir Walter Scott's *Marmion* and many of his *Tales from a Grandfather* and much of Rudyard Kipling's *Puck of Pook's Hill* were written about the Scottish Border.

The border begins on the east with dour Durham, and nowhere else is there such a solid satisfaction of a cathedral, with its round Norman pillars. Dr. Johnson said that it produced an impression of "rocky solidity and indeterminate duration." Durham is the center of smoky coal fields, but the cathedral towers above them.

Farther north, on the River Tyne, is Newcastle, known everywhere for its export of coal. It is also a center of engineering industries and shipbuilding.

A little west of Newcastle is one of the most delightful towns in north England —Hexham. From east to west it is divided by one long street, called Priestpopple in one section, Battle Hill in the center and Hencotes beyond. Hexham boasts a magnificent priory church, with Saxon remains, a building that was a medieval prison and a fine bridge.

From Hexham one can walk along part of the Roman wall and climb the fells— wild, high, almost uninhabited country. The fells are the northern end of the Pennine range, the spine of England.

The Roman wall is often called Hadrian's wall. It was planned by that Roman Emperor around 120 A.D., to keep the wild Picts out of England. It cut clear across England, a distance of seventy-three miles, between the estuaries of the Tyne and the Solway. It was eight feet thick and twenty feet high, with a rampart walk on top. Below the northern face was a thirty-foot moat, or fosse, and on the south side a military road. Along the wall were sixteen major forts, with many smaller forts—now called "mile castles"— in between, and a turret every three hundred yards. Only a small part of the wall still stands though the whole route can be traced. It remains clearly marked.

BRITISH TRAVEL ASSOCIATION

HADRIAN'S WALL, WHICH ONCE CUT ACROSS NORTHERN ENGLAND

Most of the old Roman wall has crumbled. Yet when it was built, around 120 A.D., it was a formidable barrier with forts at intervals and a wide ditch on the northern side.

North of the wall, only a few miles from the North Sea, is Alnwick. The town takes its name from Alnwick Castle, an imposing pile of medieval fortifications on a commanding site. The Scottish Border has perhaps more than its share of castles. For hundreds of years it bled in either outright war or in raids.

Nearby Chillingham Castle is a fourteenth-century structure remodeled in the 1600's by Inigo Jones, the great architect. The castle is the home of the Earl of Tankerville, who owns the last herd of wild cattle in England. They look something like the American bison, as woolly but perhaps not as humpy.

Bamburgh Castle, farther north, looks out on the North Sea from a lofty basalt crag. According to the Arthurian legends, this was Sir Lancelot's castle of Joyous Gard. The Norman keep dates from 1150.

The town of Berwick not only marks the eastern end of the boundary between England and Scotland but in all old documents has a sort of extraterritoriality. "England, Wales and the town of Berwick-upon-Tweed" runs many a writ. It did not become English until 1482.

Near the western end of the border is Carlisle, called "merrie Carlisle" in many a border ballad. The Roman wall went through a suburb to the north; and in the days of border strife the town was a formidable fortress. Mary Queen of Scots spent a brief interval of her long imprisonment in Carlisle Castle.

Some distance south, along the North Sea coast, embracing the Wash, is the Lincolnshire Fen Country. The fens were formed by the gradual silting up of a once great bay, of which only the Wash remains. (Here King John lost his baggage and treasure in 1216.) It is supposed that the Romans first tried to drain the fens. However, the deep drains and sluices constructed to reclaim the area were not completed until the 1800's. The region teems with wild fowl. Around Spalding, in the spring, one finds almost as many kinds of flowering bulb as in Holland.

The fen folk have a unique dialect, and

PHILIP GENDREAU

A WINDING STREET IN LINCOLN

Town and cathedral (a tower is visible) are on high ground in the flat Lincolnshire fens.

most families have lived for centuries in the same cottages. No English people are more sturdily independent. Lincolnshire village churches are among the loveliest in England. The whole history of English architecture may be studied here.

South of the Wash are the Norfolk Broads, as the flat, shallow lakes of Norfolk County are called. The region is a level tract of land in the shape of a triangle. It fans out from Norwich to Palling on the north and Lowestoft on the south. Within this area there are about a dozen large broads and twice as many small ones. These, together with numerous sluggish streams, drain into Breydon Water, near Yarmouth. House boats and river yachts ply them. Between Reedham, near Yarmouth, and Norwich, they are an angler's paradise, teeming with bream, roach, pike, perch and rudd. In the terrible storms of January 1953, the broads, being natural lagoons, did not suffer as much as the dykes of Holland.

Norwich, the county seat of Norfolk, was the center for the Norwich school of English landscape painters—Crome, Cotman and Constable being the most important. It is also the home of the Norwich *Mercury,* the oldest English newspaper (founded 1714) still appearing under its original name. The apse of Norwich Cathedral, which is largely Norman, is notable for its flying buttresses. Nurse Edith Cavell, World War I heroine, is buried in a plot by the cathedral called Life's Green.

Because Norfolk County is so level, one is aware of the broad expanse of sky—as at sea—and among the broads rainbows and sunsets flame with a special glory.

We have had space here to talk of only a few districts of England. There are many others each with its special charms. All of the country is inviting, and every Englishman cherishes his own corner. Rare is the visitor who can resist the spell of this storied land, no matter where he wanders on the "blessed plot."

By Anne Fremantle

Facts and Figures are given on page 64.

A LITTLE THEATER IN NORWICH WITH AN ELIZABETHAN AIR
The building is not really so old but it copies the theaters of Shakespeare's day. It has an apron (projecting) stage. Elizabethan dramas and other classics are performed here.

BRITISH OFFICIAL PHOTOGRAPH

"OH, TO BE IN ENGLAND NOW THAT APRIL'S THERE"

When an Englishman abroad grows homesick for his native land, more often than not his thoughts turn to some quiet little village. There hedgerows are white with hawthorn blossoms in the spring; and gabled Tudor houses, little changed since Elizabethan times, cling to the side of the road. This lovely view of Yalding was taken from the village church.

BRITISH INFORMATION SERVICES

"AND AFTER APRIL, WHEN MAY FOLLOWS"

It is hard to believe that this hamlet, in Essex, is only forty miles northeast of bustling London. Probably the loudest sounds the villagers ever hear are the bells in the steeple summoning them to church. It is possible that the inn, "at the sign of the fox," is even older than most of the village itself. The little bridge crosses the pond in the central green.

49

WOLLATON HALL, serenely lovely manor house built in the time of Elizabeth I.   The estate is in Nottinghamshire, where Robin Hood and his men perhaps once made merry.

"**BESIDE THE LAKE,** beneath the trees"—Wordsworth's daffodils still bloom on the banks of Ullswater, in the Lake District, inspiration of Wordsworth and his fellow poets.

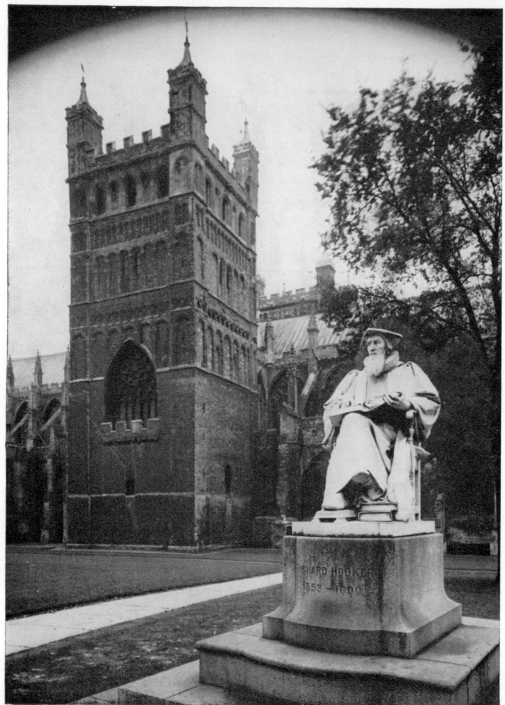

NORMAN TOWER AND ELIZABETHAN SCHOLAR

It is fitting that a statue of Richard Hooker should stand on the grounds of Exeter Cathedral. He was born near the town of Exeter and, more than that, he was a great Church of England theologian. Exeter Cathedral, begun in 1112, is one of the glories of Gothic architecture in England. The massive tower is one of two, each 130 feet in height.

A PART OF THE LOVELY BACKS OF CAMBRIDGE UNIVERSITY

The Backs are the grounds that slope down to the Cam River from the backs of some of the university buildings. In this section the stream flows past Trinity College Library. Framed in the trees beyond the bend is St. John's New Court. Out of sight there is a covered bridge, dubbed Bridge of Sighs, connecting this court with older courts of St. John's College.

TERMINAL AT SOUTHAMPTON FOR TRANSATLANTIC LINERS

The largest passenger ships that ply the North Atlantic dock at this pier, which was erected after World War II. Built of concrete, it is a two-story building 1,300 feet long. It has three double sets of gangways which can be telescoped, luxurious lounges, four escalators, twenty-one elevators and a large parking space for cars.

53

SEA AND COUNTRYSIDE meet in the white cliffs of chalk which stand out to greet those who enter England from France whether they land at Dover, at Folkestone or Newhaven. They are found where the North and South Downs run into the English Channel, and end in Shakespeare's Cliff, near Dover, and Beachy Head, near Eastbourne. Between these come the flat Romney Marshes, where smugglers once hid. We are looking here at the South Downs, near Seaford, and at the long, undulating stretch of cliff that is known as the Seven Sisters.

54

CORNWALL'S COAST is very different from that of Sussex. Here we find jagged cliffs composed of gray granite or black slate, and broken into rocky coves, deep bays or short valleys running into the high land and each occupied by a seaside town. This winding channel, filled with a swirl of white foam, is on the north coast, near Tintagel Castle.

THE SPRING OF THE YEAR IN WORCESTERSHIRE

A gracious old manor house, Priory Park, at Malvern. Its setting—old trees, flowering shrubs and borders, and velvety sward—gives us a little glimpse of the glory of spring, which seems to have a special quality in England. The west midland county of Worcestershire is a fertile region, noted for its beautiful orchards, and grows luscious apples, pears and plums.

A GARDEN SQUARE IN THE TEXTILE CITY OF MANCHESTER

Sunlight and flowers add charm to a peaceful park oasis in Manchester's Piccadilly, surrounded by the industrial buildings that play so important a part in the city's busy life. The fourth largest city in England, Manchester is a great center of cotton manufacturing. It is noted for its deep ship canal and its high-ranking newspaper, the Manchester *Guardian*.

YORK MINSTER, THE DIGNIFIED AND MASSIVE CHURCH OF ST. PETER

Famous especially for its extensive and representative series of stained glass windows, the minster
includes examples of the early English Decorated and the early and late Perpendicular styles.
On both sides of the west façade rise two richly decorated towers, 201 feet in height; in the northwest tower hangs the bell, Great Peter. The central tower rises 216 feet.

SHAKESPEARE MEMORIAL THEATER at Stratford-on-Avon. This impressive modern structure is a far cry from the little Globe Theater that Shakespeare knew in London.

THE SHINGLE BEACH of a fishing hamlet on the Devonshire coast. Some of the inhabitants of such ports are descendants of men who sailed with the bold Elizabethan sea rovers.

ALONG A QUIET CANAL, part of Britain's inland-waterway system of some four thousand miles. The leading barge has an engine and tows the second craft, which is called the butty.

DERBY DAY CRY: "I GOTTA HORSE!"

An old-time tipster, in amusing regalia, coaxes the crowd with the promise of sure bets on the races at Epsom Downs. The most famous of these races is the Derby, named for the Earls of Derby; and Derby Day is around the beginning of June. Then kings, peers and commoners flock to the course, which is in Surrey, about fifteen miles from London.

TAYLOR

THE RIVER THAMES has many aspects. As it winds under the many bridges of London, it is a muddy river, dotted with shipping. Yet only a little way beyond the city, the Thames becomes a silver stream flowing between green banks. The little craft tied up are punts. Instead of oars, they have poles. So quiet and serene does this spot look, it is hard to believe that long centuries ago, near here, Julius Caesar and his legions tried to ford the river, only to find that the Britons had driven great pointed stakes into its bed.

ABRAHAM

FROM NEAR KESWICK we look south over Derwentwater, the most beautiful lake in Cumberland, toward Borrowdale and its misty distant fells. Behind us we have the great mass of Skiddaw. The long range of hills across the lake has the curious name of Catbells, and if in the autumn we scramble up its steep, bracken-covered sides we can gather bilberries in plenty. Among the fells to the left are the Falls of Lodore, whose waters come "pouring and roaring, and waving and raving," just as Robert Southey describes them in his poem.

63

UNITED KINGDOM : facts and figures

Government
CONSTITUTIONAL MONARCHY: consists of England, Wales, Scotland, Northern Ireland, various small channel islands; monarch head of state; nominally appoints prime minister and cabinet (real executive power) responsible to bicameral Parliament; 630-member House of Commons, real legislative power; members popularly elected for 5 yrs. but prime minister may call for new elections at any time within that period; House of Lords (chiefly a revisionary body) consists of more than 900 appointed members (2 archbishops and 24 bishops of the Church of England, 22 dukes, 26 marquesses, 133 earls, 112 viscounts, 573 barons and baronesses, 16 Scottish representative peers, and judges given peerages to allow the House of Lords to function as the final court of appeals)
VOTING: universal suffrage from age 21

Area
94,279 sq. mi.
CULTIVATED: 29%
FORESTED: 6%
INLAND WATERWAYS: lakes—Lomond, Ness, Neagh; rivers—Thames, Severn, Avon, Forth, Clyde, Dee, Tyne, Tweed

Climate
TEMPERATURE: Jan. av. 39–43° F., July av. 53–63° F.
ANNUAL PRECIPITATION: London av. 24 in., Highlands over 40 in.
WEATHER PATTERN: temperate; warmed by North Atlantic Drift, a part of the Gulf Stream; mists, fogs frequent throughout yr.

Natural resources
FISHERIES: av. annual catch 850,000 tons; cod, haddock, sole, plaice, herring, mackerel, sprats
AGRICULTURE: wheat, barley, oats, potatoes, sugarbeets, dairy products
LIVESTOCK: 170,000 horses
7,000,000 pigs
13,000,000 cattle
30,000,000 sheep
MINERALS: coal, iron, barite, cadmium, salt, magnesium, zinc, small amounts of oil, tin
WATERPOWER: 2,100,000,000 kwh.

Population
53,000,000
URBAN: 80%
BIRTHRATE: 16.9%
DEATHRATE: 11.7%
ANNUAL INCREASE: 0.4%, among world's very lowest
URBAN CENTERS:

London (capital)	8,400,000
County of London	3,300,000
Outer Ring	5,100,000
Birmingham	1,200,000
Glasgow	1,100,000
Liverpool	800,000
Manchester	700,000
Leeds	550,000
Sheffield	500,000
Edinburgh	480,000
Bristol	450,000
Belfast	450,000

Language
OFFICIAL: English universal
OTHER: Scottish and Irish Gaelic, Welsh, Manx

Religion
ESTABLISHED (OFFICIAL) CHURCH: Church of England (Anglican) and, in Scotland, Church of Scotland (Presbyterian); complete freedom of religion

Church of England	53%
Roman Catholic	9.6%
Presbyterian	3.4%
Methodist	1.7%
Jewish	0.9%
Congregational	0.8%
Muslim	0.1%
Others	30.5%

Education and welfare
LITERACY: 99%; education compulsory ages 5–15
SCHOOLS AND PUPILS: 33,200 primary (5,000,000 pupils); 2,900 secondary (3,000,000); 9,000 technical (2,800,000); 170 teacher-training (43,000); 25 univ. (110,000)
WELFARE: national insurance for illness, accident, unemployment, maternity, provides for preventive medicine, treatment and care; pensions for aged, disabled and widows; family allowances for children

Commerce
GROSS NATIONAL PRODUCT: $68,000,000,000
GNP PER CAPITA: $1,280
CURRENCY: pound sterling (£); 1 £ worth $2.80 US; central banker of sterling area (25% of world's population); 50% of world trade conducted in sterling
WORLD TRADE: United Kingdom 2d only to U.S. as a world trader; carries on more than 10% of all world trade
EXPORTS: manufactured products of all kinds
IMPORTS: raw, semifinished, industrial materials of all kinds, food, fuel
TRADING PARTNERS: Common Market, Commonwealth, United States

Transportation
ROADS: 200,000 mi.
PASSENGER CARS: 6,000,000
TRUCKS AND BUSES: 1,600,000
MOTORCYCLES: 1,900,000
RAILROADS: 50,000 mi.
NAVIGABLE WATERWAYS: 2,600 mi. of canals and rivers
MERCHANT MARINE: 2,413 ships, 25,200,000 tons; fleet 2d only to U.S.; fleet carries about 25% of all world marine trade and passengers; main ports London (1 of world's busiest), Liverpool, Glasgow, Southampton, Belfast, Bristol
AIR SERVICE: 2 Government-owned lines, about 20 privately owned lines connect country with all areas of world; all major foreign lines serve nation

Communications
TELEPHONES: 8,000,000
RADIO AND TELEVISION (most stations Government-owned): 15,000,000 radios; 12,000,000 TV sets
PRESS: 114 daily papers (circulation 30,000,000); 1,300 semiweekly papers; 4,400 magazines
LIBRARIES: 3 national (9,000,000 volumes); 635 univ. (22,000,000); 1,200 special (15,000,000); 5,000 public (7,000,000)
CINEMAS: 4,000; av. annual per capita attendance 14.5

Membership in international organizations
Aid to India-Pakistan Club
Central Treaty Organization
Colombo Plan for Cooperative Economic Development in South and Southeast Asia
Commission for Technical Cooperation in Africa South of Sahara
Commonwealth of Nations
Council of Europe
European Free Trade Association
European Space Research Organization
North Atlantic Treaty Organization (NATO)
Organization for Economic Cooperation and Development
Southeast Asia Collective Defense Treaty Organization (SEATO)
South Pacific Commission
United Nations and its specialized agencies
Western European Union

For WORLDWIDE FACTS AND FIGURES, refer to Volume 7, pages 390–92

London...*metropolis on the Thames*

THE capital of England and center of the Commonwealth of Nations bestrides the River Thames thirty-seven miles above its mouth. The Thames, nine hundred yards across at London Bridge, is the link of sentiment that binds this built-up county. For London consists of two cities, Westminster and the City of London, and twenty-eight metropolitan boroughs. (Westminster is both a city and a borough.) Cities and boroughs make up the County of London. Greater London, including a ring of suburbs, covers 722 square miles. Within it live roughly 8,000,000 people, about a fifth of all who live in England. Thus Greater London is one of the largest cities, rivaled only by Tokyo and New York.

London is really a cluster of communities: the boroughs, each of which was once a village. The Londoner rarely boasts of himself as such. His loyalty is to his borough. Many of them preserve their country-village character. The heath at Hampstead, the green at Highgate, the pound at Walthamstow, and Dulwich toll gate are instances of the numerous country touches. The one true Londoner who has his roots in "London Town," who knows its stories and can sing its songs, is the cockney, the man

« LOOKING UP the Thames River toward Lambeth Bridge and the south bank. The pinnacles in the foreground are on the Houses of Parliament, in Westminster.

HOLLYMAN, PHOTO RESEARCHERS

BRITISH INFORMATION SERVICES

A BEEFEATER at the Tower of London. The Yeoman Warders
were nicknamed Beefeaters because of the hearty rations of beef they
once drew. Their uniform has not changed since Shakespeare's day.

PICCADILLY, London's "Times Square," at night is a blaze of winking advertising signs. The street is the heart of the city's fashionable West End.

CHARM IN CHELSEA, a section where many famous artists and writers have lived. The houses are a happy mixture of old and modern architectural styles.

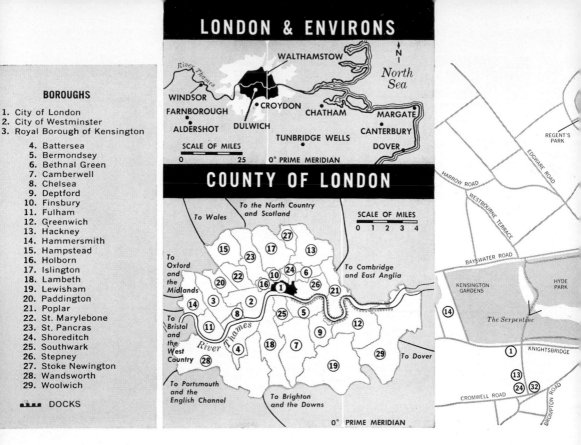

BOROUGHS

1. City of London
2. City of Westminster
3. Royal Borough of Kensington

4. Battersea
5. Bermondsey
6. Bethnal Green
7. Camberwell
8. Chelsea
9. Deptford
10. Finsbury
11. Fulham
12. Greenwich
13. Hackney
14. Hammersmith
15. Hampstead
16. Holborn
17. Islington
18. Lambeth
19. Lewisham
20. Paddington
21. Poplar
22. St. Marylebone
23. St. Pancras
24. Shoreditch
25. Southwark
26. Stepney
27. Stoke Newington
28. Wandsworth
29. Woolwich

ᴸᴸᴸᴸ DOCKS

born within sound of Bow Church bells, in the City of London. On a clear summer night this means a radius of four miles from the center of the City.

The London climate is damp and capricious. The mean summer temperature is 64° F., the winter 38°. The vapors from the river and the marshes on the east, mixed with the smoke of open fires, of which the Londoner is fond, help to produce the famous London fogs when it is hard to see a yard ahead. They are less frequent today as smoke prevention is compulsory in factories, and various smoke-free zones are being established. Showers are frequent. The annual rainfall is about thirty inches. However, the sudden changes from rain to sunshine favor the growth of flowers, even in the City. The damp accounts for the smooth park lawns and the gardens that flourish all over the county area.

Save for the cockney, most Londoners are countrymen at heart. The Londoner is anxious for a garden of his own. Where he can have no garden he makes the most of his back yard, and if there is no yard he shows his love of flowers in his window box. There are said to be more flowers in London than in any other capital, and there is scarcely a street that cannot boast a tree, most often a plane.

Reluctant to admit himself a townsman, the Londoner compensates for the crowded offices and factories in which he spends his working hours by a love of privacy in his leisure time. He so much treasures his own privacy that he hesitates to violate the privacy of others. This has its drawbacks. People in London can be very lonely. Nevertheless, the Londoner's reputation for aloofness is undeserved. Once strangers break the ice, he melts very quickly. Stress on tradition has also given the Londoner a name for snobbery. His critics say he dearly loves a lord. But equally he loves a laborer whose family has lived a century or more within his borough.

Waterloo Bridge view

London was never planned. Attempts to regulate its growth have been made repeatedly since 1610. They have always

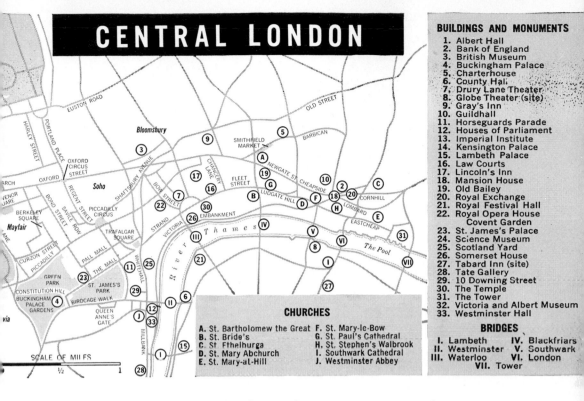

CENTRAL LONDON

failed. So the general aspect of the place is disappointing. In all the London area, which sprawls for twenty miles, there is not one imposing avenue. The closest thing to it is the Victoria Embankment, along Thameside. The finest view London offers is from Waterloo Bridge. There London's magnificence is concentrated. The Thames mirrors the towering blocks of office buildings lining its banks, the dome of St. Paul's Cathedral and the spires of Westminster Abbey, the eighteenth-century façade of Somerset House, the nineteenth-century Gothic of the Houses of Parliament.

London has certain focal points where her main traffic arteries, which mostly run east-west, converge. Cornhill, in the City, is the business center. Piccadilly Circus, in Westminster, is the center of theater and night life. Trafalgar Square, graced by the Nelson Column and at yuletide by a gigantic Christmas tree, is the common meeting place for gatherings and demonstrations.

Though London has no fine thoroughfares, it has a multitude of small and gracious streets, squares and terraces, many unaltered since the early 1700's. Some are even older. Lincoln's Inn, Holborn, is a composite dating from 1530; New Square, adjoining it, from 1689; Queen Anne's Gate, St. James's, from 1714; and Great James Street, Holborn, from 1720. Cheyne Walk, in Chelsea, Church Row, in Hampstead, and Bedford Square, in Holborn, are unspoiled examples of eighteenth-century brick architecture. Individual buildings of even greater antiquity, such as Staple Inn, in Holborn, and the Charterhouse, in the City, stand isolated among large office blocks of the 1950's.

The square-mile City

The City of London covers one square mile. It has only five thousand residents and five private residences. Yet every day a half million office workers converge upon this central business area. This does not ease the London traffic problem which seemingly defies solution.

The City is the nucleus of London, which first appeared in history in A.D. 61. A brave Queen of the Britons, Boadicea

70 **TRAFALGAR SQUARE** and the Nelson Column. Behind it is the National Gallery. Church spire at right is that of St. Martin-in-the-Fields.

ST. PAUL'S, London's treasured cathedral designed by Wren. World War II
bombs flattened the area around it, leaving the superb edifice open to view.

(properly Boudicca), sacked what seems to have been a Roman fort on the site. She took poison rather than yield to the invaders. Her statue stands by the river in Westminster. Nothing remains of this first London save its name, from *Londinos,* an ancient Celtic word meaning "fierce," which the Romans latinized to *Londinium.*

London was turned into a walled city by the Roman Emperor Hadrian in A.D. 120. The Romans also built the first bridge across the Thames. Part of the wall, uncovered by the bombings in World War II, survives in London Wall, a busy City thoroughfare. Other relics of the Roman occupation have been uncovered through the centuries. Most notable are a fine head of Mithras, set up in the Royal Exchange, and a Roman galley preserved by Thames mud. Upon the highest hill within the Roman city there stood a temple to the goddess Venus. From the same site, St. Paul's Cathedral dominates the City today.

Most of the ancient city has been destroyed in two great fires. One was the Great Fire of 1666, after which much of the City was rebuilt. Most famous of the architects of this period is Sir Chrisopher Wren (1632–1723), who skillfully adapted the style of the late Italian Renaissance —baroque—to London. The old St. Paul's was razed in the 1666 fire, and the present structure, a marvel of baroque, is Wren's work. Admiral Nelson and the Duke of Wellington are buried there.

The second holocaust was the result of a rain of incendiary bombs that fell in December 1940. This time St. Paul's was spared. Londoners felt that its preservation among a waste of ruins was an act of Providence. But Providence helps those who help themselves. In December 1940 St. Paul's had its private corps of volunteer fire watchers, headed by the Dean, who pounced on the bombs and quickly put them out. The fire had one fortunate result. Until then St. Paul's had been hidden in a warren of office buildings, and the fire disclosed the structure in its full glory. It remains open to view.

Other City churches were less fortunate. Of those that survived, wholly or in part, among the most interesting are:

TENNIS COURTS at Wimbledon (on London's outskirts), scene of world championship matches.

A RIGHT ROYAL GAME outside Buckingham Palace. The children are playing cricket—as enthralling to them as baseball is to their American cousins.

St. Bartholomew the Great, by Smithfield Market, which was raised by Rahere, court jester to Henry I, in 1123; and fifteenth-century St. Ethelburga, Bishopsgate, the smallest City church. Wren's surviving churches include St. Mary at Hill, Bishopsgate; St. Mary Abchurch, in Cannon Street (with Grinling Gibbons's altarpiece and painted dome); St. Bride's, in Fleet Street; and St. Stephen's, at Walbrook, held to be Wren's masterpiece.

The civic buildings of the City fared no better than its churches. Of thirty-four halls belonging to the City, or livery, companies—originally guilds, whose members elect the lord mayor—three only were undamaged: the Ironmongers Hall, destroyed in 1917 and rebuilt in 1925; the Vintners, in Upper Thames Street; and the Stationers, on Dowgate Hill. The medieval Guildhall, the "town hall" of the City, in King Street, was damaged but has been skillfully restored.

Other outstanding City structures include Mansion House, official residence of the lord mayor, little altered since it was built in 1742; and, facing Cornhill, the Bank of England, designed by Sir John Soane in 1778, and the Royal Exchange. Among the City courts and narrow alleys stand delightful old-time houses, many of them once inns.

Just east of the City stands the Tower of London. It was once a Roman fortress. Within the battlemented walls of the Tower there are several tower struc-

tures, erected between the eleventh and fifteenth centuries. Today the Tower is at once a barracks, a state prison and a microcosm embodying in stone a thousand years of English history. The keep, or White Tower, dates from the time of William the Conqueror. In the Wakefield Tower, dating from 1354, the crown jewels are kept. Elsewhere there is a valuable museum of armor, and until 1828 the Tower could boast a zoo, the only one in England. The lions at the Tower were for eight centuries the greatest of all London marvels.

Most famous of the prisoners who died within the Tower walls were King Henry VI, in 1471; the two young Princes, Edward and Richard, for whose death in

QUEEN ELIZABETH awards a prized cup to the captain of a winning soccer team.

BUCKINGHAM PALACE, home of the British sovereign. It faces an ornate memorial to Queen Victoria. There The Mall begins, which leads to Trafalgar Square.

HENRY VIII steps out of the past, part of a group in Madame Tussaud's famous waxwork museum.

POMP AND CIRCUMSTANCE—one of the royal landaus in which the monarch rides on ceremonial occasions. Red-coated footmen and handsome horses add to the spectacle.

MAJOR DONALD D. JULIN

FPG

WESTMINSTER ABBEY, witness to a thousand years of English history. The oldest part dates from the eleventh century, the main Gothic structure from the 1200's.

1483 their uncle, Richard III, is usually blamed, perhaps unjustly; Anne Boleyn, the second wife of Henry VIII, in 1536; and Sir Walter Raleigh, in 1618. Their dungeons are still shown. Karl Lody, a German spy, was the last person to be executed in the Tower, in 1915.

Prisoners were brought by water, down the Thames, to the Traitor's Gate. The barge passed beneath the gate, then the portcullis fell and very few came out again. Only one prisoner ever escaped, Lord Nithsdale, in 1746, a leader in the last attempt to restore the Stuarts to the throne. He passed the sentries undetected, dressed as a woman in clothes that had been smuggled in to him.

The Tower remains a barracks for the Foot Guards and the Royal Fusiliers. It is not an envied station in the British Army. At night the place seems to brood under the weight of unhappy memories and has an eerie atmosphere. By day, however, the Tower is thronged with visitors who come to see the gabled houses facing Tower Green, the giant ravens and the uniforms of the Yeomen warders.

«

A STATUE of Peter Pan, Sir James Barrie's immortal character, entrances young visitors to Kensington Gardens.

Their full dress, worn only on state occasions, is similar to that of the Yeomen of the Guard, who are on duty at St. James's Palace. The handsome uniform is of scarlet cloth heavily laced with gold. It has changed hardly at all since Henry VII founded the Yeomen. They carry halberds and are the royalist counterpart of the City's Honorable Artillery troop of Pikemen.

Across the Thames, on the southern (Surrey) side of London Bridge, is Southwark. Of all the London boroughs this is the most ancient and is still known simply as the Borough. At one time it was the haunt of rogues and vagabonds. The Tabard Inn, a meeting place for pilgrims bound for Canterbury, is mentioned by Geoffrey Chaucer in his *Canterbury Tales*. A modern building occupies the site of the inn and keeps the ancient name. In Trinity Square stands London's oldest statue, of Alfred the Great, dating from 1399. The George Inn, in Borough High Street, is London's one surviving coach and posting house, a timbered building with open galleries around the yard. Only one side remains.

There in Southwark, on Bankside (the south bank of the Thames), stood the Globe Theater and the Rose, its rival. In these oval wooden houses the plays of Shakespeare, Marlowe and other Elizabethan writers were first performed. Shakespeare acted in his own plays—one role was as the Ghost in *Hamlet*—and in his leaner years minded the horses of wealthy playgoers. Something lingers of the Elizabethan raffishness today. In Southwark and in Lambeth, west of it, the cockney congregates. He plies his barrow with his donkey. On holidays he drives out in his donkey cart, his suit and cap completely covered with mother-of-pearl buttons, his wife beside him decked in ostrich feathers. Cockney slang, purposely incomprehensible to strangers, is still spoken. These last vestiges of London's past are dying out, however, as modern housing blocks replace the narrow alleys and courts, and wider education destroys cockney speech.

The city of Westminster developed around Westminster Abbey and the court. It was the stronghold of the monarchy. The Palace of Westminster was the residence of English kings and queens from the eleventh century until the early 1500's. Little remains of it except the banquet hall (Westminster Hall) of Norman times. It is noted for its roof of hammer beams. Charles I was tried in the palace and there condemned to death. The court, a rump Parliament, was probably irregular. "Two things alone be certain," one of his friends remarked. "No court can try the King and this court can try no one."

Generally today the Palace of Westminster refers to the Houses of Parliament, which adjoin the Norman hall. The House of Commons and the House of Lords are joined by a great lobby. The Gothic-revival building is long and lofty and covers 8 acres of land beside the Thames. It has 11 quadrangles, 100 staircases, a river frontage of 900 feet, and 3 tall towers, of which the best known is the Clock Tower. It is 320 feet high and the clock is 20 feet across. Called Big Ben, after Sir Benjamin Hall, who designed it in 1858, the clock is London's best-known landmark. A small light burning in the tower shows that Parliament is in session.

Westminster Abbey

Facing Parliament across the road is Westminster Abbey, the hallowed shrine of England. Started about 1050 by the last Saxon king, Edward the Confessor, it was not finished until 1745 when Nicholas Hawksmoor completed its famous twin towers in the Gothic style. There almost every king and queen of England has been crowned, from William I (1066) to Elizabeth II (1953). Most English sovereigns and many notables are buried there. The Abbey architecture is predominantly Gothic, the richest part being Henry VII's Chapel. West of the Abbey, the Cloisters are perhaps the most beautiful of all the London monuments. The

AT DAWN only a swan ruffles Kensington Gardens' Serpentine. Later, boats will crowd it.

Chapter House was the assembly place of the first English Parliaments.

Westminster has many other noteworthy buildings: St. James's Palace; Buckingham Palace, the reigning monarch's residence; the various ministries; the residence, 10 Downing Street, of the prime ministers since 1731. The Horse Guards, headquarters of the London (military) Command, is guarded by sentries of the Household Cavalry.

Perhaps the most thought-provoking structure of all, and surely the most ugly, is the concrete fortress, mercifully covered with ivy, on the Horse Guards Parade. It was run up in 1940, after the fall of France, and there it was assumed that King George VI and his chief ministers would make a last-ditch stand against invading Nazis. Whether it would have worked that way is uncertain. But in that "finest hour," when London was the last fighting capital of a free Europe, King George and his Prime Minister, Winston Churchill, stayed in the heart of Westminster, both armed with Sten guns. The daily sight of Britain's royal standard floating high above the palace, which was badly bombed, the King escaping almost by a miracle, inspired the capital to hold when Britain's cause looked hopeless.

In Holborn, immediately north of West-

THE CENTER SPAN of Tower Bridge lifts to allow a ship to pass down the Thames River. Though the structure looks medieval, it was built between 1886 and 1894.

WHERE JUSTICE REIGNS—the imposing Law Courts. They face The Strand. Just beyond the courts The Strand becomes Fleet Street, newspaper-publishing center.

WESTMINSTER BRIDGE and the Houses of Parliament. Big Ben booms from
the Clock Tower. The bell's voice has rarely been stilled since it began to mark
the hours in 1859. Mellow chimes ring out just before the hour strikes.

OVER THIS COUNTER passed the first pound of tea to be sold in the City of London, in 1657. The store still handles a thriving business.

minster, are, in part, what remain of the Inns of Court—four separate areas, each with its gardens, library, hall, common room and, until 1940, chapel. These Inns have for five centuries been colleges where law students and members of the English bar meet for lectures, dinners, debates, mock trials and other solemn or convivial occasions. To practice at the English bar a man or woman must be "called" by the Bench, the self-perpetuating governing body of one of these Inns. The four are Gray's Inn, on the site of the fourteenth-century town house of the Lords Grey de Wilton; Lincoln's Inn, where the bishops of Lincoln had their London residence; the Inner Temple, that is, within the City limits; and the Middle Temple, part in the City. The temples were once a commandery of the Knights Templars. At Temple Bar (Fleet Street), the entrance to the City is marked by a griffin.

All except Lincoln's Inn were largely destroyed in 1939–45. They have been reconstructed since behind replicas of the old fronts but now afford elevators and central heating. The medieval Church of the Knights Templars, one of four round churches in England, has survived with its choir built in 1240. So too has Middle Temple Hall where Queen Elizabeth I saw the first production of Shakespeare's *Twelfth Night*.

Of Gray's Inn there is only a remnant of the ancient structure, chiefly the seventeenth-century gate. Though the hall was gutted, the old inner walls have been restored, and the stained-glass windows and the minstrels' gallery, which were saved, have been put back.

Also in Holborn is the vast gray pile of the British Museum and a good part of the Bloomsbury district, made famous by the group of intellectuals that included Virginia Woolf.

Chelsea, immediately west of Westminster, is still a charming riverside borough, well known for its sixteenth-century Physick Garden, the Royal Hospital for veterans, designed by Wren, and the former Duke of York's School, now headquarters of the London Territorial (militia) Garrison. This borough always was a favorite with artists and writers. Sir Thomas More, Jonathan Swift, Smollett, Carlyle, Meredith, Swinburne, Turner, Whistler, Oscar Wilde and Henry James all made their homes there. Charles Dickens was married in its parish church, St. Luke's, in 1824.

Lambeth, cockney borough

Lambeth, a working-class borough teeming with racy London characters, faces Westminster from the south bank of the Thames. Lambeth Walk is a favorite cockney shopping center. Close by stands Waterloo Station, the best-equipped, most modern railroad station London boasts; the Royal Festival Hall, center of London musical life, set in gardens running to the riverbank; and Lambeth Palace, official residence of the archbishop of Canterbury.

Greenwich, downstream from the City, once famous for fish dinners at the Ship Inn, preserves the salty character of the great days of sail. Its park of 912 acres was topped by the seventeenth-century Observatory until 1948. The Royal Naval

College is on the site of the old palace where Elizabeth I was born.

London is rich in open spaces, all tended with care. The royal parks on the west—St. James's (92 acres) and the adjoining Green (53 acres)—are gay with flowers and center around a pond frequented by exotic ducks and pelicans descended from birds brought by Charles II.

Hyde Park and Kensington Gardens form a continuous whole of some 600 acres. The boating and bathing lake, the Serpentine; the dell with owls and rabbits; Kensington Palace with its orangery and formal seventeenth-century garden—all give Londoners a satisfying illusion of being in the country. At the Speaker's Corner by the Marble Arch, at the northeast entrance, every conceivable opinion on every imaginable topic, including both theology and politics, is aired publicly every Sunday afternoon.

Regent's Park (472 acres) is perhaps the most countrylike. The inner circle of the park displays one of the most extensive rose gardens in the world.

Below Tower Bridge begins the Pool, where ocean-going ships can anchor. The Pool stretches on to London Port (which covers 4,000 acres, 670 of them water) and includes five separate docks, which handle 50,000,000 tons of shipping a year. Heavily bombed in 1940 the dock area lost with its crowded squalor much of its fascinating cosmopolitan character. The little area of Chinatown (Limehouse) was utterly obliterated.

London's most dubious quarter is Soho, an area of eighteenth-century houses, small foreign restaurants, and night clubs, encroaching on the theater district around Piccadilly Circus. Soho has an attractive, Bohemian aspect, most so at night.

The leveling tendencies of the war years have evened out the once distinctive grace of Mayfair and Park Lane, today largely given over to business blocks. Bond Street still has its enticing shops. St. James's Parish, which includes Pall Mall and St. James's Street, is well known for its clubs and smart shops for men (tailors on Savile Row).

As one might expect of such a great city, London has educational institutions of a high order. The University of London is grouped in Holborn and South Kensington. Unlike Oxford and Cambridge, London University is mostly nonresidential. In Holborn stands the Senate House, the London School of Economics, University College, and the School of African and Oriental Languages, with London House, where students from the Commonwealth reside. King's College (the Strand), housed in a wing of Somerset House, offers courses in the arts and sciences. The Royal Colleges of Art and Music are both in South Kensington.

Many learned societies enrich the intellectual and cultural life of London. The Royal Society, the Royal Geographical, the Royal Institution of Great Britain, the Royal Institute of International Affairs, and the Zoological Society—complete with its own comprehensive zoo and aquarium—are perhaps most notable.

To explain London's government, we

QUEUES are an everyday part of London life. Stools help a long wait.

AN UMBRELLA, rain or shine, and a Homburg or bowler (derby) mark the City of London man.

TOTING CAMERAS, the photographers walk Fleet Street toward their newspaper office.

DALE WHITNEY

A PALACE GUARDSMAN, un-
aware, excites admiring imitation.

The variety of
London faces

A VENDOR of birds, in the
East End, gives a sales talk.

THE STAMP of character and intelligence
—Lord Chief Justice Goddard, in his wig.

THE MUSTACHE is
cultivated with pride.

BEARING a carcass—a merry porter
in Smithfield Market.

HENRI CARTIER-BRESSON, MAGNUM

BRITISH LION and British sailors on shore leave, in Trafalgar Square.

A SENTINEL stands watch amid the statuary adorning Buckingham Palace.

AT HYDE PARK a Sunday-afternoon orator harangues a tolerant crowd.

must return to the City. It grew up as a mercantile community, extremely jealous of its privileges against the royal power. Throughout the struggle with the monarchy, which reached a climax in the Civil War, 1642–52, the City's main defense lay in its own militia, the train (trained) bands formed of spirited young apprentices who fought for Parliament against King Charles I. They were the best-trained troops in England. Against the military dictatorship (1653–58) of Oliver Cromwell the train bands were as vigorous as they had been against Charles I. They welcomed King Charles II in 1660 with joy. Their present-day descendant is the City regiment, the Honorable Artillery Company, formerly the Guild of Archers of St. George, a corps of volunteers. In both world wars this company (artillery and infantry) fulfilled its ancient purpose, of training officers, and also fought in France in 1914 and in North Africa in 1942. The members form a Guard of Pikemen, in the uniform of Civil War days, which marches in the lord mayor's procession on November 9.

Since medieval times, when its merchants and guilds were growing powerful, the City has had a unique system of government. It is not under the London County Council but the Corporation of the City. This body elects, for one year, the lord mayor, the City's chief magistrate. The City also has its own police, who wear a distinctive uniform.

London, outside the City but including Westminster, is administered by the London County Council, elected every three years. There is no mayor of London as a whole, only the chairman of the council. Each borough, however, has a mayor besides a Borough Council, town hall, and library. The Metropolitan Police are responsible to the home secretary of the British Government. The police commissioner's office is at Scotland Yard, in Westminster. (Police do not carry arms in London.)

Many other aspects of London are no less inconsistent than its government, making for charming incongruities. In one street there is neon lighting, in another gaslight. Plate-glass show windows gleam beside hand-rolled glass panes, a fifteenth-century tower is neighbor to a twentieth-century block of steel and concrete. The cockney's donkey and the brewer's dray horse thread their way among rushing high-powered cars and towering buses, while overhead a jet plane roars its way to an airport.

The Left Wing council of a Labor borough (St. Pancras) runs up the Red flag on May 1 but hoists the Union Jack beside it. The judges of the High Court still wear seventeenth-century full-bottomed wigs and scarlet robes; the Household Cavalry (Life Guards in scarlet, Horse Guards in blue), wearing breastplates, ride mounted through traffic to the Changing of the Guard at Whitehall. Labor Party mayors wear crimson robes and golden chains of office.

All this is not for show. The man who dons ancient robes or a traditional uniform does so with a sense of responsibility and feels a strange compulsion to be worthy of these symbols. His fellow Londoners are well aware of this. The sight of the traditional costumes comes as reassurance of integrity and continuity.

A thousand sights and sounds endear London to its inhabitants as though it were a sleepy country village. On gold October evenings, flocks of starlings gather round the spire of St. Martin's in the Fields, in Trafalgar Square. The call of screech owls echoes though Holborn's office blocks on summer nights. The yellow lamplit back streets are silent save for the hand-rung bell of muffin sellers. The mile-long traffic jam around Cornhill, the queues at tubes (subways) and bus stops in the rush hour, the moments snatched away to sprawl upon a deck chair with a book among the roses in Regent's Park, where London's traffic roar is barely heard—all form the composite of London.

Aptly did a fond Londoner—his name was Dr. Samuel Johnson—say in 1777, "When a man is tired of London he is tired of life, for there is in London all that life can afford."

By George Edinger

Wales
...land of song

On an outline map of Britain, Wales looks like an afterthought of nature, an undistinguished hump about 140 miles long by 100 miles wide, tacked on to the Atlantic coast. But on a relief map it appears as a geographical unit in its own right. From its craggy mountain core the peninsulas of Lleyn, in the north, and Pembrokeshire, in the south, push out to grasp a great sweep of the Irish Sea in Cardigan Bay.

The geographical center of Wales lies somewhere along the bay coast where the boggy hills of Cardiganshire roll back from the sea. But the true heart of Wales lies to the north, in the mountains of Snowdonia, at the base of the Lleyn Peninsula. There the five peaks of Snowdon tower over three thousand feet above the sea, not an impressive figure perhaps but an impressive sight. For the grinding of ancient glaciers has carved steep-sided valleys and sharp-edged ridges to give a tremendously rugged landscape. Chill lakes lie in some valley floors, locked in for eons by the encircling crags.

Here the Welsh made their last stand against English conquest six hundred years ago, after many centuries of defiance. The view from the summit of Snowdon shows why the struggle lasted so long. The area is defended first by a belt of rounded uplands, some two thousand feet above sea level, which extends from the Harlech dome to the south through the Berwyn Mountains to the Hiraethog moorlands to the east. The second line of defense is the rampart of moorland extending from Denbighshire, about thirty miles to the east of Snowdonia, to Pembrokeshire, some seventy miles to the south. On a clear day you might be able to make out the bastions of South Wales: Radnor Forest, Brecon Beacons and, beyond, the Black Mountains.

Though lofty this southern massif is more accessible than the northern one by reason of the many valleys leading down to the lowlands flanking the River Severn and to the coastal plain of the south. Consequently South Wales has always been more open to English influence and to industrial development. Today the South holds the bulk of the population in the ports and industrial cities of the coast, like Swansea and Cardiff, and in the mining towns of the Rhondda Valley area. Though these communities are intensely Welsh and faithful to the Methodist

85

ALARM FIRES once blazed from these two Brecon Beacons, known as "Arthur's Chair," to give warning of invasions.

Church, which has become so much their own, the people as a whole must still seek inspiration in the northern mountains, which safeguarded their culture and language for so long.

The border with England runs down the edge of the uplands but it is a little vague. Monmouthshire, officially in England, is usually considered part of Wales. This is an echo of the old medieval border, the Marches, a broad boundary with its own law, part Welsh and part English. Insulated by the Marches the Welsh have always turned toward the sea.

Today Milford Haven is a great oil port. It is the latest link in a chain of maritime tradition reaching back to Madoc, the legendary figure said to have discovered America before the Norsemen. Another link, the Welsh buccaneer Henry Morgan, is associated with the settlement of Jamaica, in the West Indies.

Lying off the northwest shore of Wales is the island of Anglesey. It forms a county of 276 square miles and is joined to the mainland by two bridges. One is a tubular railway span, built by Stephenson in 1850. The other is the beautiful Menai Suspension Bridge, constructed by Telford in 1826. For many years it was customary to pay a toll when crossing the latter bridge. A certain sum was exacted for a cart and an appropriately smaller amount for a pedestrian or a sheep or a cow. This custom was dropped in 1941, though there are still a few bridges in Wales for whose use tolls are asked.

When William the Conqueror set foot on England in 1066, it took him some time to subdue the whole country. To each of the friends who served him best, he gave a certain portion of land. Thereupon the Norman lord built a castle or fortress to keep the troublesome natives in order. The border country between Wales and England (the Marches) was particularly turbulent; and all along this line today can be seen the remains of the castles of the Marcher lords. Fortresses were erected at strategic points, on a commanding height or at the ford of a river. Once-impregnable Caerphilly, with its leaning tower, is every child's ideal of a heroic battlement. Caernarvon, not far from Mount Snowdon, is still a noble structure. Here the first Prince of Wales, an infant "who spoke no English," was presented by his father, Edward I, to the Welsh chieftains. Thus the conquest of Wales was completed in 1301. Romantic, turreted Conway, overlooking a sandy estuary and with a medieval-looking bridge, has an irresistible suggestion of the poetic days of chivalry. Unbelievable Harlech, towering on its crag, calls to mind the most tragic of Welsh legendary figures, Branwen, the princess whose voyage to Ireland as a bride ended in ill treatment and shame. The little bird that brought her sad message back across the Irish Sea to her kinfolk in Britain was the harbinger of revenge and of a great slaughter of the warriors of both kingdoms. In its essentials, Branwen's story is a Celtic equivalent of that of Helen of Troy.

Legends and Poetry

Like Greece, Wales is rich in legend. Though the word "Mabinogion" is little known outside Celtic and scholarly circles, everybody has heard of the tales of King Arthur and the Round Table. These stories are to be found in old Welsh manuscripts, from which modern scholars have produced such volumes as *The Red Book of Hergest*. The legends were told a thousand years or so ago by wandering minstrels at the courts of Welsh chieftains. Gradually they worked their way into the broader stream of European literature. Malory retold them in English in his *Morte d'Arthur* and centuries later Tennyson drew upon these sources for his *Idylls of the King*. Scholars are agreed today that the idea of chivalry and the figure of the knight-errant have their origin in this little Celtic country.

One of the earliest Welsh poets is said to have prophesied of his people:

Their God they shall praise;
Their tongue they shall keep;
Their land they shall lose,
Except wild Wales.

It is curious how that prophecy has held

A BEVY OF GIRLS on a road near Llanberis, North Wales, wearing steeple hats over frilled caps. The headgear is part of the national costume, rarely seen now except on fete days.

good. The Welsh are to this day a religious-minded people with a strong mystic element. Some have clung tenaciously to their language in spite of its suppression and of its uselessness for trade. Though once they possessed the whole of the British Isles (as such place names as Dover—Welsh *Dwr,* water—and Medway—*way* in Medway comes from the Welsh *wy,* a river—prove), they were never dislodged from their mountain fastnesses in the west.

We know that in ancient times the Celts were to be found in many parts of Europe. When the Romans came to Britain, they found a Celtic culture there. Julius Caesar was the only contemporary reporter to describe the rituals of the druids. This he did in his *Gallic Wars,* as many a schoolboy can affirm. Anglesey, where the druids made the last stand for their religion, has been inhabited since prehistoric times. Proofs of this are to be found not in books but in the soil of the county that the Romans called "the granary." In 1943 a number of Celtic bronze and iron weapons, implements and personal adornments of great style and beauty were unearthed near Holyhead.

Regarded as the most important finds of pre-Roman antiquities yet made in any part of Britain, they can now be examined in the National Museum of Wales at Cardiff.

The Roman conquest of south Britain and Wales was for some time successfully opposed by Caractacus, son of Cymbeline. In A.D. 78, however, Wales was overcome. Communications were opened up by the construction of military roads from Chester to Conway in the north, linking up the Roman settlements of Caerleon and Caerwent with other centers in the south. Roman pavements and traces of villas can still be seen, and so can many of the roads. Latin words such as *porta* (gate or door) and *fenestra* (window) filtered into the Welsh language, as the Celts adopted from their conquerors both new objects or devices and the Latin names for them.

Christianity was introduced during the Roman occupation, in the fourth century. After the withdrawal of the Roman garrison, the faith was kept alive and carried to the Hebrides and the northernmost islands by Celtic missionaries. So when St. Augustine landed, probably in A.D.

STRANGE PARTNERS—a frowning medieval fortress and a railroad bridge. Conway Castle, built in the thirteenth century, is a mile in circumference and is girdled with twenty-one round

595, there was already a native British church in existence.

In the fifth century, the Saxons and other northern European tribes invaded the shores of Britain. After a long struggle, they drove the natives westward and northward into the mountains. The Celts were pushed into Cornwall, Cumberland, southwest Scotland, and Wales, and were renamed by the invaders *Waelisc,* or Welsh. Ironically enough, the meaning of that Anglo-Saxon word is "foreigner." And yet there was a certain element of accuracy in the description, for even to this day the Welsh have retained a distinct nationality. It is this foreign quality that adds interest to a visit to Wales, even for the neighboring Englishman.

Nowhere is the Welsh distinctiveness more clearly seen than in the way the people amuse themselves. A Welshman enjoys a few things above all others: singing, poetry, talk, preaching and rugby football. All are arts that give full scope to the individual, and thus make a strong appeal to the Welsh character. Also, they are, generally speaking, arts that a poor man can follow. Wales has never been a rich country. Its people have been mainly of the peasant type; and the pastimes that have been cultivated are ones that do not depend on material riches. So you will find in Wales no tradition of theater or opera or of instrumental music. All these require patrons and wealth for their support.

Welsh singing is famous the world over, so that Wales has earned the name

towers. The wrought-iron span belongs to the early days of railway bridge building.

of the Land of Song. Welsh poetry is of a technical complexity far beyond that of English; and Welsh preaching has touched off great revivals. The printed sermons of the "eight-inch nails" (as the great preachers of the past were called) have with their power and cadences shaken readers in their study chairs today. The dramatic sense of the Welshman, which is very strong, has, in default of a theater, burst through into the pulpits.

In this present century, Wales has nevertheless contributed directly to the theater, in the persons of such actors as Gwen Ffrancgon Davies, Dame Edith Evans, Richard Burton, such playwrights as Emlyn Williams and such composers as Ivor Novello. Among the Welsh

poets of our day are W. H. Davies, the "tramp poet," and Dylan Thomas, who died in New York in 1954. Both of these wrote in English. There are many more poets whose main work is in the Welsh tongue—Williams Parry and Parry Williams, W. J. Gruffydd, Crwys and Gwili. Wales's greatest orator in the twentieth century was the incomparable Lloyd George. His magnificent language and melodious voice could charm a bird off a tree. Every year he held an audience of thousands spellbound during his speech on the Chairing Day at the National Eisteddfod, the climax of the festival.

Eisteddfods Big and Little

The Welsh Eisteddfod is a competitive festival of literature and music. It is unique, and it may well prove in its latest form, the International Eisteddfod, the greatest single contribution this little country has to offer the family of nations. Every village has its Eisteddfod, at which the competitors are weeded out for the National. The National is a wandering jamboree—that is, one year it is held in North Wales, and the next year in South Wales, always during the first week of August.

In its present form, the festival dates back to the last decades of the 1800's. However, the custom of holding a competition in music and letters has been current in Wales for centuries. The picturesque ceremonies of the Crowning and the Chairing of the Bard and the ritual of the Gorsedd Circle do not, as some imagine, derive from the druids of antiquity. Nevertheless they are a colorful form of pageantry and add something to the enjoyment of the Eisteddfod.

Llangollen, Festival Host

The International Eisteddfod is held in the same place every year—the small town of Llangollen in North Wales. It was founded in 1947, and the attendance in a recent year was 143,000. Among the winners was the Yale Glee Club, which competed against eighteen male choirs from England, Wales, Spain, Norway and Germany. Overseas visitors are

89

DRILLING FOR A BLAST, in one of the numerous slate quarries near Mount Snowdon.

coming in increasing numbers to see young people from all over Europe and sometimes from America competing against each other in folk dancing, singing and choral work.

Nationalism was the spring that set the older Eisteddfod in motion. The newer version has internationalism as its driving force, and it is catching on in a remarkable way. The sense of fellowship is demonstrated when a spontaneous collection of £100 is taken up for a competitor who had sold his piano to raise enough money to make the journey to Llangollen.

The word *eisteddfod* must cause trouble to all the non-Welsh who try to pronounce it. The sound *dd* is approximately that of English *th* in "think," but the only accurate equivalent to the sound is found in Arabic. Many Welsh place names begin with *llan,* and the meaning of the word is "church." Thus Llangollen is the "church of Collen"; Llanfair is the "church of Mary"; Llantrisant is the "church of the three saints."

As one travels through Wales it is fascinating to work out the meaning of

LLANDUDNO, a charming resort on Colwyn Bay, an arm of the Irish Sea. There are fine beaches and a half-mile-long pier for strolling. A side-wheeler is docked at the end.

CAERNARVON CASTLE RUINS provide a dramatic backdrop for an Eisteddfod. Participants wear the costume of the ancient Druids, who originated the festivals revived in modern times.

the different place names. A very slight knowledge of Welsh often yields the necessary clues. *Aber* (mouth of) is often followed by the name of a river, as in Abertawe—mouth of the Tawe; Aberbach—little estuary. *Caer* is the Welsh word for a fortress and, as might be expected, occurs pretty frequently, with a word tacked on at the end that adds to the meaning; for example, Caerfyrddin (Carmarthen)—the fort of Merlin. The old magician of King Arthur is said to have founded Caerfyrddin, and a fragment of a tree said to have been Merlin's is still preserved in one of the streets. *Pont* (bridge) occurs frequently in place names and so does *rhyd* (a ford).

The Welsh Tongue Still Heard

The language spoken in Wales is mainly English, though about 30 per cent of the inhabitants can also speak the Welsh tongue. In rural areas there are a few persons who still speak only Welsh.

It is supposed to be very difficult for a stranger to learn. Yet children sent to Wales during World War II learned it with some success. Its pronunciation, which is phonetic, presents no difficulties. But its grammar is somewhat complex, and the variations at the beginnings of words are obstacles to those who do not speak it regularly.

An example of this is the word for mother, which is *mam*. "Her mother" is *ei mam;* "his mother" is *ei fam;* "their mother" is *eu mham*. Thus the word *mam* changes three times according to the word placed in front of it. Many scientific and technical words, as in modern Hebrew, have to be invented. Thus, for instance, when television reached Wales, there were numerous names suggested for it, such as *teledu, radio-olwg, radio-lygad* and (by the frivolous) *teli-weli*. It appears that *teledu* has been accepted, both as noun and verb.

Though television came to Wales some years later than to the Midlands and north of England (and many years later than to London), this was not because the principality lagged behind in technical matters. It was simply that Wales is farther from London, where the first TV transmitter was built in the British Isles, and because reception was difficult due to the mountainous nature of much of the country, which set up a barrier.

Women in Industry

The greater proportion of the population of Wales is engaged in industry. The rural and coastal areas have their tourist trade, but by far the greater part of the earnings of the Welsh come from heavy industry and from factory work. One significant change since the 1930's has been the increasing employment of women in industry. Around 1850 women had worked in mines and steel mills. With the approach of more enlightened ideas, however, both women and young children were spared heavy and unsuitable labor of this kind. So, almost until the second World War broke out, the Welshwoman was usually found at home or, at most, in a schoolroom or an office. Then, as man power became scarce due to the demands of the conflict, women's contribution to industry became increasingly vital. New factories were built, into which women and young girls were absorbed in considerable numbers. Here they worked on armament production—turning out important equipment ranging from switchgear to heavy guns.

Light Industry Fills a Need

In the years between the two world wars, many new light industries were established in Wales. Their aim was to absorb the army of unemployed laborers and also men who had become incapable of working in heavy industry because of industrial injuries or occupational diseases. One of the worst of these last was lung inflammation resulting from inhaling dust.

It was during this period that what is called a trading estate was established at Treforest, near Cardiff. With the cooperation of the Government, factories were put up by refugee industrialists from Germany and Czechoslovakia. In this way, new industries were introduced and the Welsh workers were taught new skills. As a result, Wales today produces, for example, watches and clocks, nylon yarn and radio sets. With a variety of light industries, the economy of Wales is becoming more stable.

In the old days, when the whole economy was geared to coal and steel, a slump in those two industries was bound to hit the greater part of the working population, all at one time. In the depression of the 1930's, for instance, there was great hardship and suffering in Wales.

Today the general level of employment is high. In a recent year, only four out of one hundred workers were idle. Though many men lost their jobs when the steel and tin-plate industries were reorganized, they soon found places in other fields.

South Wales continues to produce more than 99 per cent of the tin plate in

COCKLES TAKE MUSCLES. The arduous task of collecting the mollusks in Caermarthen Bay is women's work. After the cockles are boiled, they are easily sifted from their shells.

BRITISH INFORMATION SERVICES

SWANSEA, as seen from the air, is an intricate pattern of docks, shipyards and breakwaters. The busy port is on the Bristol Channel, not far from the open Atlantic Ocean.

the United Kingdom and more than half of its sheet steel. The men engaged in the hot-rolling mills of the Abbey Works at Margam and in the cold-reduction and tin-plate plant at Trostre have moved on into a new phase of Welsh industry. Where sweat and grime was the lot of the worker in the old tinworks, today he runs precision machinery of the most fabulously modern kind.

Coal production in a recent year was 26,600,000 tons from the South Wales coal field (48 per cent mechanically cut and 88 per cent mechanically transported) and 2,100,000 tons from the North Wales field. South Wales production included 2,900,000 tons of anthracite —"black diamonds." This Welsh "steam coal" is of incomparable quality and is in demand all over the world.

A plan for reconstruction, put forward in the 1950's, will transform the anthracite mining area of west Wales. The two main projects are the opening of pit shafts at Cynheidre, near Swansea, and at Abernant, near Neath. They will employ more than five thousand men between them, and both plants will be engaged on large-scale "horizon" mining at a depth of half a mile. This is a kind of shaft mining in which the shafts stay on a level instead of following a seam up or down. It is done where the seams incline toward the vertical. Though the formation is a common one in hilly Wales, the method had not been tried before in the anthracite district.

Other schemes for reconstruction in the coal field also aim at increased efficiency and output. It is estimated that by 1964 the same number of men will be producing 50 per cent more coal. Besides this, measures are being taken to reduce the danger to the health of the workers from dust. Estimates of the reserves of this valuable anthracite coal in several areas indicate that they are sufficient to last for more than a century.

Though most of the wealth of Wales comes from industry, the little country has been fortunate in retaining, to a remarkable degree, its rural charm and beauty. In the industrial valleys of Glamorgan and Monmouthshire and in parts of Carmarthenshire, the mountains are still untouched by the smoke and grime that heavy industry so often brings in its train.

The capital city, Cardiff, which with Swansea and Newport handles most of the overseas trade, is an exceptionally clean and elegant place. It has a civic center that reminds one of Washington, D. C. Half the population of the whole country is to be found in industrial Glamorgan; and the people of the valley towns use Cardiff as their shopping center and playground.

The largest towns are Cardiff, Swansea and Rhondda. Each of the first two has a college of the University of Wales. Other colleges of the university are at Aberystwyth and Bangor.

In the rural areas, farms are in general small by North American standards. Yet agricultural production is increasing steadily. There is more and healthier livestock, and crop yields are greater than of yore. The Welsh Plant Breeding Station at Aberystwyth has developed improved strains, particularly of grasses, which are used nowadays in many parts of the globe. In Wales, more than 65 per cent of the cattle are in attested herds— that is, they have passed tests for tuberculosis. The corresponding figure for all Great Britain is 42 per cent. The native breed of cattle, the Welsh Black, has remarkable resistance to disease, probably because it has long been used to outdoor life at mountain altitudes.

Thanks to its incomparable scenery— its beautiful mountains, lakes and rivers and its indented seacoast—Wales is becoming more and more popular as a holiday center for visitors from England and abroad. Seashore resorts and health-giving spas offer sports and other amusements. Not least among Wales's charms in this troubled world is the utter peace of its mountain tarns.

By Nest Bradney

WALES: FACTS AND FIGURES

THE COUNTRY

Forms a peninsula on the west coast of England. It is bounded on the east by England, on the south by the Bristol Channel, on the west by St. George's Channel and on the north by the Irish Sea. The total area, comprising 12 counties, is 7,466 square miles and the population is 2,597,000.

GOVERNMENT

For purposes of government, Wales is associated with England, and is subject in local administration to similar conditions. Separate organizations deal with health and education. There are 3 boroughs and 12 counties, excluding Monmouthshire which is technically part of England although often included with Wales for statistical purposes.

COMMERCE AND INDUSTRIES

Commercial and industrial activity is located chiefly in South Wales and the district around Wrexham. The shipping industry of Cardiff and Swansea and the anthracite coal deposits in South Wales are the chief sources of wealth. Slate quarries are numerous. Other minerals include limestone, iron, copper, tin and lead. A large portion of Wales is pasture and grazing land. Sheep are by far the most numerous of the world-famous livestock.

COMMUNICATIONS

The important docks at Cardiff, Barry, Port Talbot and Penarth and the railroads associated with them have been under the control of British Railways, a nationalized concern, since 1947.

RELIGION AND EDUCATION

The Church of England in Wales and Monmouthshire were disestablished in 1920 under the Welsh Church Acts of 1914 and 1919, and Wales was created a separate Archbishopric. Education is compulsory between the ages of 5 and 15 years. The University of Wales comprises the 4 colleges of Cardiff, Aberystwyth, Bangor and Swansea. The National School of Medicine is also at Cardiff.

CHIEF TOWNS, POPULATIONS

Cardiff, 253,300; Swansea, 163,300; Rhondda, 106,400; Newport, 104,200; Merthyr Tidfil, 59,300. All except Rhondda are county boroughs. Some of these towns are losing population with the decline of the coal-mining industry.

Scotland

...rugged land and proud people

THOUGH Scotland occupies the northern two fifths of Britain, it contains only about a tenth of the island's population: five million out of a total of fifty million. The bulk of that five million is concentrated in a lowland industrial area that is a mere tenth of Scotland's total. Emigration and a low birth rate have kept the population from increasing much in the last half century. By and large, Scotland remains sparsely settled and isolated.

Human communities have survived many centuries, betraying diverse origins in their dialects: the soft lilt of the Hebrides, of pure Celtic origin; the accents of the southeast, of Anglian origin; and the broader cadences of the southwest, once occupied by a Welsh people. But even without these varied ethnic backgrounds, the special demands of each area would still have produced great contrasts.

For the country is divided into four well-defined regions, distinct in appearance, economy and population. The northernmost section, comprising the counties of Caithness, Ross and Cromarty, Sutherland and half of Inverness, is in effect an island, cut off from the rest of Britain by the Great Glen: a long, natural cleft that runs slantwise down from the Moray Firth to the Firth of Lorne. Through it flows the Caledonian canal, which joins several lakes, including Loch Ness, to form a continuous waterway from Fort William to Inverness. This northern area is a desolate mass of mountains, eternally scoured by wind and rain. They rise as they near the Atlantic, looming some three thousand feet above the multitude of fiords that indent the coastline. By contrast, the eastern coast of the area, in Caithness, is lower and flatter, supporting some agriculture and a few fishing towns. These occasionally shelter Scan-

dinavian and Russian fishing vessels and the people have always been open to influence and even rule from the north.

The people on the other side of the Great Glen are far less open to outside influence. Their villages are separated by great tracts of uninhabitable moorland and mountain. Towns are rare though a few have grown up as tourist centers, capitalizing on the beautiful scenery. The Grampian Mountains, which occupy the whole of this section of Scotland down to Strathmore, at the edge of the central lowland plain, are the Highlands of legend and travel brochures. The placid surface of the tarns mirrors majestic, heather-mantled mountains under a soft northern sky. Old villages huddle in narrow glens, like Glencoe, or sprawl down in straths, broad valleys, like Strathmore. For many Highlanders the chief occupations remain fishing, farming patches of arable land by the coast or in the valleys and home industries, like weaving tweed fabrics.

Where the Highlands are poor in all except beauty, the central lowlands are rich. The coal fields of Ayrshire, the Lothians and Fife, and the iron deposits in Ayrshire and Lanarkshire supply a great industrial area. Heavy industry is supplemented by many lesser, more specialized ones: jute and marmalade in Dundee; woolens in Stirling and Clackmannan; linen around Dunfermline, Ar-

broath and Montrose. Rich agricultural land is available in the east, in Perth, Angus, Fife and the Lothians. This rich area has been the womb of Scottish civilization. Here the Scots built their towns —Edinburgh, Glasgow, Greenock, Paisley —and established their government.

Finally, there are the southern uplands: the Border country and the southwest. A tamer version of the Highlands, they too are beautiful but more like northern England. Streams do not tumble through rocky glens; they flow through grassy dales. There sheep graze, wandering in Tweeddale or Teviotdale, Eskdale or Nithsdale. Even industry is spreading from the north into the western dales. Though the area has few towns it has a distinct culture, exemplified by the work of Robert Burns and by the Border Ballads, heritage of a history not unlike that of the Highlands.

Local differences have long been eroded by the church, education and, more recently, by industry. Today there is an aluminum industry in the Highlands, based on hydroelectric power. A very advanced nuclear reactor has been built at Dounreay in Caithness.

Industry everywhere in Scotland can count on a labor force that couples native astuteness with a good education. Parish schools for all have been widespread since the end of the seventeenth century. St.

Andrew's, Glasgow and Aberdeen universities are about five hundred years old, and Edinburgh almost four hundred. Educational standards have always been high making Scotland less class-ridden than England. Indeed England and the empire owed much to the enterprise of Scottish emigrants. It is the boast of one British Prime Minister, Harold Macmillan, that his grandfather was a Scottish crofter.

The democratic temper of the people, like their independence of mind, shows in their Church (Presbyterian) in which all ministers are of equal rank. For hundreds of years the differences between England and Scotland have found expression in differences between their Churches. Where the English have bishops, the Scots have assemblies, ranging from the Kirk Session, in each parish, to the General Assembly, for the whole nation. Where the English doctrines are vague, the Scottish are uncompromising. The elaborate ritual and hierarchy of the Church of England are all very well for the English, but they do not suit most Scotsmen, with their dour taste for the austere.

A NEW DAY DAWNS: the Dounreay nuclear reactor takes shape on the chill north coast. The installation, of advanced design, started operations in 1959.

THE LOCH LEVEN in western Scotland (there is also an eastern Loch Leven) is really an arm of the sea, reaching in between the shires of Argyll and Inverness. At the head of the placid waterway, where the short Leven River rushes in, there is a hydroelectric-power station.

A PICNIC ON THE MOORS mid the heather, in Aberdeen, a Highland county on the east. Nearby are castles, mansions and lodges, some of them built by early Scottish chieftains.

"Does nobody in this country ever laugh?" inquired a visiting girl with a Scottish name.

She admitted that she had been in Scotland for only eight and a half hours when she asked the question. Yet in that time she had met and tried in vain to hold cheerful conversations with many dour Lowland Scots—with a dozen officials at Prestwick Airport; with a flight of taxi drivers, a brood of shopkeepers, several helmeted Glasgow "bobbies" and a score of other men and women. All spoke an almost incomprehensible dialect and their names more often than not began with "Mac." They seemed alert, intelligent and busy but hardly gleeful.

Like most visitors to Scotland, she had come in through the back door, through the coal and iron belts of southwest Scotland, the most depressing industrial area in the world. Along dismal sooty roads, for mile after mile, lie the huge slag heaps of mines and foundries—the "bings," as the Scots call them. In the communities that line the way the only clean things are the stone doorsteps and brass door handles of the tiny houses, scrubbed and burnished daily by the miners' wives in defiance of the sordid, smoke-filled panorama.

Like most of the thousands of visitors who come to Scotland every summer, the girl had ended her first day there in the "fierce black city" of Glasgow. This city is one of the major ports and industrial cities of the world. It is far too big for little Scotland. It should have a hinterland with unlimited natural resources. Instead it has behind it a rocky little peninsula and some clusters of islands—Scotland—which juts out toward the Arctic Ocean and is kept from freezing only by the friendly Gulf Stream. To feed and support Glasgow and supply it with energy to keep its industrial wheels turning, it should have at least twenty million people in the country behind it, not a mere five million occasionally industrious Scots.

One third of the people of Scotland are clustered in and around the Glasgow area. The result is that the slums, the material and spiritual squalor of the city seem, at first sight, as bad or worse than in any other allegedly civilized place on earth. No wonder the people do not laugh.

Perhaps, however, it is a good thing after all that foreigners should have their first glimpse of Scotland through the smoke of the industrial part of the Lowlands. It cannot fail to make them realize with an abrupt jolt that Scotland is not a happy little agricultural and pastoral land like Denmark—as they had envisioned it —but a land scarred by intensive industrial activity. Best of all, by entering Scotland through the back door, the visitor will see, much more strikingly than in any lonely Highland glen, the personality contradiction that is the modern Scot.

There in that Clyde Valley, home country of James Watt and the nursery of the industrial revolution, the Scot first brought coal and iron and steam together and started wheels turning without the help of horses or flowing water—and he has regretted it ever since. Naturally he is proud of his engineering achievements —and not without reason. The Queen Mary and the Queen Elizabeth are only two of thousands of great vessels that have been designed and wrought on Clydebank. When anything happens to his ships, as, for example, when the Queens lost the Blue Riband for the fastest Atlantic crossing, the Clyde shipwright feels it as a personal blow and a challenge and goes straight back to his drawing board to design something even more spectacular.

Yet his heart is not truly in his work. The industrial worker of the Scottish Lowlands is not a natural wage earner or paid hand. He is a peasant-mechanic. His hand is shaped for the plow rather than the wrench. He may live in a back room up several flights of stairs in an appalling tenement and may never have seen a hill or a loch or a really green field. Yet the hay is still sticking in his hair and the sound of clear running water is still tinkling afar off in the depths of his mind. He has an ever present urge to get back to the way of life of his ancestors.

Edinburgh—the clean, aristocratic, cultured capital of Scotland, on the other side of the country—has always been a center of learning. But Glasgow is stealing its reputation today. Much of the original thought, many of the new and progressive ideas are coming, not from the academic halls of Edinburgh, but out of the soot-laden pall of smoke that has covered Clydeside and the industrial belt of Scotland for more than a century.

However—the criticism is just—few even of the young people of southwest Scotland are laughing. Be it remembered, however, that they are only now recovering from three or four generations of undernourishment and bad living conditions. Be it remembered also that they are busy on serious matters—cleaning up Scotland's back door and letting light into the lives of one third of Scotland's inhabitants. If their efforts are successful, the time for laughter will come.

By the Banks of Loch Lomond

Perhaps, however, the reorganization and resurgence of industrial Scotland, like the area itself, is of less interest to non-Scots than the features and life of the rest of the country. The most attractive part is, of course, the well-known Scottish Highlands. Only twenty miles from the heart of industrial Glasgow, one enters the fringe of the Highlands by the "bonnie banks of Loch Lomond." Geologically, the mass of rock and granite is one of the oldest parts of Europe. It was there many eons before England "arose from out the azure main," and it is likely to be there many eons after England has sunk back again, for the British Isles are tilting. England is slipping a few inches lower into the sea every century, while Scotland is being pushed farther upward. The Highland massif shows the scars of the battles it has fought through the ages with snow and ice and exploding volcano. Yet its basic rock has survived and gives to the grandeur of the scenery an aura of incredible age and indestructibility.

"I to the hills will lift mine eyes, From whence doth come mine aid" is the song of praise that is sung in Scottish churches probably more than any other. One need only look up from the doorway of practically any little Highland church to see why this is so.

The Scottish Highlands are usually thought of as a land of moor and mountain and isolated glen. But there are many such places in every land, and the Highlands have other features that make them unique. For example, it is impossible anywhere in Scotland to travel farther than about forty miles from salt water. The sea surrounds and indents Scotland as it does no other country. The coastline of the peninsula alone is about 2,300 miles. There is no part of the country where one does not find sea gulls, and few are the places where, with an appropriate wind, one cannot smell the sea. Though he is usually thought of as a landsman, the soul of the Highlander is, like his land, soaked through with salt sea water.

In spite of Scotland's small size, there are areas so isolated and hard to reach that they seem as remote from the world as the Antarctic or the central African forests. In many places it is still possible

A HIGHLAND LASSIE swirls in the difficult sword dance with youthful grace and agility.

MC LEISH

THE TOLBOOTH, with its conical turrets and projecting clock, stands in the Canongate in the old town of Edinburgh. It is all that remains today of the medieval prison described by Sir Walter Scott in *The Heart of Midlothian*. The jail, however, occupied only the ground floor; upstairs was the court room, which also served as the city council chamber.

URQUHART CASTLE stands on a spit of land jutting out into Loch Ness, mid the wild beauty of the Highlands. A modern legend has made the lake famous. It is supposed to be the haunt of a very shy monster.

MARVEL of engineering—the Firth of Forth Bridge. It leaps the wide inlet a few miles inland from Edinburgh.

to walk for days without seeing a sign of man or his works, and there are a thousand lonely glens where one could lead a Robinson Crusoe life and see no other person for years on end.

Are the Highlands of Scotland then a spectacular but useless collection of colorful, heather-clad rocks on a barren, sub-Arctic peninsula? Certainly they are not today, although fate, history and the strange ways of men have all tried to make them so in the past.

Where the Romans Were Halted

Having conquered the greater part of North Africa, the Near East, Europe and south Britain, the Romans tried to conquer the Highlands of Caledonia—Scotland as it is today—and failed. Rome ruled the country that is now England for four hundred years, but it never ruled Scotland. One or two "punitive expeditions" against the fierce red-headed Caledonians it tried. Each time the grandeur of Rome retreated quickly southward to shelter for another hundred years or so behind huge defense works built against the Highland barbarians.

Some today see this failure of Rome as a bad thing, and think that at the beginning of its history Scotland might have been the better for a few hundred years of the discipline to which the rest of Europe was subjected. Others—Scots themselves included—see it as a good thing, the root of the passionate independence that has marked the character of all who have inhabited Scotland ever since.

The story of the 1745 rebellion is well known. At the call of their chiefs, the Highlanders rose to follow Prince Charles Edward (Bonnie Prince Charlie), and frightful pillage and massacre followed his defeat and flight. But disaster, natural or man-made, is an accepted part of life in Highland places, and recovery began. Life in the glens was peaceful for almost the first time in history. Roads were built. Small townships took shape. The land, as someone has said, was emerging at last from the Middle Ages.

Then the chiefs of the ancient clans—whose followers had given a breath-taking

EDINBURGH'S FAMOUS MILE—Princes Street, which is just one mile long. Shops and

example of loyalty and devotion through centuries—suddenly realized that in the new industrial age sheep had become more valuable than men. So the Highland clansmen and their families were forced to leave the glens where their ancestors had dwelt for centuries. They heaved their simple belongings on their shoulders and departed—forever. Where they went can be found out today by consulting any telephone directory in the United States or Canada, Australia, New Zealand, or South Africa, under the sec-

office buildings line one side. Opposite are gardens and lawns and the soaring monument to Sir Walter Scott. Crowning the crag beyond are the battlements of ancient Edinburgh Castle.

tion—always many pages long—devoted to the "Macs."

Only a small handful of shepherds and gamekeepers remained in the once well-populated land. The Highlands were conquered at last . . . by sheep!

"But what," asked the visitor in exasperation, "have these old tragedies got to do with the condition of the Highlands in modern times? Why do you Scots keep harping on the past?"

The answer is: The tragedies of the past have well-nigh everything to do with the condition of the Highlands today. A land that is almost totally stripped of its people twice in a century takes more than a century to recover. However, much is being done to improve things in the present and to make the future history of the Scottish Highlands far happier than its past has been.

Ultimately the chiefs and their heirs gained little. Sheep lost much of their value in Scotland when wool began flooding the world's markets from the huge farms of Australia and Wyoming—farms,

EDINBURGH CASTLE as seen from gardens on
Princes Street.   Mary Queen of Scots lived and
bore her son, James I of England, there.

HOLYROODHOUSE, the official residence of the British sovereign in Edinburgh. It began as a guest house for an abbey, now in ruins, founded by King David I of Scotland in 1128. A vision had appeared to him of a stag with a cross (holy rood) between its horns.

PIPE MAJOR of the famous Black Watch regiment. It dates from the 1700's and was named for its somber tartan (black and green). Since Queen Victoria's time the Black Watch pipers alone have worn the Royal Stewart tartan (in the pleated, mostly red kilt).

107

justly enough, that were often built by the displaced Scottish Highlanders.

In some cases it is the grandson or great-grandson of an evicted Highlander who has come back home from the Western Hemisphere or the Antipodes, and come full of far-sighted ideas and a determination to do for Scotland as Scotland should have done by his forebears. Some of these former exiles are starting experimental farms, new industries. Already such projects are pumping new life into the Highland community. One of these men has taken over a famous Scottish newspaper. Another has started a cattle ranch in the Highlands, which he proposes to run on Western lines. More important than these individual efforts, industrial concerns are beginning to take an interest in the Highland area. Most significant of all, 75 per cent of the Canadian and American firms that have set up branch factories in the United Kingdom since World War II have chosen Scotland for their locale.

In other cases it is a board of Scots, mainly of the peasant-mechanic type from Glasgow, who, with or without government support, are initiating huge projects capable of unlimited expansion. If these are successful, they may well make Scotland the happiest and most prosperous small country in Europe.

Turbines in the Highlands

One such plan is the north of Scotland hydroelectric program. It was already well ahead and showing results in a big way in the mid-1950's. This scheme, backed but not financed by the Government, aims to turn the almost unlimited water power of the Highlands to productive use. The dams and artificial lochs, the man-made tunnels, torrents and turbines, and the great humming, smokeless palaces of power they are erecting have become a welcome feature of the Highlands, fitting with good taste into the landscape. They attract visitors away even from the old romantic scenes and give hope to the handful of people still remaining in the Highlands and the many who yearn to return there from the over-

crowded black areas of the south.

Another equally important project is a forestry commission, under government control. This body has been working quietly for some years, repairing the shocking damage done to the once magnificent forests of Scotland. Though the damage will certainly take a century or more to repair, spectacular results are already apparent. Glens, hillsides and whole mountain ranges—which the middle-aged Scot remembers as a boy to have been a sorry, barren waste of bog or an impenetrable jungle of ancient tree stumps and undergrowth—are today green with young pine, spruce and fir trees. The "Forestry Chaps" are now familiar residents of nearly every Highland village. And before he dies, the middle-aged Scot will see his country clad once more in its natural raiment of noble trees—trees such as were the admiration of all visitors to the Scottish Highlands from the time of Tacitus until the visit of Dr. Johnson.

Riches from the Sea

There are also men watching the fisheries of Scotland—men who realize that the Highlanders and islanders of this rocky peninsula on the edge of the Gulf Stream have a harvest off their shores potentially as valuable as any they will glean on land. These men are scientists, trained in the marine laboratories of the proudly ancient but superbly up-to-date and progressive Scottish universities. They are developing new conservation methods, wise restrictions and productive uses for Scotland's immensely rich fishing grounds. Every economically useful swimming thing—literally from the whale to the sprat—is engaging their attention. Whaling has been a major industry in Scotland for nearly two centuries and is still so today. Two Scottish whaling expeditions, each consisting of some twenty ships, sail way into the grim Antarctic every year to bring back a rich cargo of protein, fats, vitamins and the hundreds of by-products for which the modern world is still dependent on the whale. The little herring in the home waters is

FROM GLASGOW'S SHIPYARDS are launched some of the world's mightiest vessels. Here a freighter, in the process of being painted, lies in one of the basins along the Clyde.

MC LEISH

GLASGOW UNIVERSITY has a beautiful situation on a tree-covered hill overlooking the River Kelvin. Although the buildings are of a later period, the university, founded in 1451, is the second oldest in Scotland. Many distinguished Scots, such as Thomas Campbell, the poet, and Lord Kelvin, the scientist, have been connected with it.

IN PEEBLESHIRE the steep valley sides, watered by the many small tributaries of the Tweed, are planted with oats, rye and barley although the stony ground makes hard plowing. The rolling, grass-covered hills of this Lowland county afford good grazing for sheep.

REID

HIGHLAND CATTLE, which roam among the western mountains, in a half-wild condition, are akin to the wild oxen that used to live in Scotland long ago. They are hardy, fierce-looking little creatures with shaggy red hair, and are much smaller than ordinary bulls and cows.

nearly as important to Scotland, and the fishery experts are determined that new methods of harvesting and processing shall make the little fish an important factor in the country's economic recovery.

The men dedicated to saving Scotland through its fisheries, like the others who are thinking about and planning the future development of the Highlands, are not dealing in trivialities. They are not considering the advantages and profits of next year or the year after. They are thinking in decades, and in some cases in centuries. Their aim is not to preserve Scotland as it is but to give it some kind of future; to make a Scotland that Scots can work for and take pride in, though many alive today will never see the results of the work. These broad development schemes will go on, even though some beautiful things like the gray seals and some romantic, traditional things like the medieval trappings of the Highlands are partly sacrificed to make way for them.

For its immediate recovery, Scotland is banking strongly on its tourist trade. Scotland is one of the most romantic parts of the British Isles, and the tourist board is out to exploit that fact to the full. It has worked out a long-term policy to improve the hotel, catering, amusement, traveling and sight-seeing facilities.

Other products on which the Scots are basing the immediate commercial recovery of their country are whisky and tweeds. Neither product needs any introduction to the markets of the world. Taking its name originally from the frontier river between Scotland and England, the famous Scottish tweed is known wherever there are men and women who are cold and want garments that will stand rough usage. The world is apparently so cold today that all the looms on the Borders and in the Highlands working overtime cannot produce sufficient genuine tweed to satisfy the demand. And where in the civilized world does one not find skirts, coats, shirts, scarves, hats and a host of other garments made from Scottish tartans?

All this development and progress is not really spoiling the older, traditional, more romantic and more widely known

PHILIP GENDREAU

PORT ASKAIG is a tidy hamlet on lovely Islay, southernmost of the Inner Hebrides Islands. Islay was the former seat of the Lords of the Isles—the Macdonalds and the Campbells.

CULCROSS, IN FIFESHIRE, on the eastern coast, is an ancient village that still wears a medieval look. Mercat Cross, on the left of the market square, was erected in 1588.

and loved features of Scotland.

"I won't feel I've had even fifty cents for my tourist's dollar," said the visiting girl, "until I've heard your bagpipes, watched your brawny Highlanders tossing cabers, tasted haggis, seen Highland cattle standing in a misty loch, heard some Gaelic songs and some fairy music, walked the Road to the Isles, sailed Over the Sea to Skye, and spent at least one night in a cave where Bonnie Prince Charlie, or Robert the Bruce, or Rob Roy or somebody has spent a night hiding from the English dragoons!"

It is still easy to show her all these things and many more. Some of them, too obviously laid on and sugar-coated, the Scot is almost ashamed to show. To make up, however, there are many other lesser known, more intimate, more real and therefore more truly romantic things he could show her in the Highlands to-day. Instead of massed bands of pipers in fancy dress, he could show her occasional lone pipers playing the music of their ancestors for their own enjoyment, far up glens where they thought they would not be heard. Instead of the caber tossers, throwing telegraph poles about for large money prizes, he could show her equally brawny Highland men erecting pylons and other more important "cabers" far away in the middle of desolate moors, to carry electricity to remote villages where even the oil lamp is still regarded as a modern innovation. The Gaelic songs she can hear in almost any Highland village at night. If the villagers should not happen to be holding a ceilidh —or impromptu concert—the Highlanders' main amusement today as it has been for centuries—then she need only turn on the wireless and hear the best of the Gaelic music from the B.B.C. studios in Glasgow. The fairy music she must listen for alone far up a glen—and if, as she claims, she has Scottish blood in her veins, she will hear it. The road through Tummel and Loch Rannoch and Lochaber, which leads ultimately to the isles, is as lovely today as when men wrote songs about it, though very few visitors cross it, for no car or bicycle has ever been that wild way. A Highland "high tea," even

FAST TRAINS to Edinburgh rumble over this graceful arched bridge that spans the River Tweed. The lower course of the stream marks the east border between Scotland and England.

MELROSE ABBEY is in the Tweed Valley, near Abbotsford, Sir Walter Scott's home. The abbey is only a lovely shell today—the ruins of a Cistercian monastery established in the 1100's.

A VIVID LENGTH of tweed rolls from a loom. The name does not refer to the River Tweed. It is said that a clerk wrote "tweeds" instead of the Scottish *tweels*, meaning a weave—twill.

BEN NEVIS, HIGHEST SUMMIT (4,406 feet) in Great Britain, overlooks the Water of Nevis. From the top on a clear day there is a magnificent view of rugged hills and shining sea.

HIGHLANDS "CAPITAL"—Inverness, which is on the narrows between the firths of Beauly and Moray. Once the town resounded to the clash of clan warfare. Macbeth's castle was here.

though haggis is not served, is an adventure in gourmandry she will not ever forget. Especially—as is likely—if every single ingredient of the meal except the salt and pepper and the tea leaves has been produced in the glen in which she sits. Her cave? When a Highland Scot finds a cave, he keeps the knowledge to himself . . .

But our visitor must not dally too long in the Highlands, even though she has at last found some Scots who laugh. There are many parts of Scotland she has not yet seen, and many—neither very ugly like the Clyde Valley nor very beautiful like the Highlands—that she must see if she is to leave with a balanced and complete picture of the little country.

There are the islands—each one, or at least each group, almost a separate country of its own. The Hebrides, where Gaelic is still the natural tongue, and many children even today learn English at school as a foreign language. The Orkneys are the poultry house of Scotland and have often served as a naval base. The Shetlands were a Norse colony longer than they have been a part of Scotland. This is where the famous little ponies come from and where the people

still talk of "going abroad to Scotland!" Shetlanders have always manned the British whaling fleets.

More important than these delightful places is the eastern seaboard of Scotland, with its two ancient towns, Aberdeen—the Granite City—and Dundee—the jute and marmalade city.

Between and around these towns are the "straths" of Scotland—agricultural country limited in extent but with a depth of soil and a wealth of pasture that are the envy of farmers everywhere else. The proof of that claim is to be seen on most beef-cattle ranches and in every stockyard where the butcher is the buyer—the black, stocky, beefy little Aberdeen Angus stirk, which is native to the country between Dundee and Aberdeen.

The visitor must see Edinburgh, the capital of Scotland, before leaving the country, even though Edinburgh is dissociated in most ways from the remainder of the country. Some would say—not without justice—that it is the only Anglicized piece of Scotland; others would say that it is a once great city living on its past reputation. Friendly enemies have called it: an attractive museum; the town that is "east-windy and west-endy"; and,

MC LEISH

LOCH LOMOND, its placid surface starred with green islands, is encircled by wild, rugged country and lofty mountains. At one time it would not have been safe for a farmer to allow his black-faced sheep to graze on this sunny hillside near Luss, since round the shores of the loch and on some of its islands lived unruly Highland chieftains and their robber followers. All that has long since been changed, however, and pleasure boats cruise on the clear waters of Loch Lomond and bring crowds of tourists to the hotels and inns throughout the district.

IN THE TROSSACHS are many wooded glens where all is peaceful in the leafy shade. Ben Venue's barren slopes enhance by contrast the rich loveliness of the glen. The Trossachs district, between Loch Katrine and Loch Achray, is one of the most beautiful in Scotland, and is famous as the scene of Sir Walter Scott's poem *The Lady of the Lake.*

A HYDROELECTRIC PLANT on the banks of Loch Lomond, part of a large system to provide electricity throughout Scotland. Through the hillside pipes flows water from Loch Sloy.

pithiest of all, "Auld Reekie." To critical friends it is the "wise gray woman by the rock"; the "Athens of the North"; "Edina, Scotia's darling seat." Supreme compliment of all (though it was an exiled Scot who paid it), one of New Zealand's largest cities is named Dunedin, which is the old name of Edinburgh.

It is undoubtedly one of the most beautiful cities of the world. Seen in the sunshine—which is seldom possible, the Scottish climate being as it is—it is no exaggeration to say that Edinburgh is breathtaking. Its main thoroughfare, Princes Street, is one mile long, and nowhere else is there such a street. On one side are the headquarters of Scottish businesses; on the other, gardens and green lawns, statues of Scotland's greatest men, and—the only two buildings—the Scottish art galleries and one ancient kirk. Every business, Scottish or foreign, that has anything to sell in Scotland, struggles fiercely for space on the north side and blazons there its name and the worth of its goods. But all the pounds in the sterling area or dollars in North America

could not buy a single square yard on the other side of the street for commercial purposes.

Beyond the gardens rises a precipitous crag with an impregnable fortress atop it—Edinburgh Castle, Scotland's most famous and probably its most ancient building. One can wander about in that castle for days and still see only the half of it, for it contains the whole of Scotland's history within its battlements. One can enter a small chapel and flit back into the twelfth century, wander into medieval dungeons and great halls of feudal times, see the scars and relics of Scotland's five-hundred-year war against the English, or visit a modern barracks filled with kilted troops. On the pinnacle of the rock is Scotland's national shrine—a hall and a chapel containing the story of the country's agony and sacrifice in the two world wars. No country has a finer temple to contain its national gods than Scotland has in Edinburgh Castle, and nowhere else is the soul of a country so fully and fittingly depicted in stone.

At the other end of Old Edinburgh

stands Scotland's royal palace of Holy-roodhouse, today merely a week-end stopping place for the British Royal Family. Though Scotland's capital has a Parliament House with a democratic tradition as old or older than that of Westminster, no parliament has met there since about 1700.

Edinburgh has a university and is an academic center that is honored and respected wherever there are men who think. Edinburgh sponsors and organizes an International Festival of Music and Drama.

Among Scotland's other unique sights are the spectacular bridges that span the firths (sea inlets) of the Forth and Tay. The bridge over the Forth is the highest and the one over the Tay is longest of all the railway bridges in the world. There are the famous lighthouses. Some, like the storied Bell, or Inchcape, Rock, are built on rocks far out to sea. There is Scotland's oldest university, St. Andrews, which was a seat of learning when most of Europe still languished in the Dark Ages.

Having seen all the wonders and paid homage at all the shrines, the visitor will leave Scotland by way of the Borders. The Border country has been famous for its sheep as long as the Highlands for its men. Just as every cattleman today knows the Aberdeen Angus, so every sheep man knows the Cheviot. It was on the Scottish slopes of the Cheviot Hills that this breed was produced in early medieval times, and continues to be bred today.

The Border people are as old a stock as the sheep they breed. Being Scottish peasants who have never been displaced from their land by industrial upheaval or arms or by treachery, they are a happy people.

It is they, yet another type of the ever contradictory Scots, who will bid the visiting girl farewell, ushering her out of Scotland's front door, and sending her on her way . . . laughing.

By R. B. Robertson

SCOTLAND: FACTS AND FIGURES

THE COUNTRY

Occupies the northern portion of the island of Great Britain, with the Atlantic Ocean on the west and north, the North Sea on the east and England on the south. Total area, including adjacent islands (186 in number) 30,405 sq. mi.; pop., 5,225,000. The islands belonging to Scotland are the Orkneys and the Shetlands on the north; the Inner and Outer Hebrides along the west coast; those in the estuary (firth) of the Clyde—Bute, Arran and some smaller ones.

GOVERNMENT

As a part of the United Kingdom, general laws are made by the British Parliament in London, in both houses of which Scotland is represented, but for matters which concern the country alone there is a Secretary for Scotland. Health matters are under the Scottish Board of Health. Local government is under the county councils of each of the 33 civil counties. Law is under the Court of Session (civil) and the High Court of Justiciary (criminal).

COMMERCE AND INDUSTRIES

The Firth of Clyde, near valuable coal and iron deposits, is a shipbuilding center of world rank. Dundee is the center for jute, linen and hemp manufacture. Heavy industries include iron and aluminum works and machinery. Light industries include tweed cloth, carpets, shawls, silks, hosiery, paper and spirits. Fishing and stock raising are important industries, and Scotland is the original home of some famous breeds of cattle and sheep.

COMMUNICATIONS

Railway, road, water and air transportation are all important in Scotland's communications system. Its chief international airport is at Prestwick in Ayrshire, and the chief centers of sea and air communications for the Orkney and Shetland islands are at Wick and Thurso in the north. There are 184 mi. of canals, including the Caledonian Canal, 60½ mi. long.

RELIGION AND EDUCATION

The established church is the Presbyterian, which dates back to 1560. Education is compulsory until the age of 15, and it is encouraged until at least 18. In addition to regular primary and secondary education, there are continuation schools for defectives, schools for the blind and deaf, industrial schools and reformatories. The 4 universities are St. Andrews, Glasgow, Aberdeen and Edinburgh. There are also Presbyterian and Catholic theological colleges and training schools for teachers.

CHIEF CITIES, POPULATIONS

Edinburgh, capital, 467,000; Glasgow, 1,088,400; Aberdeen, 186,800; Dundee, 178,500; Paisley, 95,800.

RUSSET-COLOR CALVES, offspring of sturdy Highland cattle, amble about on wind-swept North Uist. This is one of the islands of the Hebrides, in the open Atlantic west of Scotland's mainland. From the Hebrides comes one of the most famous tweeds of all—Harris tweed.

MENDING NETS on a fishing smack in the harbor of Oban, a little port on the Firth of Lorne. Long ago, in its days of glory, Oban was the stronghold of the mighty lords of Lorne.

RAIN is the price paid by the little town of Ballyjamesduff, County Cavan, for the rich, beautiful land surrounding it. So the drizzle does not bother the farmer or the greyhound trainer.

Ireland ...*fabled island*

THE legendary boldness and charm of the Irish shone in the period of English rule, which was marked by famine and bloody rebellions bloodily suppressed. They shine today in the period of independence, which is marked by rebellion against the tyranny of an economy dominated by backward agriculture. In both periods they have sustained the swarm of Irish emigrants to England and the United States. Above all, these qualities have brightened the whole world through the brilliance of Irish dramatists.

Since 1921 the Emerald Isle has been divided into the six counties of Northern Ireland (part of the United Kingdom) and the independent twenty-six southern counties, the Irish Free State. In 1927 this became the Republic of Ireland and in 1949 it broke all ties with the Commonwealth, though its citizens still have free entry into Great Britain. This is the es-

sential Ireland: it is little industrialized; it is against English rule; it is officially Gaelic-speaking; and it is Roman Catholic to the core. Northern Ireland, however, is pro-English, entirely English-speaking and mainly Protestant.

When we talk of Ireland we usually mean the Republic, which is strange because an economist would describe it very unfavorably. He would say that Ireland lost half its population between 1850 and 1950; that losses from emigration were not made good because of late marriages and a low birth rate; that per-capita income is low—less than a fourth of America's; that the home market is small enough to discourage domestic industry but large enough to unbalance foreign trade; and that agriculture is unmechanized and hampered by old-fashioned farming methods. Finally, he would say, industry is insufficiently diversified. Nevertheless the underdeveloped, population-starved Republic yet manages to bewitch the visitor and turn out a stream of great men, poets and patriots.

Northern Ireland is much smaller than the Republic and though it has considerable unemployment, it enjoys a higher standard of living. Of course there is plenty of room for economic expansion but power facilities and skilled labor support the venerable linen and shipbuilding industries and encourage foreign investment. Though some of its farming is backward the people enjoy the benefits of British social services.

It was not until the late 1950's that the Republic bestirred itself to attract foreign investment and improve its economic lot. In 1956 the national treasury found itself in serious trouble when a drop in cattle prices cut back exports. "We are within sight of national bankruptcy," announced the *Irish Times*. Well aware of the gravity of the situation, Eamon de Valera, who became prime minister at the next election, took steps to speed up industrial development. Food subsidies were discontinued, taxes were increased on luxury items and incentives were offered to export manufacturers. Foreign investors were promised tax concessions and government grants for plant construction and employee training. The response, particularly from West German and American firms, was encouraging. In 1959 a three-company American combine put up Ireland's first oil refinery. However, there is still a long way to go. As the Mayor of Dublin has remarked, "The great task is how to find work for people and stem our heavy emigration . . . We are trying to change an agricultural country into one that is self-sufficient, with a balanced economy, with well-developed industries."

Serious though they are, economic difficulties do not dominate politics. The electorate still remembers the "Time of the Troubles" which preceded independence and in which many political leaders —Eamon de Valera among them—established themselves. Although a new generation has arisen since the bad old days

of fighting the English and the men of Ulster, an Irishman can still say, "All our politics are determined by who shot up whom forty years ago."

Every political party in the Republic is dedicated to union between North and South, ranging in fervor from De Valera's moderate Fianna Fail to the fiery Sinn Fein, some of whose members have been accused of association with the terrorist Irish Republican Army. All parties are strongly nationalistic. One of the Fianna Fail's main planks remains the universal adoption of Gaelic, the ancient Irish tongue. The strongest opposition to the Fianna Fail has come from the Fine Gael, a conservative "businessman's party." It was able to break De Valera's grip on the Dail (the lower house) twice between 1948 and 1957 by joining an opposition coalition and thus gaining a majority.

In foreign policy the Republic has been consistently, almost rigidly, neutral. Its refusal to join any military alliance with Great Britain kept it out of World War II, though large numbers of Irishmen enlisted under the British flag. Its refusal to enter into a Mutual Security Pact with the United States, which would have granted aid in exchange for a promise to join in defense of the free world, has kept it out of the cold war. This neutralism stands the Republic in good stead in the United Nations, where its representatives hold several key posts. In 1960 it sent a contingent to the Congo on behalf of the UN and in the same year an Irishman, Frederick Henry Boland, was president of the General Assembly. Both East and West cannot fail to be impressed by the independent position taken by this little country, despite its bitter history and its close cultural ties with the United States and Great Britain.

The People and Their Past

In the same cold, foggy latitude as Labrador, Ireland gets its climate from North America—from the Gulf Stream—the warm mass of air that flows across the Atlantic from the Gulf of Mexico and strikes the Irish coast so that tropical plants and fuchsia hedges grow in Con-

MODERN HOMES in the suburbs of Dublin, on the Sallynoggin Estate at Dun Laoghaire.

SHOPPING CENTER of the Sallynoggin development, acclaimed by foreign architects.

A GREAT DAY in Dublin—the horse show in August. It is Ireland's peak social and sporting event, drawing visitors and horse fanciers from the far corners of the earth.

A QUIET STREET of well-kept residences in Dublin. Many of the city's loveliest houses were built in the early 1800's, in the Georgian style.

ST. LUKE'S CANCER HOSPITAL in Dublin. The modern structure is well designed and equipped for its purpose and is a leader in its field.

nacht, and arbutus and palm trees luxuriate in Munster. Shaped like a saucer, with mountains all around the coast and a hollow in the middle, the island has such an indented coast line that no part inland is more than sixty miles or so from the sea. The majestic Atlantic washes its rugged coasts on the north, west and south and the Irish Sea erodes its eastern side.

It has been said that the men who fly from Shannon airport today are one in mind and spirit with the people who have inhabited this island outpost for countless centuries. There the ancient and the modern blend. Streamlined buses roll over roads that seem to lead to fairyland. You talk with a friendly Irishman in the dining car of the express train from Killarney to Dublin and may be asked for your opinion of everything from leprechauns to tweeds. At Shannon's airport, men from Israel or India mingle with the people of Clare or Limerick while changing planes for North America.

To Ireland, archaeologists and anthropologists have come to solve the riddle of the origin of its people. Mounds have been dug, raths (hill dwellings), tombs, forts, duns (fortified residences) have been explored, crannogs (curious refuges in lakes or bogs) have been laid bare. Yet the Irish continue, like the Basques,

IRISH, the first language of the Republic, is a form of Gaelic, an ancient Celtic tongue.

as a fascinating ethnic puzzle. In the flowering of the Elizabethan age, the poet Edmund Spenser tried his hand at solving the origins of the Irish people. According to him, the first inhabitants were Gaels, the same people who once occupied Britain. Then Scythians, from far eastern Europe, inhabited the north of Ireland. Later, Spaniards settled in the west, Britons in the east, and Gaels from Belgia (the Lowlands of the Continent) in the south.

In any event, central Europe was once covered by a great Celtic empire. The members of the family occupying Ireland were known as Hibernians, Scots or Gaels. By 800 A.D., we are assured, the Gaelic invaders had become masters of Ireland. In the meantime St. Patrick, a Romanized Celt, brought Christianity to the Irish, in the fifth century. The Romans and their proconsuls never put foot in Ireland. Some say this was a pity as the Romans were great organizers and builders. The Irish look upon it as a happy thing. They are strongly individualistic, and the Romans were regarded as dictatorial steamrollers obsessed with state organization.

Legends of Hospitality

In the third century A.D. reigned one of Ireland's greatest and wisest kings, Cormac MacArt. He built the banquet hall at Tara, which was the center of government. The hall was 300 feet long, 100 feet broad and 45 feet high. King Cormac said that a worthy chief should be generous to guests. Houses designed for public entertainment were a feature of

128

early Irish social life. King Connor was told that if he brought all the men of Erin with him all would be welcome to food and gifts. A frequently repeated pattern in Irish storytelling is that such and such a festival lasted so many days and so many nights and the last night was better than the first. Various hospitality centers are described thus: every man there is a good chess player; there is good company that knows no stint, and the door is never closed to strangers; the leaders love the chase and are good feast givers.

In the Ulster epic cycle of stories, mention is made of Bricriu of the Evil Tongue, the disturber of meetings and maker of quarrels. He invited King Connor and other chiefs to a feast at his new house. The feast took a year to pre-

pare. As was customary, a special place was set aside for the foremost hero in the hall. The hero's prizes were a seven-year-old pig, a seven-year-old cow, a hundred cakes of corn covered with honey, and a vat of wine large enough to hold three warriors. Incidentally, into their pagan paradise of wassailing and joy the ancient Irish admitted women, in contrast to some pagan nations which restricted their blessings to men.

Finn MacCool is the great hero of early Ireland—a sort of King Arthur. Were the brown leaves of Woodland made of gold or the white billow of silver, Finn would have given it all away. Finn was entertained at a feast for a year.

When monasteries came with the Christian Era, it was impressed on the monks that the Lord Himself was re-

CRUMBLING WALLS are all that remain of the Abbey of SS. Peter and Paul, just outside of Trim, in County Meath. Founded in 1206, the abbey fell under the ban of Henry VIII in 1536.

SHANNON AIRPORT, a familiar scene to those who fly the Atlantic. Almost all the passenger planes on the route between North America and Europe stop there. It is in County Clare, on the west coast of Ireland.

KING JOHN'S CASTLE and Thomond Bridge at Limerick, at the head of the estuary of the River Shannon. The English King John ordered the castle built in the early 1200's. It has been much altered since those days.

FRESH MILK for the town of Cong, in County Mayo, is loaded at a nearby dairy farm. The cottage—low, whitewashed and with overhanging eaves—has a charming air of welcome.

131

THE HEART OF DUBLIN—famed O'Connell Street. In the center is the 134-foot-high Nelson Pillar. The street merges into O'Connell Bridge, the chief span across the River Liffey.

ceived when a guest was entertained. "I will not close my house against any one lest the Lord close His house against me." "If you have a guest in your house and conceal anything from him 'tis not the guest that will be without it but the Lord Himself." So run the rules in ancient Irish manuscripts.

The Venerable Bede, the English historian, tells us that in the plague toward the end of the seventh century, great crowds of Anglo-Saxons flocked over to Ireland. The Irish treated them as guests—gave them food, books to read and instruction without fee from Irish masters. Outstanding men entertained all ranks of society without distinction. Open house was kept for scholars, and patrons of learning were numerous. A certain philanthropist was styled "the servant of generosity." Scrooges were rare and one was lampooned as "the head of inhospitality of Ireland" because he swore he would never serve guests with butter and bread together. In 1433 Margaret O'Carroll invited Irish and Scots to two of her feasts. About three thousand people, from the most prosperous to the poorest, came to the great banquets.

"A Hundred Thousand Welcomes"

Many are the feet of all the flies in the world; many are the stars of the sky and the waves of the sea, but the guests of O'Donnell are far more numerous. So goes an old poem. Proverbs continued: A generous person never went to Hell. Three things cannot be learned: a voice for singing, poetry and generosity. John O'Twomey, an Irish poet of the eighteenth century, hung out a sign from his inn, stating that even if people lacked the price of refreshment they were still welcome within. An Irish poet of the fourteenth century, Carrol O'Daly, addressed his beloved Eileen Kavanagh, as he carried her over the doorstep, with "a hundred thousand welcomes." Shakespeare introduced the phrase, now a familiar form of welcome, into a play. It is often quoted in Irish as *cead mile failte*—a hundred thousand welcomes before you. Christmas cards in Ireland frequently portray a candle in a window and an open door, symbols of Ireland's ancient hospitality—for St. Joseph, the Blessed Virgin, the Divine Child and every wayfaring mortal on the pilgrimage to eternity.

Ireland's Dramatic History

History is a subject dear to the Irish mind. Tacitus in his life of the Roman General Agricola describes how the Romans looked across the Irish Sea and decided that a spectacle should be made of the Irish by inflicting Roman liberty upon them. The Romans never came. But the Normans did come and they brought some Roman ways with them.

From the fifth to the end of the eighth century the Irish had enjoyed their own Celtic ways. Then Norsemen from Scandinavian lands disturbed them and came to dwell in their midst, giving Norse names to towns such as Wexford, Waterford and Wicklow. Sad tales are told of what happened to the Gaels in these times. At last Brian Boru, Ireland's hero and high king, defeated the Northmen in the battle of Clontarf near

IRISH TOURIST BUREAU

ABBEY THEATRE, Dublin, landmark in the history of the theater. It was burned in 1951.

133

WILD BEAUTY in County Wicklow—the rolling Vale of Glendalough. St. Kevin founded a monastery there in the sixth century, which became a renowned center of medieval learning. A round tower shows above the trees in the center.

QUAYS LINE THE RIVER LEE at Cork, which has one of the best natural anchorages in the world. Ships that ply the Irish Sea dock there. The oldest part of the city is on an island in the middle of the River Lee.

THE BLARNEY STONE is set high in the hoary castle's square keep. To kiss the stone—which confers eloquence—one must hang down from the top.

DUBLIN'S DIVIDING LINE is a lovely river banked by quays. Like the Seine in Paris, the Liffey separates Dublin into two nearly equal parts. Within the city, twelve bridges cross the

Dublin in 1014. In the piles of slain they identified the dead King Brian by his precious crown of gems and gold.

Dermot MacMurrough, king of Leinster, was in trouble with his people in the twelfth century when he eloped with the wife of Prince O'Rourke. She was a Helen of Troy to Ireland. To justify himself, Dermot brought in the help of adventurous Norman knights from Wales whose prowess had already been displayed from England to southern Italy and Palestine. Richard FitzGilbert, nicknamed Strongbow, was the leader. England and Celtic Wales had fallen. Celtic Ireland was now besieged. The Normans made headway but they could never really conquer the Isle of Destiny. Norman blood mingled with Gaelic.

Names with Fitz and De blended in marriage with names from the stocks of Mac and O. Ireland had swallowed up a number of peoples and made of them one —"the indomitable Irishry," as the poet, Yeats, says, molded from seven hundred years of history. We are told that the Normans became more Irish then the Irish themselves. Names such as Fitzgerald, Fitzmaurice, Fitzsimmons, Fitzgibbon, Butler, Burke, De Courcey, De Lacey mixed with O'Donnell, O'Neill, O'Connor, O'Connell, O'Brien.

The Gaelic language jostled for pride of place with Norman French and in later times became almost extinct except along the seaboard from Cork and Kerry to Connemara and Donegal. Although as late as 1600, Irish was the sole tongue of

stream. Dublin's Gaelic name *Baile Atha Cliath*—means "The Town of the Hurdle Ford."

the native people. The upper classes began to neglect the Irish tongue in the seventeenth century. The middle classes were dropping it in the eighteenth century. In the nineteenth century the battle was fully on to make the masses of the people speak English only. Today Gaelic is restored as the first official language of the Irish Republic.

The old Irish laws—the Brehon laws—gave way to the Roman law system of the Norman French invaders. At this time the Normans were the ruling group in England, though on the way to blending with the Anglo-Saxons. So for quite a while after the Norman invasion, English law and customs were enforced within the district called the Pale—the counties around Dublin. The Pale was like a piece of political rubber, which stretched or contracted as English power rose and fell. The phrase "beyond the Pale" came into existence, as meaning outside the law. Even in the reign of King Henry the Eighth, who was the first to style himself King of Ireland, Irish ways still prevailed outside the narrow Pale. This was in the face of stern laws made to force English laws, dress, customs, language and traditions on the Irish.

Long Locks Defy Henry VIII

The Irish way of growing beards and hair was forbidden. The early Irish loved to cultivate a beard and were sensitively proud of their long flowing hair. At Glendalough, an ancient church center of St. Kevin in Wicklow, one may still see on the capital of a pillar a youthful head with flowing tresses. A statute of Henry VIII obliged the Irish to cut off their long locks. Defiant poems were written against Henry's tyranny. To this day an air survives, perhaps the most tender in Irish minstrelsy, called the *Coolun*. A *coolun* means a long lock of hair hanging down the back and this is how an Irish maid wished to see her young man. At crossroad dances today you may hear this plaintive melody bewitchingly wailing from a violin.

With Henry VIII and Queen Elizabeth I also came changes in religion. The Irish remained on the whole steadfast in the Catholic faith, which today is the creed of over 90 per cent of the people in the Republic of Ireland. However, the constitution of Ireland, approved by the voters in 1937, established religious freedom for all and the state grants full facilities to the schools of all faiths.

Many of Ireland's great national leaders were Protestants—Henry Grattan, Charles Parnell, Lord Edward Fitzgerald. The first president of modern Ireland, who took office in 1938, was a Protestant, Dr. Douglas Hyde. In 1893, he had started the Gaelic League to restore the native language, and early in the 1900's went abroad to collect funds for this work. From Ulster, a province about two-thirds Protestant, came na-

ANGLERS TRY THEIR LUCK for salmon in the short stream that flows from Lough Corrib into Galway Bay, on the Atlantic coast.   In the distance is a man-made salmon leap, or ladder.

KYLEMORE ABBEY has a lovely setting, overlooking the three Kylemore lakes, in County Galway. Though it looks quite old, the mansion was built in the late 1800's.

ON INISHMORE, largest of the three Aran Islands, thirty miles offshore from County Galway. Craggy and with little soil, the islands have few spots as invitingly green as this.

139

WORK IN PROGRESS on a passenger coach in a railroad shop at Inchicore. The community is an industrial suburb of Dublin, with paper mills as well as coach factories.

tional leaders such as Wolfe Tone, and the United Irishmen who were pioneers in the demand for an independent Ireland.

The Protestant Dean of St. Patricks Cathedral, Dublin, Jonathan Swift (1667–1745), is regarded as the founding father of the Sinn Fein movement that began in the early 1900's—*sinn fein* meaning "ourselves," or "Ireland for the Irish and the land for the people." Swift, who wrote *Gulliver's Travels,* also is hailed as the father of Anglo-Irish literature. His strange tales in English seem like a continuation of old Gaelic voyages and of the visions of the early monks with their fantastic legends. One of those, the story of St. Brendan's voyage, was translated into other European tongues and reached libraries during the Middle Ages. The Saint journeyed for seven years over the seas in quest of Paradise and is said to have reached the shores of North America.

After the first World War ended in 1918, the Sinn Fein Party renewed its efforts to free Ireland. The party had the backing of the people, the majority of whom had voted for separation. At Easter, in 1916, there had been an uprising led by Patrick Pearse. This had scarcely been quelled when the Irish re-

publicans were on the march again. The Anglo-Irish conflict that followed was ended by a treaty with Britain in 1921. Pearse is hailed as the father of modern Ireland.

The names of other heroes such as Robert Emmet, Parnell, Daniel O'Connell, great at they are, pale before the appeal of the romantic figure of Pearse, who was schoolmaster, poet, commander-in-chief, lawyer and, for a few days, president of the "Irish Republic." When the Easter rebellion failed, he was executed, at the age of thirty-six, by British forces for having signed Ireland's declaration of independence. Born in Ireland of an English father and an Irish mother, he was to exert more influence than any other person on the future of the Isle of Destiny. He had founded his ideal school outside Dublin where boys were taught the noblest principles of Ireland's long line of heroes. Gentle was Pearse too. He placed a solemn vow on his pupils never to hurt God's creatures, be they birds or butterflies. Any grinding system of uninspired education only in facts he called "the murder machine."

The Irish Free State born in 1921 was regarded as a dominion. Six counties of Ulster (in the northeast) voted against joining the new state. They set up a par-

140

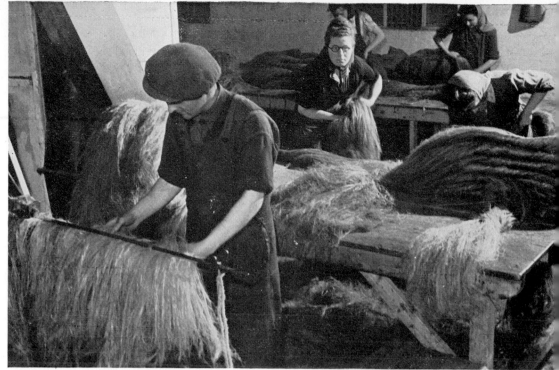

FLAX FIBERS are taken from a scutching machine, which separates the woody fibers from the flax. In the background, girls tie the flax into bundles. From it will be woven the famous linen.

COLLINSTOWN AIRPORT is about five miles north of Dublin. From Collinstown one can make connections with Shannon Airport, near Limerick, where transatlantic planes call.

141

CATTLE WAIT PATIENTLY to be sold on market day in a Northern Ireland village. Irish breeds of cattle are well known the world over.

A LONG AVENUE leads from a statue of Lord Carson (who helped to keep Ulster in the United Kingdom) to the Parliament in Belfast.

PLEASANT HOMES for working people in Belfast. Clay, from which bricks are made, is abundant around Belfast, which gives the impression of a city built of brick.

BELFAST'S SHIPYARDS are enormous. Many celebrated liners have been built there, including the ill-fated Titanic. Shipbuilding leads among the city's many industries.

143

liament and government of their own and their territory is known as Northern Ireland. This is a part of the United Kingdom. As an Irish historian observes, the forces that attract the men of one nation together are greater than those that hold them apart. So some day perhaps North and South will eventually be united as they were in the days of the Ulster Chieftains O'Neill and O'Donnell.

Eamon de Valera became the head of the Irish Free State. He was born in New York in 1882 of an Irish mother and Spanish father. Though he had fought as an officer in the rising of 1916, his life had been spared. In 1937 he proposed a new constitution which was approved by vote the same year. Under it, the name of the country became Eire, which in the Irish language signifies Ireland. In 1948 the Government proclaimed the Republic of Ireland, its official name today.

National Symbols

Orange, white and green are the colors of the Irish Republic flag. The harp is the official national emblem. This musical instrument runs through the whole of

IRISH TOURIST ASSOCIATION

SNUG LITTLE HOMES on the stormy shores of Achill Island. It is part of County Mayo and the largest island off the Irish coast. The people wrest a difficult living by farming and fishing.

A SUNNY DAY on Achill Island is used for mending nets, a constant task for those whose livelihood depends on the sea. The island has a wild beauty—*achill* in Gaelic means "eagle."

RICH, LIGHT SOIL and a mild, moist climate make Ireland an ideal place for agriculture. The Irishman's love for his own bit of land has made it a country of many small farms.

Irish history. There were small harps used by ladies. Bishops, abbots and other clergymen had small harps on which to sing their hymns. Large harps were used by the bards. Double chords could be played on the large harps, which suggests that the ancient Irish may have understood counterpoint. Some harps had twenty-eight strings and later thirty-three. Reputed to be the oldest Irish harp in existence is that of Brian Boru, now in Trinity College, Dublin. Henry VIII put the harp on the coins of Ireland in the sixteenth century. In the nineteenth century, Thomas Moore lamented that the harp of Tara no longer sounded for chiefs and ladies bright. But it has come back as a national symbol.

The Irish Theater

Modern Ireland is noted for its drama, its playwrights and the famous Abbey Theatre in Dublin. Rather oddly, there are no traces of interest in the theater in what is known of ancient Ireland.

Drama is usually one of the first forms of art to appear in the history of a society. In the dances of the early Irish some features of a primitive ballet may be traced. Of course the classical ideas of comedy and tragedy did not arise even in England till the time of Henry VIII. To mark his becoming king of Ireland, medieval plays—mysteries and moralities—were performed in Dublin. But such performances were confined to the Pale.

With the rise of Anglo-Irish literature the name of Irish playwrights graced the London stage—Richard Brinsley Sheridan (1751–1816) and Oliver Goldsmith (1728–74), Oscar Wilde (1856–1900) and Bernard Shaw (1856–1950). Early in this century, John Millington Synge (1871–1909) gave us such plays as *Riders to the Sea* and *The Playboy of the Western World*. In them the native Gaelic form of expression was so deftly used in English that they started a new style. William Butler Yeats (1865–1939) and Lady Augusta Gregory (1859?–1932)

TRANS WORLD AIRLINES

HORSE AND DRIVER rest for a moment on a street in Adare, a pretty village in County Limerick. In the Republic of Ireland, most of the road signs are in both Gaelic and English.

BESIDE A KILLARNEY LAKE a jaunting car carries passengers comfortably on either side above the wheels. No visit to Ireland is complete without a ride in one of these vehicles.

made the Irish theater world-famous. Lord Dunsany (1878–1957), of *Night at an Inn* and the *Glittering Gate,* added further luster. Sean O'Casey (1884–), one of the outstanding playwrights of our time, turned from the romanticism of the early Abbey Theatre to the realism of revolution in the rebirth of Ireland. Maud Gonne MacBride (1866–1953), one of Ireland's most beautiful women, inspired Yeats and acted in his plays. His was an Ireland of queens, heroic chieftains, fairy lore, poetry and youth. O'Casey's dramatic world is peopled with grim young Irish rebels, devoted slum mothers, wastrel husbands, outcasts—amid the motley of city tenements. But as in Irish life the worker has his hands to the plow and his eyes to the stars, so in O'Casey, tragedy and comedy dance on one another's heels. Temple Fielding in his modern *Travel Guide to Europe* writes of the Irish: "The people courtly, warmhearted, gay; brimming with humor, laughter and outlandish superstitions; handsome, healthy, athletic, sturdy; rigidly devout and moralistic; hard-drinking, hard-fighting, argumentative; an honest, hard-working, God-fearing people, stubborn, charming, graceful and lovable." Some four hundred years ago, Holinshed, in his *Chronicles of England, Scotland and Ireland,* wrote of the Irish: "The people are thus inclined: re-

ligious, frank, amorous, sufferable of infinite paines, verie glorious; excellent horsemen, delighted with wars, great alms-givers, passing in hospitality."

There is drama even in the ordinary speech of the country folk. Take the jarvey (driver) in the jaunting car in the days of Ireland's agricultural reform at the turn of the century. Then absentee landlords drew racking rents from properties in which they took no interest. A traveler observed that there were many places with the name of the Devil in them —the Devil's glen, the Devil's punch bowl, the Devil's gap, the Devil's bit and many more—and remarked that the Devil must own a lot of property in Ireland. "But he lives abroad," said the jarvey.

Ancient and Modern Arts

In the Metropolitan Museum of Art in New York may be seen replicas of many of Ireland's ancient art objects which are still preserved at home. Many treasures have been lost through the centuries of successful invasions. Enough has been saved, however, to point to a long tradition of artistic achievement. The Cross of Cong, a gem of medieval beauty, was discovered in the last century. So was the Tara Brooch—an ancient ornament found accidentally by a child on an east coast beach. The Ardagh Chalice was dug up

BENBULBEN, in County Sligo. The curious flat-topped mountain figures in many old legends. Here Diarmuid was slain during a boar hunt. Tales and scenery both inspired W. B. Yeats.

DRUID PRIEST and Christian convert struggle—a scene from a pageant of St. Patrick's life.

in a field; it is supposed to stem from the same period as the *Book of Kells*.

The *Book of Kells* is one of Ireland's most glorious possessions. It contains the four Gospels in Latin, though some parts are written in Gaelic and Hebrew. The pages are illuminated with miniatures painted in vivid colors and in gold and silver. The exquisite volume is also known as the Gospel of St. Columba or Columcille. Its popular name, *Book of Kells,* comes from the fact that originally it was preserved in the monastery of Kells in County Meath. Saint Columba of the O'Donnell family may have been its author and it was probably done between the sixth and eighth centuries. During the Norse invasions it was stolen from Kells, lost and then found in bogland with its gold cover gone. Restored to Kells, it was moved from there in the sixteenth century when Henry VIII abolished the

CUTTING TURF from a peat bog. Dried peat burns well in open grates and makes superior charcoal. It is the fuel most used at home, for Ireland has only a little coal of poor quality.

ARAN ISLANDERS don their best clothes to greet the steamer arriving from Galway. The bleakly beautiful islands, at the entrance to Galway Bay, are pounded by Atlantic rollers.

monasteries. Gerald Plunkett, nephew of the last Abbot of Kells, then acquired it. From him it passed into the hands of the Protestant Archbishop of Dublin—Archbishop Ussher—who finally placed it in Trinity College, Dublin. There it rests, and a page a day is turned for viewers. Considered the queen of all the books in the Western world, it is so beautifully wrought that it is sometimes called the Book of the Angel because it was thought that only angels could have achieved its fineness of line and illumination.

From Ulster comes the delicate porcelain called Belleek. This, too, is artistry of a high order though for practical use.

In recent Irish painting there stand out Sir John Lavery, Sean Keating and Sir William Orpen. Orpen painted a record of the peace conference at Versailles, in 1919. Irish artists such as Daniel Maclise and Sir Martin Archer Shee were closely connected with the early Royal Academy in London.

In music the names of Balfe, Wallace, Stanford, Sir Hamilton Harty are notable. As in the nineteenth century Thomas Moore put the name of Ireland on the lips of the world with his immortal melodies, so did John McCormack with his beautiful voice, in the early 1900's, bring Irish songs to every continent. In Ireland

SHAGGY DONKEYS are the beasts of burden on the Aran Islands. Barren and swept by **gales,**
the islands have little soil. Vegetables are grown in narrow crevices between the rocks.

many a festival of music, or *feis* (pronounced *fesh*), commemorates the competitions of the bards at Tara, in pagan days. According to tradition, the skilled performers of the old Irish dances are supposed "to dance with death in their faces and lightning in their feet."

Love of Learning

In the Republic of Ireland there are two universities: Trinity College, or Dublin University, dating from the sixteenth century; and the National University of Ireland founded in the present century. There are university colleges (associated with the National University) at Cork and Galway, and at Maynooth for ecclesiastical students taking degrees. In Northern Ireland is Queen's University, Belfast.

During the seventeenth and eighteenth centuries many Irish students went abroad, to Italy, Spain and France, to be educated as Catholics were forbidden to have schools. During that time in Ireland the outlawed Hedge Schoolmasters flour-

ASSOCIATED BRITISH AND IRISH RAILWAYS

THE GIANT'S CAUSEWAY is part of a headland on the coast of County Antrim. Its thousands of basalt columns, 15 to 20 inches across, resulted from underground volcanic disturbances.

QUEEN'S UNIVERSITY in Belfast was established, as Queen's College, in 1849 and became a university in 1908. The stately buildings are in the Tudor-Gothic style of architecture.

DONEGALL QUAY, near the center of Belfast, accommodates vessels that connect Northern Ireland with Scotland and England. A deep-water channel leads to Belfast's seven miles of quays.

ished. For want of buildings they taught their pupils by the hedgerows in summer and in hillside huts in winter. They managed to teach Latin and Greek well. Without texts, masters and pupils had to rely on memory. Not until the nineteenth century did these banned hedge schools disappear, when a system of public education was finally approved by the British Government.

From the busy hum of linen manufacturing and shipbuilding in industrial Ulster to the remote world of Connacht, Ireland is a land of change and yet of unfading traditions. The Irish still go on pilgrimages to St. Patrick's Purgatory in Donegal for example. St. Patrick's is a lovely shrine on an island where people have fasted, prayed, walked barefoot and kept vigils through the centuries. Dante (the Italian poet who wrote *The Divine Com-*

edy) is said to have been inspired by the vast literature that grew up around this ancient shrine. Shakespeare himself mentioned it in *Hamlet*. Thither had flocked pilgrims from all parts of Europe in the Middle Ages.

During the days of the wandering Irish scholars in Europe, as they sometimes sat in a monastery library copying the Gospels they would turn to the edge of their manuscripts and write notes and poems on the Ireland for which they were homesick. George Bernard Shaw should have known why for he was one of them. Said Shaw: "There is no magic like that of Ireland; there are no skies like Irish skies; there is no air like Irish air; the Irish climate will make the stiffest and slowest mind flexible for life." There let it rest. For the Irish mind the half-said thing is the dearest.

By MAURICE LEAHY

IRELAND: FACTS AND FIGURES

THE WHOLE ISLAND

Island in the Atlantic, west of Great Britain, from which it is separated by North Channel, the Irish Sea and St. George's Channel. Territorially it has long been divided into four provinces: Ulster with 9 counties; Leinster with 12; Connacht with 5; and Munster with 6. Politically it is divided into Northern Ireland and the Republic of Ireland (Eire). Total land area, 31,839 sq. mi.; est. pop. 4,256,000.

NORTHERN IRELAND

Comprising 6 of the 9 counties of Ulster, it is a part of the United Kingdom but has considerable self-government. Representatives are sent to the British Parliament, but the local Parliament of two houses meets in Belfast. The cabinet is responsible to Parliament, and the Queen is represented by a governor. Area, 5,238 sq. mi.; est. pop., 1,403,000. Capital and chief city, Belfast, 443,670. Agriculture is important and wheat, barley, turnips, mangels, oats, flax, hay and potatoes are raised, besides considerable livestock, but the principal industries are the manufacture of linen, shipbuilding, aircrafts, engineering, ropemaking, and distilling. There are 13,736 miles of roads. Air and sea services operate to chief centers in Great Britain. The majority is Protestant. Primary, secondary and special schools. Queen's University is at Belfast; Magee University College, Londonderry, is associated with Queen's.

REPUBLIC OF IRELAND

Includes Leinster, Munster, Connacht and 3 counties of Ulster. Area, 26,601 sq. mi.; est. pop., 2,853,000. Independent since 1921, Ireland became a republic in 1949 with its own constitution and no ties with the Commonwealth of Nations. The constitution provides for a president, elected by direct vote for 7 years; a prime minister, in whom is vested executive power; and a legislature of two houses. Each of the 26 administrative counties and the 4 county boroughs has a council for local government. Agriculture and stock raising are the principal occupations. The chief crops are rye, potatoes and other root crops, oats, wheat and barley. The exports are livestock, meat, eggs, butter, beer and whisky. Imports: machinery, electrical goods, textiles, vehicles and parts, and fats and oils. Railway mileage, 2,579; inland waterways, 571 miles; 50,585 miles of roads; air service operated by Aer Lingus. Over 90% of the population is Roman Catholic, but the constitution guarantees freedom of conscience. Free elementary and technical schools; secondary are mostly private. Gaelic is the language of instruction in the national primary schools. The University of Dublin has one college, Trinity; and the National University of Ireland has 4 constituent colleges: Dublin, Cork, Galway and St. Patrick's, Maynooth. Principal cities, with est. population: Dublin, capital, 534,476; Cork, 80,011; Limerick, 50,886.

Atlantic Islands ...*the peaks of submarine mountains*

THE dominant feature of the Atlantic basin is the presence of an underwater mountain range, the mid-Atlantic ridge, almost exactly in the center of the ocean. It follows the S-shape of the continental coasts. The average depth over this ridge is about 1,100 fathoms, but much greater depths are found on each side. The existence of such a ridge has been known since the 1870's. In 1957, however, geologists traced a deep rift in the range. This rift is a center of earthquake disturbances, which may be felt as far north as Iceland.

North of the equator the ridge breaks the surface of the water to form the Azores archipelago; and south of the equator, Ascension, Tristan da Cunha and Gough islands. All of these consist of volcanic rocks.

Because the Atlantic is so far-reaching —it touches the polar regions north and south, and the equator is a little below its center—we find its clusters of islands in both cool and in warm waters. There is naturally a great variation in their form and appearance. Many are volcanic in origin, that is, they have been thrown up from the ocean depths by some convulsion of nature in past ages. Others are made of coral. Some of the islands are well covered with vegetation and are fertile and beautiful; others are little but bare rock, rugged specks of land in the immensity of the ocean.

Some of the larger islands, such as Iceland, Newfoundland, the Bahamas and others of the West Indian group are described elsewhere. Here we shall discuss the less known but interesting islands that are scattered over the Atlantic from the Azores in the north to South Georgia at the opposite extreme. We shall thus follow in the wake of sea rovers who centuries ago made daring voyages from Europe in their small vessels. Most of these islands were discovered during the early attempts to reach India and the (East) Indies by sailing around Africa or westward across the Atlantic.

The Azores lie athwart a natural route between North America and Europe. The Canaries and Cape Verde Islands intersect the European sea route to the West Indies. The Falklands, deep in the South Atlantic, not only stand in the path of ships rounding Cape Horn on the way from the Pacific to Europe but early became a busy whaling center. Even such lonely specks of land as the Tristan da Cunha group, St. Helena and Ascension islands, all of them scattered between South America and Africa, were sighted

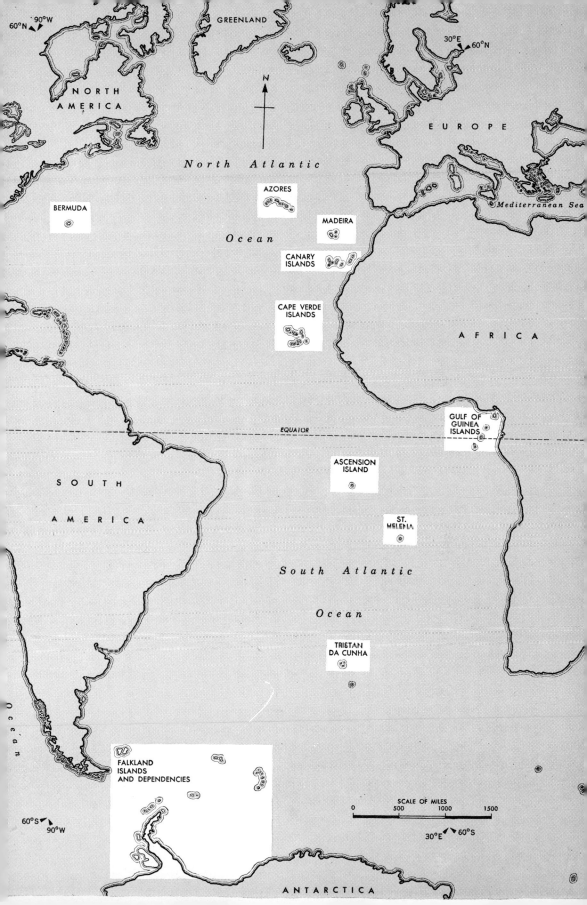

and used by ocean voyagers early in the Age of Discovery.

Such accidents of geography give these islands what little importance they enjoy. For centuries they have been the "service stations" of the Atlantic, replenishing ocean-going vessels with food, water and coal. The advent of the air age has not yet diminished this importance. During World War II, in fact, some of the islands played vital roles as allied air bases. The Azores today are a steppingstone for air as well as sea travel. Crucially located at the center of the great-circle route from northeastern United States to the Mediterranean, the commercial airfield at Santa Maria is one of the most traveled-through spots on earth. Since 1944 the United States has had use of the base at Lajes, on Terceira, for refueling military planes crossing the ocean. Though none of the other Atlantic islands is in quite so fortunate a position, the mobility that the airplane and other forms of modern transportation have brought is affecting all of them. Among other results, they are benefiting from climbing tourist revenue.

This is especially true of the Bermudas and Madeira. Bermuda, a British colony some 580 sea miles off the United States coast, has been a vacation land for years. Today an airplane can transport visitors from New York to Bermuda in a matter of hours. To meet the tourist demand the island Government has embarked on an extensive redevelopment program, restoring ancient landmarks and expanding such facilities as golf courses.

Madeira is not much farther from Europe than Bermuda is from the United States and offers something of the same appeal: superb food, refreshing scenery and a moderate climate. In 1960 an airport was opened on Pôrto Santo Island to service scheduled flights to the islands.

Modern communications may yet give the islanders themselves a chance to see something of the outside world, but up to 1960 most of them were still quite isolated, outside the mainstream of world events. Two exceptions, under unhappy circumstances, were the Azores and the Falklands. In late 1957 off Faial, one of the

smaller members of the Azores group, an active volcano emerged. It rose abruptly and spread until it actually touched the shore, spouting smoke and red-hot ashes. The "island" made by the eruption was claimed by the Portuguese on October 12; by October 30, though, it had sunk back into the sea. About three thousand persons, many of whom lost their homes for good, were forced to flee the area.

The Falklands' share of the spotlight has not been much more pleasant. These islands—and particularly their dependencies—the South Orkneys and South Georgia—are the base of operations for British exploration in Antarctica. Argentina and Chile dispute Britain's right both to Palmer Peninsula and other parts of Antarctica; and Argentina claims the Falkland Islands. All three countries base their claims on prior discovery and exploration. Only the British, however, can point to a long record of "effective occupation" in the Falklands. The quarrel has been referred to the International Court of Justice but Chile and Argentina have refused to join the proceedings. The British, meanwhile, are going ahead with plans to develop new roads, schools and plants to process the products of the islands' chief industries: sheep raising and whaling.

The historical background of the Atlantic islands is spare but colorful. The Azores were given their name by the Portuguese seamen who reached them in the fifteenth century. The word *azores,* which means "goshawks," was applied to the flocks of buzzards that were found there. The archipelago, as it is styled, really consists of the summits of a chain of submarine volcanoes. At one period, according to scientists, the islands were widely covered by forests, but now there are large areas of open land. These are under cultivation on São Miguel, the largest of the group, and on Terceira, Pico and Faial, which are next in importance.

An interesting fact in connection with the Azores is that they play an important part as a meteorological station. They would seem to have been placed out in the Atlantic to serve as a sentinel for the

ONE WAY OF MEETING LIFE'S UPS AND DOWNS ON MADEIRA

Many of the streets in town as well as country lanes are rugged on the island of Madeira, and the hammock-taxi offers to the weary tourist the best means of transport. Because of its mild climate, which does not vary much from season to season, the island is popular as a health resort. Funchal, the capital and a seaport, has a number of fine modern hotels.

purpose of warning Europe of storms that are brewing in the ocean. There are observatories at Ponta Delgada in St. Michael's, on the island of Flores, and at Horta, in Fayal, all under the supervision of the Portuguese government.

One of the ocean phenomena for which the observers at these stations are on the watch is the "houle." This is the name given to a remarkable wave that rises out of the sea, apparently without cause, somewhere between the Azores and Iceland. It gathers strength as it goes, and sweeps, at a speed that varies from four to twenty miles an hour, upon some coast hundreds of miles distant.

The houle does not always announce its coming by a storm or similar sign. It will arise suddenly on a calm day, when the sky is cloudless, and ships riding at anchor in open roadsteads may be flung high up on the beach and wrecked. When the warning of this treacherous wave is given, vessels at sea in the vicinity of the Azores have several good harbors in the islands to which they can flee for safety.

From 1580 to 1640 the Azores, as a part of the Portuguese kingdom, were subject to Spain. At that time the islands were a favorite stopping place for ships on their way home from the Indies, and it was off the island of Flores that the battle took place between the English ship Revenge, commanded by Sir Richard Grenville, and a fleet of fifty-three Spanish vessels. In the early days of commercial transatlantic flying service it was an important stopping place.

Supposing that we were not venturesome enough to sail so far into mid-ocean, but were content to make a shorter voyage from the Spanish or Portuguese coast, we might turn our vessel's head in the direction of Madeira. This beautiful, well-wooded island is one of a group of five islands, of which only two are inhabited. It is a Portuguese possession, but a curious story is told in an old chronicle which attributes its discovery to an Englishman. According to this account, a certain Robert Machin, in the year 1370, fled from England in a small boat, taking

159

A STURDY SHEPHERD WHO ROVES THE STEEP HILLSIDES OF MADEIRA

Only a few miles from the lush, banana-growing coast of the island one enters a region of bare uplands, good only for the pasturage of sheep. It can get very cool among these hills and the shepherd is protected against the weather with a sweater and an ear-covering cap. Instead of a crook, he carries a long, straight staff with a sharply pointed end.

CAMACHA, A VILLAGE HIDDEN AWAY AMONG MADEIRA'S MOUNTAINS

Though the village seems so remote, it is only five miles from Funchal and has many visitors. They come to enjoy the sweeping grandeur of the view and also to buy wickerwork. Almost every inhabitant of the hamlet earns his living by fashioning various articles of wicker—furniture, baskets, trays—that find markets all over the world.

160

"ORCHIDS TO YOU"

Flower vendors are on hand to greet the tourist in Madeira. Exotic orchids and fragrant gardenias are often tossed into the lap of a delighted visitor, who hastily throws back a coin from his car to the trusting salesman. The incongruous "beanie" perched on the head of the young woman at the left may be causing the mirth that both girls are trying so hard to suppress.

a lady. He intended to sail for France, but instead, he was blown out of his course and came to Madeira. Here the lady died and was buried, and Machin erected a cross to her memory. In 1420 the island was re-discovered by the Portuguese.

To most people Madeira is familiar as a popular health resort. It is a warm and sunny island which has much to at-

tract the visitor. The loftiness of the mountains, often snow-covered, the sharpness of the ravines, the pleasing contours of the coast and the proximity of the sea afford many scenes of glorious beauty. In addition to the picturesqueness of its gorges and woods, its caves and bubbling springs, the island possesses a very fertile soil, on which coffee and tobacco flourish amid an abundance of

A FOUR-FOOTED FREIGHT CARRIER OF THE CANARY ISLANDS

The people of the Canary Islands make use of camels for a great variety of domestic and agricultural purposes. These strong and patient animals are especially useful in transporting the produce that is grown in the interior of the islands to the coastal ports. This camel is carrying a load of fruit in a wooden container. Mules are also used as beasts of burden.

fruit and flowers and tropical ferns. For centuries the vine has been grown on the island and Madeira wine has been famous. Sugar-cane growing has been attempted, but with limited success.

The chief town of Madeira is Funchal, and here there takes place annually a very curious celebration. On the last day of the year, shortly before midnight, the whole of the valley in which the capital lies seems to burst into flame. It is a magnificent firework display, in which the entire population joins. Colored lights gleam on all sides, rockets, Roman candles and fountains of fire flash into brilliance here and there, while an added effect is given by the illuminated boats which dart about the harbor. No one who has seen Funchal thus lit up can forget the sight.

Very near to Madeira, to the southward, are the Canary Islands, which were known to the Romans. One was called Insula Canaria—the isle of dogs—after a species of dog supposed to have been found there. Thus the group got its name. From the Canaries first came the little yellow bird which has been given the name of the country in which it dwelt. In its native home the canary is colored like a greenfinch.

Known to the Romans also as the Fortunate Isles, the Canaries have had a stirring history. They have been fought for by French, Spanish, Portuguese and English. In the early 1800's they were created a province of Spain; later their ports were declared free; and in 1883–84 the laying of the submarine cable linked up these ocean islands with the rest of the world.

The Canaries are of volcanic origin, like the Azores and most of the other Atlantic islands. Pico de Teide, the volcanic peak that rises from the center of the island of Tenerife, has often been active. During various disturbances outlets were made some distance below the

PONTA DELGADA, thriving Azores seaport, is on the island of San Miguel. It has an excellent man-made harbor, which is sheltered by a breakwater almost one mile long.

WASH DAY ON A HILL ABOVE TENERIFE IN THE CANARY ISLANDS

The basins follow the shape of the hill by steps and are solidly built of concrete. For housewives who have no running water in their homes, such a place is a big convenience.

crater itself, and from these there often come little puffs of smoke and steam, which are lively evidence of its hidden fires.

If the Canaries were of old the "Fortunate Islands," they might very properly now be called the "Fruit Islands," for from them comes a great banana supply. The islands are also rich in other fruits, and, as in Madeira, the grapevine has been grown for centuries.

One notable feature of these islands is the large herds of goats to be seen there, and we may sometimes see an extraordinarily athletic feat performed by the men who look after them. In the gorge known as the Great Caldera of La Palma, for instance, where the rocks are very steep and dangerous, the goat-herd will jump after a troublesome goat that has got away to some crag many feet below. As he descends he will strike at the animal with his "lanza," a long wooden pole, but even then will be able to break his fall

by sliding down the "lanza" the moment it touches the ground. It is said that these men are so expert in pole-jumping that they can even spring from the top of a house into the street without injuring themselves.

The people on the neighboring island of Gomera are among the world's most expert whistlers. They are able to imitate the exact qualities—tone, timbre, pitch, rhythm and so on—of spoken speech; and their whistled conversations carry for a much longer distance than even shouting would. The islanders have had this remarkable ability for centuries.

Let us sail still farther south, where the Atlantic makes a sweep round the coast of Morocco, until we come to Cape Verde, in Senegambia. Off this part of West Africa, three hundred miles out at sea, lie the islands named after the cape. They are fourteen in number. Being of the same volcanic character as the Canaries, the islands present a bare and un-

ST. HELENA, WHERE NAPOLEON SPENT HIS LAST DAYS

Lying twelve hundred miles from the nearest continent, Africa, this small, volcanic island in the South Atlantic must have been a dull dwelling place for an emperor. Jamestown, in a narrow ravine, is its only town and seaport. St. Helena is mountainous, and although once covered with forests, it is now largely barren, with wretchedly poor soil.

ST. JAMES CHURCH IN JAMESTOWN, CAPITAL OF ST. HELENA

Jamestown is the only town on the island, and more than half the population lives here. In 1658, the East India Company erected a fort here called James, named for the Duke of York, and around it the community of Jamestown grew up. It has an excellent harbor, and was an important port of call for ships sailing round Africa to the Orient, until the Suez Canal was opened.

LONGWOOD, ISLAND HOME OF AN IMPERIAL EXILE

In this simple dwelling on St. Helena, an island in the South Atlantic Ocean, Napoleon I passed the years of his exile until his death in May 1821. The house is three and a half miles southeast of Jamestown and is named for the Longwood Plains in the northeast part of the island. It was presented by Queen Victoria to the Emperor Napoleon III in 1858.

inviting appearance as viewed from the sea. This is deceptive; on landing, we find that the valleys of the interior are green and fertile. The Portuguese have introduced eucalyptus, baobab and dragon trees to replace the trees cut down for timber. A volcano, Pico do Cano, is still active on the island of Fogo (fire). Its crater, which stands within an older crater, is three miles in circumference and may be seen from a hundred miles at sea. Coffee is largely grown here; the biggest Cape Verde island, Saint Jago, has a good export trade in this berry.

Far more interesting to us, however, is the island of Ascension, that lonely rock which rises steeply from the South Atlantic, about half-way between the continents of Africa and South America. This island, so scientists say, is probably only the summit of a huge volcanic mass, and whatever animals or plants it may have possessed at one time have been completely exterminated by the lava from eruptions.

In history, Ascension has a particular connection with Napoleon. When, after Waterloo, the fallen French emperor was sent in exile to St. Helena, over eight hundred miles away to the southeast, it was feared that Ascension might be used by his friends with a view to effecting his rescue. So Great Britain occupied the island, and since then it has been one of her Atlantic possessions. Before that date, 1815, Ascension had remained uninhabited, except for a short period when Dampier, the buccaneer, and his crew lived upon it after they were shipwrecked. But the most picturesque feature of this ocean rock is the fact that for a long time it was under the control of the Admiralty. It actually figured in official books as a ship—H.M.S. Ascension—lying at anchor, so to speak, in latitude 7° 57' S., longitude 14° 22' W. Its commander was a naval captain, appointed by the governor of Gibraltar, and under him was a ship's company. This peculiar state of affairs came to an end in 1922, when the Admiralty handed over Ascension Island to the Colonial Office.

A LAND OF TROPICAL SUNSHINE AND GAY VACATIONS

Bermuda sunshine creates a pattern of light and shade along Hamilton's Front Street, the main business avenue of the capital city. The buildings face the bustling waterfront, busy with the constant arrival and departure of ships. Automobiles have been allowed in Bermuda since December 31, 1946, but the bicycle and the patient horse are very much a part of the scene.

CRYSTAL CAVE—AN UNDERGROUND FAIRYLAND

The magical beauty of thousands of stalactite "icicles" is reflected in the calm waters of Crystal Cave. Through the ages, water containing calcium carbonate has dripped through the roof of the cave. This constant dripping has left deposits of lime which have gradually formed the stalactite needles. Visitors are guided through the cavern on a pontoon bridge.

ST. GEORGE—BERMUDA'S OLDEST SETTLEMENT

Narrow, winding streets, fringed by ancient walls and picturesque houses, are typical of the town of St. George, which was founded in the year 1612. This little town is the oldest Anglo-Saxon settlement in the Western Hemisphere to be continuously inhabited since its beginnings. Until 1815, when the government moved to Hamilton, it was the capital of Bermuda.

169

BERMUDA NEWS BUREAU

A BERMUDA ROAD WITH WALLS OF CORAL

A two-horse team steps smartly along a narrow road that
has been cut through a hillock of solid coral limestone.
The coral consists of both marine animal deposits and
coral fragments blown and packed down by the wind.

by the Portuguese explorer who
discovered it, and whose name
it now bears. From a distance
it appears to be a single mountain rising from the sea, so narrow is its coastal plain and so
lush is the vegetation which covers its volcanic slopes. Torren-
tial streams have cut deep beds
down the mountainsides, forming many beautiful waterfalls
and ravines. Oil-palms, tree
ferns, African oak, mahogany
trees and a variety of fruit trees
grow in abundance. Cacao is
an important export from the
island of São Thomé; to-day
the population is largely composed of descendants of the
slaves who were brought from
Africa to work on the cacao
plantations in the latter half of
the nineteenth century. The descendants of the original settlers control about one-eighth of
the land.

St. Helena, the island which
we are next visiting, is another
of the extinct volcano type. It

It is a lonely rock; the population consists of the officials of the cable station
and a hundred or so colored people from
the Guinea coast. The naval garrison
which used to be stationed here has been
withdrawn. About thirty-four square
miles in extent, the island has little vegetation, save grass and shrubs which have
been planted by colonists. Around the
coast there is enough to support a few
thousand sheep. Were it not for the
turtles which frequent its shores the inhabitants might fare badly. These creatures find their way to Ascension to lay
their eggs, and enough are killed to keep
the islanders in turtle meat.

The islands in the Gulf of Guinea, to
the northeast of Ascension Island, are
surprisingly different. The Portuguese
possessions of Saint Thomas and Prin-
cipe, touching the Equator, and the Spanish island of Fernando Po are covered
with luxuriant vegetation. Fernando Po
was christened Formosa, "the beautiful,"

is simply a point of rock rising straight
from the depths of the ocean. As it is
approached there is no sign of a sloping
beach or shore, and it presents, indeed, a
gloomy and forbidding appearance in the
outlines of its coast. Nor does a closer
examination do much to dispel this impression. There is very little soil on St.
Helena that is suitable for growing flowers
or vegetables. Only here and there, in
some of the valleys between the great
chasms in the rock, can any earth be
found.

In the olden days, when the East India
Company's ships used to pass that way,
they called at the island to obtain fresh
water. Nowadays its chief point of interest is its association with Napoleon,
who was kept a prisoner here from 1815
until his death six years later. "Longwood," the house which he occupied, is
now visited every year by numbers of
the emperor's admirers, mostly French
people, of course. The house and

LANZAROTE WOMEN wear deep straw hats, tied over head wrappings. The islanders are a Spartan people, keeping to old customs and little influenced by the outside world.

LANDSCAPE ON THE MOON? No, it is Lanzarote, one of the Canary Islands. The crescent-shaped rock piles shelter grape vines, planted in volcanic ash, from ever blowing winds.

ART NEEDLEWORK, AN IMPORTANT HOME INDUSTRY OF MADEIRA

On a terrace amidst a semitropical garden, diligent ladies ply their deft needles. They stitch the beautiful floral patterns that have made the embroidery of their islands famous.

FURNISHING THE INTRICATE PATTERNS FOR THE EMBROIDERERS

In a bright drafting room of a Portuguese textile house, careful workmen plot and trace designs that will be transferred to cloth and then embroidered in countless homes and factories.

AN AZORES FARMER ON MULE-BACK LOOKS OVER THE DRYING FLAX

Flax fibers, used for rope, are an important export from the mid-Atlantic Azores Islands, owned by Portugal. The rich, fertile land also produces oranges, bananas, tea and coffee.

grounds, with the tomb in which he was first buried, have been transferred to the keeping of France, so that that country holds a piece of territory in St. Helena.

Hundreds of miles south of St. Helena is its dependency, Tristan da Cunha, a group of four islands—Tristan, Nightingale, Inaccessible and, 250 more miles to the southeast, Gough. Only Tristan was settled. Its inhabitants were descendants of shipwrecked sailors and the handful of British soldiers who elected to remain after a temporary garrison was withdrawn about 1817. Only a few acres were farmed, but at times seal hunting was found profitable. In October 1961 the British evacuated the total population of 260 to England when a volcano on the island began to erupt. Homesick, the colonists hoped to be allowed to return after the volcano quieted.

For our next Atlantic islands let us sail up into the warmer region above the West Indies. Here lie the Bermudas, of whose "still vexed" waters Shakespeare wrote in *The Tempest*. Even so far back as the poet's day these islands had an unenviable reputation for storms.

It was during one of these hurricanes, in 1609, that Admiral Sir George Somers was shipwrecked there while on his way to Virginia. This disaster led to the settlement of the group and a Bermuda Company was formed three years later to send out colonists. On some old maps we find the name of the islands given as Somers; their more general title of Bermudas serves as a reminder of the Spanish seaman Juan Bermudez who first visited their shores early in the sixteenth century.

The Bermudas are coral islands, thus they are distinct from the others with which we are dealing. They are some three hundred and fifty in number, but the total area does not exceed twenty square miles. All round them are reefs, to a distance of thirty miles from the main group.

It is a remarkable fact that such coral-built islands should exist so far from the equator, surrounded by living coral reefs, but they are right in the track of the Gulf Stream and so the surrounding waters are warm. The Bermudas are unique, further, in that no native people

LANDING SUPPLIES ON THE BLEAK SHORE OF GRAHAM LAND

Graham Land is the tip of Antarctica that reaches toward South America. It is included in the Falkland Islands dependency, a British colony, though Argentina also claims the territory. The boats are coming ashore at Hope Bay with supplies for a British expedition. Extensive surveys of the dependency have been made in recent years and permanent weather stations established.

A WELCOMING PARTY IN FULL DRESS AT HOPE BAY

Penguins flourish mid the ice and snow of the Antarctic mainland and islands, where few other animals could survive. But even some of the penguins move a little farther north before the dark winter closes down. Adélie penguins like these, for instance, spend only the summer on the Antarctic ice. At other times they can be found on the rocky coasts of the Falklands.

or traces of them were found upon the islands.

Vegetation grows rapidly and the islands are almost perpetually clad in green; the shores are fringed with mangrove; prickly pear grows in the most barren spots and sage bushes spring up wherever they are allowed. The charm of these islands is fully appreciated by the people of northeastern United States who flock to them during the winter months.

Passing the little, isolated islands of Martim Vaz and Trindade, in the South Atlantic, we reach the Falklands, which lie off Patagonia, the southern extremity of South America. The principal islands are the East and West, but there are hundreds of smaller ones clustering in the straits between these two. Their treeless slopes are swept continuously by winds and heavy rainfall. Nevertheless the islands are well adapted for grazing and many cattle and sheep are bred here.

First sighted in the sixteenth century the Falklands were alternately ruled by Great Britain, France and Spain. In 1829 the Argentinians claimed possession as an inheritance from Spain, but an 1833 expedition put the islands in Britain's hands for good.

Farther south, nearing the Antarctic, are South Georgia and the bare, windswept islands of the South Shetlands and South Orkneys. All are attached to the British Crown Colony of the Falkland Islands as dependencies.

ATLANTIC ISLANDS: FACTS AND FIGURES

THE AZORES (*Western Islands*)

An archipelago in the North Atlantic Ocean, 800 mi. off the coast of Portugal; divided into 3 groups; administered as an integral part of the Republic of Portugal. Total area is 888 sq. mi.; estimated population, 318,700. Populations of chief towns: Ponta Delgada, 22,700; Angra do Heroismo, 10,500. Chief exports: fruit (especially oranges), wine, cheese and coarse linens.

MADEIRA

A group of islands in the North Atlantic about 400 mi. from the coast of Africa. Administered as an integral part of the Republic of Portugal. Total area, 308 sq. mi.; population, 267,000. Chief exports: sugar, fruit and particularly wine and embroidery for which the islands are noted. Funchal, the chief town, population, 37,215.

CAPE VERDE ISLANDS

An archipelago belonging to Portugal about 350 mi. off the west coast of Africa in the North Atlantic Ocean; administered by a Governor. Total area, 1,557 sq. mi.; population, 195,000. Chief products are castor beans, coffee, mustard, oranges and brandy. There are 120 primary schools. Praia is the capital of the islands.

SÃO TOMÉ (ST. THOMAS) E PRINCIPE

Two islands in the Gulf of Guinea about 125 mi. off the west coast of Africa. Portuguese province administered by a Governor. Total area, 372 sq. mi.; population, 62,000. Chief products of the islands are cacao and coffee.

BERMUDA

British colony in the North Atlantic Ocean about 580 sea mi. east of the United States. Administered by a Governor assisted by an Executive Council, a Legislative Council and an elected House of Assembly. Consists of 20 inhabited islands and numerous uninhabited islets; area, 21 sq. mi.; estimated population, 44,000. Chief products are drugs and vegetables. Excellent telephone and telegraph communication. Education government-aided. Population of Hamilton, capital, 3,000.

FALKLAND ISLANDS AND DEPENDENCIES

British Crown Colony in South Atlantic 300 mi. east of Strait of Magellan. Area of Falkland Islands, 4,618 sq. mi.; population, 2,250. Dependencies are South Georgia, South Shetlands, South Orkneys, South Sandwich group and Palmer Peninsula. Sheep farming and whaling are carried on.

British possessions in the South Atlantic include the island of St. Helena, 1,200 mi. off the west coast of Africa (area, 47 sq. mi.; population, 4,800); Ascension Island, 700 mi. northwest of St. Helena; Tristan de Cunha, a small group of islands halfway between the Cape of Good Hope and South America.

CANARY ISLANDS

An archipelago in the Atlantic Ocean about 60 mi. west of the African coast. Considered as part of Spain for administrative purposes. Total area, 2,808 sq. mi.; population, 810,000. Bananas, tomatoes, potatoes, onions and sugar are exported. Schools are numerous. Population of Santa Cruz de Tenerife, 115,000.

FERNANDO PO

Spanish island in the Gulf of Guinea about 25 mi. from African coast. Under a governor. Area about 779 sq. mi.; population, 45,000. Santa Isabel, capital of Spanish Guinea, has a population of 11,000.

"EXPORT" read the labels on the windows of these light trucks. The endless quest for fresh markets is leading the Netherlands to expand its automobile industry. It finds ready buyers in Latin America, Asia and Africa as well as the rest of Europe.

The Netherlands

.. a land won

from the sea

THE Dutch have always been great seafarers. Crowded into a small corner of Europe, most of the area naturally low, marshy land, they have made up for this handicap not only by reclaiming land from the sea but by energetic exploration and development abroad. In the seventeenth century, the golden age of the Dutch, they leaped ahead in commerce, exploration, industry and art. Dutch command of the sea lanes, their monopoly of the rich trade in spices flowing from the East Indies brought immense wealth to busy seaports like Amsterdam and Rotterdam, which grew with trade.

Though rivalry with England and wars with France and Spain brought about a decline of Dutch power in the eighteenth century, the Dutch held fast to the East Indies. The spice trade became somewhat less important but other island resources came to the fore: rubber and, in this century, oil. As we tell you in the article on Indonesia, the Netherlands lost its Indies empire after World War II.

In 1956 Indonesia repudiated the economic and financial agreements that had been made with Holland in 1949. Also, in 1956 Indonesia announced that it would no longer honor its debts to the Netherlands. There were still about 146,000 nationals working in the islands and Dutch business interests there were valued at $1,000,000,000. Dutch companies dominated banking, insurance, oil refining, rubber, tea and shipping. In 1958 the Indonesian Parliament nationalized all Dutch enterprises. Practically all Dutch nationals have left Indonesia since.

The loss of the East Indies was a jolting political blow but, as matters have turned out, had a much less devastating effect on the Dutch economy. Toward the end of the 1950's Holland was waxing more prosperous than ever before. There are several reasons for this. Practically all of Western Europe made an amazingly swift recovery from World War II, helped by the generous Marshall Plan aid from the United States and a variety of international co-operative agencies such as the Organization for European Economic Co-operation. The loss of the East Indies made Holland more receptive to such collaboration with its neighbors. At the same time, because of industrial expansion, Holland's trade has been exceptionally well balanced. This was achieved by a low-tariff policy which made it possible to buy the lowest-priced goods available abroad. Meanwhile, inflation was kept in hand at home by employer-trade-union agreements and other measures. As a result the Netherlands was able to produce cheaply and export a higher proportion of its national output (50 per cent)

than any other industrialized country.

The trend toward European co-operation began shortly after the end of World War II when Holland joined Belgium and Luxembourg to form the Benelux customs union. This was only the first of several co-operative ventures, culminating in the European Economic Community (Common Market) treaty signed by the Benelux nations and France, West Germany and Italy early in 1958.

The Dutch are not altogether happy about their participation in the Common Market, whose tariff policy may conflict sharply with their own. Some of their industrialists fear that the absence of tariff protection will drive them out of business. But after signing the treaty, Dutch Foreign Minister Luns remarked: "The alternative, in my opinion, is certainly less attractive for many countries, and for the Netherlands in particular."

Close alliances characterize Dutch foreign policy too. Holland is a charter member of NATO and a partner in the United States Mutual Security Pact. Relations between the Dutch and the Americans have been a little strained, however. Holland resented Washington's refusal of support during the struggle between Dutch and Indonesian troops. When the United States made friendly gestures toward Indonesia after its independence, Dutch anger increased. The forces that bring Holland and the United States together, though (a common defense system —NATO—and a common culture), are stronger than any divisive force. Dutch-American relations seem bound to improve.

At home the Dutch have redoubled their efforts to defend and win more land from the sea. As we shall see later, this struggle began and has continued from ancient times. With the aid of modern engineering methods, though, advances are being made that the early Dutch could never even have dreamed. In 1954 the Government announced a $500,000,000 plan to protect the maze of islands and the coast in the delta of southwestern Holland from the ravages of the North Sea. In 1953 this area had been the scene of a disastrous

THE BROAD-VANED ARMS of windmills still sweep Holland's sky, but the windmills themselves have earned a rest. Most of their work is done today by high-powered pumping stations.

KOSTICH

ON THE SHIP CANAL from Flushing to Veere, in Zeeland. Because most of the maritime province of Zeeland is very low, its people wage a never ending battle against the sea.

179

flood causing over 1,500 deaths. Today the area is being more strongly fortified against the sea by a number of ingenious dikes (some resting on foundations that consist in part of nylon and other plastics) that dam three of the widest arms of the sea. On the north the massive Ijssel Lake (Zuider Zee) reclamation project continues to make headway. There vast stretches of land are being uncovered and built up as the sea water is pumped out. These stretches will amount to 550,000 acres of new fertile land when the project is finally finished.

With such achievements bolstering Holland's widespread prosperity the appeal of radical political parties has lessened in the Netherlands, much as in Belgium. The Dutch Labor Party remains quite strong, but its socialist program has been watered down through the years. In coalition with the Catholic People's Party the Laborites held power in the lower chamber of parliament from 1946 far into the 1950's. In 1958, however, Labor lost ground in the provincial elections due to its unpopular deflationary policy. The new cabinet that was formed on the national level at the same time excluded Labor for the first time in twelve years. A number of minority parties have made strong showings in recent elections, making it practically certain that Dutch politics will continue to produce coalition cabinets for some time.

Victory over the Enemy, Water

"God created the world, but the Dutch made Holland," runs an old saying, and in a sense it is true.

If you could have flown over Holland some thousand years ago, high enough to see all of it, you would have noticed a long strip of sand dunes on the western coast which faces the North Sea. Just behind this, toward the east, you would have seen many swamps and lakes, and then— beginning at about the middle of the country—higher land covered with rolling moors and forests. Today, on this same flight, you would find that the swamps and inland seas have disappeared almost completely, and in their stead there are rich farm lands, crisscrossed by canals and dotted with prosperous villages. This great change was the work of the Dutch people.

Their struggle with the sea produced the spirit of endurance and self-reliance that enabled little Holland to be an international power.

Whether you approach the Netherlands by sea or by air, the first thing you notice is the tremendous natural sea wall of sand dunes that protects the country against the fury of the stormy North Sea. This wall is the first line of defense, and a constant watch is kept over it. Wherever the sea might break through, the wall is reinforced with strong dikes; and wherever shifting sands might weaken the structure, helm grass is planted, which forms a mat that holds the dunes in place.

Three times in history the sea has invaded large sections of Holland's southwestern area which consists mostly of a group of islands and therefore is more exposed. In 1421 and in February 1953 (as we have mentioned) huge storms whipped up such large waves that they broke through the dikes and swept the sea far inland. During World War II these same islands were flooded for strategic purposes after the population had been evacuated.

What are dikes really? When people first came to the Netherlands, more than two thousand years ago, they settled on only the high parts of the land. However, as the population grew, it spread to the more swampy sections in the western area. Here, in order to protect themselves and their cattle from the ever-present water, the people built small, artificial hills, called *terpen*. Not long afterward they invented an even better way to remain dry, and this was simply to surround a section of swamp or a lake with a dike and then to pump the water out across the dike. As steam or electric engines had not yet been invented, they used the one source of power that was always available: the wind. So tall towers were erected. To each of these a large propeller was attached, and this in turn was connected, through a series of gears, with a water wheel. These structures were the first windmills. Thus the steady winds were made to serve the Dutchmen in their fight against the water, which will seep through even the sturdiest dikes. Through the centuries, more and more of the swamps and lakes were pumped dry. Such a drained area is called a polder. The last major project of this kind is the draining of the former Zuider Zee, started in 1919. By 1962, over half of the planned 550,000 acres had been reclaimed and three of the five polders were being cultivated.

At first, the water pumped out of the polders was led into the rivers. Soon, as more and more swamps were reclaimed, the distances to the rivers became too great, and a series of canals was dug next to the dikes to carry off the water. The level of these canals had to be higher than that of the polders and the rivers, in order that the water might flow away to the sea naturally. (It is forced up to the level of the canals by the pumps.) So there is the curious spectacle, familiar to everyone who visits western Holland, of seeing a large river boat calmly sailing along at the level of roof tops. Houses are hardly ever built right on the dikes but usually in the polders themselves, which actually lie below

LAND OF THE THRIFTY DUTCH

sea level because they are really the bottoms of the one-time swamps. On the top of the dikes are Holland's highways, and thus both water and road transportation often run parallel. The level of the water is controlled through a series of locks which enables the Dutch to irrigate the land as well as to keep it dry, providing exactly the right amount of moisture for the lush meadows and fertile cropland. The locks controlling the sea exits of the canals are closed during high tide.

How Water Helped the Dutch

Water contributed to Holland's development in another way—this time as an ally, not as an enemy. Soon after the first settlers came, fishing villages began to appear along the rivers, lakes and seashore, and today fishing still is an important source of income for the Dutch people. The fact that there were villages on both the North Sea and the rivers Rhine, Meuse and Scheldt almost forced the Dutch into trade and shipping. For the North Sea gave them free access to the rest of the world, and the rivers gave them cheap highways of transportation with western Europe. From the beginning of the sixteenth century, Dutch ships sailed ever farther and farther. Discoverers and traders roamed to America and South Africa and as far as the East Indies, carrying with them goods from Europe and bringing back the riches of those far-off lands. The Dutch thus became a people of farmers, fishermen and traders, with a merchant marine that today ranks as the sixth largest in the world.

Signs of Holland's Golden Era

Windmills, although mostly replaced by pumping stations powered by electricity or steam, still are very much in evidence, lending the Dutch landscape its peculiar charm. In addition, the beautiful houses of the merchant princes of Holland's "golden seventeenth century" can be found in every city. Thus, one is always reminded of the past.

Dutch history, however, began at a much earlier date. Of prehistoric men and others of the very earliest people in The

THE AMSTEL, a canalized river, flows past the shopping section in Amsterdam, Holland's principal city. It is from this river that the busy commercial center takes its name.

IN THE HEART of Amsterdam's business district stands the Royal Palace, formerly the town hall. It was built in 1648–55 but was not used as a home of royalty until 1768.

KOSTICH

TRANQUIL WATER reflects the dignity of the Peace Palace, one of The Hague's many fine buildings. Once a hunting seat of nobility, The Hague is now the home of Holland's court.

THE SOARING ARMS of a windmill mark the course of these skaters. Skating over the frozen surfaces of the canals has long been a favorite winter sport in the Netherlands.

A ROAD that is constructed along the crest of a dike. The dike and the canal to its left are very much higher than the polder, or fertile reclaimed land, which lies to the right.

Netherlands, not much is known. However, about 50 B.C. Roman legions marched in and, after some considerable difficulty, subdued the hardy people they found there. In the ninth century, after invasions by various tribes and races, Holland found itself part of the great empire of Charlemagne. You can still find the remains of one of his castles near the city of Nijmegen, in the eastern part of the country. During the Middle Ages, the section of Europe that is now The Netherlands and Belgium consisted mostly of the feudal states of local dukes and barons who, during the fifteenth century, came under the rule of the Dukes of Burgundy. Through various intermarriages of the Burgundy family with the Austrian and Spanish royal families, The Netherlands became a possession of the Habsburg (or Hapsburg) dynasty under Emperor Charles V. Under this monarch the Dutch did not fare too badly, but during the reign of his son, Philip II of Spain, the country passed through what was possibly the worst time

in its entire history. Beginning in 1568, the Dutch fought a war against this foreign power that was to last for eighty years. The burghers of the Dutch towns, proud of their accomplishments, refused to bow to the power of an overlord from far-off Spain with its feudal system. It was a struggle, also, for spiritual freedom by a people who had adopted the new Protestant religion. Their revolution was led by a man who became the founder of Holland's independence and of the present Royal House, Prince William of Orange-Nassau, called William the Silent. When the war was concluded by the Peace of Münster, in 1648, it was established once and for all that a people have the right to decide their own future and their own government—a right that the rulers and kings of Europe were forced to accept.

Holland now became the Republic of The Netherlands; the Princes of Orange were given the title of Stadtholder. They had no sovereign power or status and were in effect the "servants" of the States-

AERO-PHOTO NEDERLAND

THE SEA, mighty foe of the valiant Dutch, gains a temporary victory. Early in 1953 furious waves smashed through the protecting wall of dikes and caused immense destruction.

ROBERT LEAHEY, SHOSTAL

CHEESE-CARRIERS of Alkmaar, the center of cheese export, north of Amsterdam. The red straw hats and gleaming white suits make up the traditional costume of their profession.

TULIP BLOSSOMS, from carefully cultivated bulbs, spread a flaming carpet across a field near Lisse. Dutch bulbs are prized all over the world for the quality of their blooms.

187

IN THE HAGUE, Parliament opens each year in the ancient Ridderzaal (Hall of Knights).

General (or Parliament), who were the representatives of the Dutch people. Actually, the Princes were the chief magistrates of the Dutch Republic, and a democratic system was established.

A period of great prosperity followed, and arts and sciences flourished. Philosophers and scientists from every country where independent thought was suppressed came to Holland as the only haven of freedom in the Europe of the time. It was no mere accident that some of the Pilgrims first set out for America from a port in The Netherlands. Even as Dutch mariners discovered and Dutch pioneers settled new lands, so did Dutch artists and scientists break new ground.

Frans Hals, Rembrandt, Vermeer and others depicted the beauty of the country and the sturdy quality of its people. Joost van den Vondel became its greatest dramatist. The University of Leiden, founded

PHOTOS, BLACK STAR

A GOOD EXAMPLE of Dutch tidiness. Orderly bundles of carpet-beaters made of supple willow wands are neatly displayed during the day, along a village wall.

THE FLAT ROOFS and angular design of the Town Hall of Hilversum, a city in central Holland, illustrates the strong Dutch trend toward very modern styles in architecture.

THE RAVAGES of World War II left this area in Rotterdam largely an empty space. Today stores and other commercial buildings flank the sidewalks, which are unusually broad.

189

TWO LITTLE GIRLS of Marken, in northern Holland, enjoy dressing up in colorful old costumes. A dike links Marken, once an island in the former Zuyder Zee, to the mainland.

THE STURDY FARMHOUSES that dot the Dutch countryside are well kept and comfortable. Much of the fertile land on which they stand has been reclaimed from the sea.

TYPICALLY DUTCH in architecture, the trim houses that overlook a placid canal in Edam, North Holland, illustrate the orderliness that is a characteristic of the Dutch people.

wars with the British, rivals of the Dutch at sea, and with Austria and France. Toward the end of the eighteenth century, Napoleon conquered Holland and established his brother as King. Upon Napoleon's defeat at Waterloo in 1815, The Netherlands became an independent kingdom under a descendant of William the Silent, King William I. The southern provinces, however, which had always remained different from the north, revolted in 1830 and formed a separate kingdom under the name of Belgium.

World War II Brought Suffering

Essentially a peace-loving people, the Dutch remained neutral during World War I. However, Holland was invaded by Hitler's nazi armies in 1940, after which a period of suffering followed that can be compared only to the persecution under Philip II. Since the war, The Netherlands, through stubborn hard work and careful management, is once again taking a prominent place among the Western nations.

Holland is both a kingdom and a democracy. In other words, it is a constitutional monarchy, which means that the powers of the ruler are limited by a constitution. Executive power and responsibility is in the hands of the Cabinet, which is selected by whatever party has a majority in Parliament. Legislative power is vested in the States-General (Parliament) of which the lower house is elected by popular vote. The upper house is elected by the Provincial States, the representative council of the provinces. The seat of the Government is at The Hague, but for many purposes Amsterdam is the capital of The Netherlands.

BLACK STAR

FARMING in the North-East Polder, one of the most important arable regions of Holland.

The Character of the Dutch People

A long history has given the Dutch special character traits. They are peaceful and inclined to be silent, slow to make up their minds but amazingly stubborn when they have done so. They are clever in business and trade, thrifty and hardworking. These qualities are especially true of the Dutch of the northern provinces, where the predominant religion is

in 1575, became a center of enlightened, modern thought. Hugo Grotius, the father of international law, wrote about principles and practices that are still the basis of the relationship between civilized nations. The philosopher Spinoza, the scientist Huygens and many others spread Holland's fame to the far corners of the civilized world.

Then, however, there followed a time of

© E. N. A.

ARNHEM, IN GELDERLAND, lies in a wooded and slightly hilly country, the beauty of which has long attracted many people. This avenue of lofty beeches was mowed down in the tank drive on Arnhem during World War II. About the people of this province there runs a proverb, "Great in courage, poor in goods, sword in hand, such is the motto of Gelderland."

AMSTERDAM'S diamond-cutting industry employs thousands of highly skilled workers.

more talkative; their religion is mostly Catholic. A recent census showed that the population of Holland is 43 per cent Protestant and 38 per cent Catholic.

The Dutch woman has always played an important role in national life. Not only has The Netherlands in recent history been ruled by two queens but ever since the seventeenth century Dutch women have been outstanding in literature and in the arts and sciences. In the home, too, the woman shares the responsibilities of family life as an equal partner with her hard-working husband. Home life in Holland is very important, and people go out comparatively little. Because of the short distances, the father can usually come home for lunch, as do the children.

Official school age begins around the sixth birthday. Elementary school takes six years, while regular high school takes five and the classical high school, or gymnasium, six. In secondary schools, in addition to Dutch and the regular courses, French, English and German are taught. After graduation, young people may go to

Protestant. In the south, below the rivers that divide The Netherlands approximately in half, the people are somewhat gayer and more easygoing, and certainly

BECAUSE HOLLAND is such a flat country, bicycles are a popular and economical means of transportation. Droves of them compete with automobiles during the rush hour in Amsterdam.

any of Holland's six universities. Holland has a 0.2 per cent illiteracy, one of the lowest illiteracy rates in the world.

New Designs for Living

The Dutchman is usually an orderly person and one who likes comfort. His home is essentially a place for good, simple food, reading, music and the other advantages of family life. As in everything else, the Hollander is very practical when designing his house. In the seventeenth century, along the stately canals of Amsterdam and other cities, the Dutch merchant built himself a combination office, home and warehouse, where even the hoist to convey goods to the upper floors for storage was built as a permanent part of the structure. Some people still live in such old houses, but today most Dutchmen live in very modern homes. Dutch architects were leaders in modern European styles. They created new designs and used newly developed building materials for homes as well as for factories, schools and office buildings. Sound city planning, with broad, shaded streets, special shopping centers and large park and play areas, was developed in Holland. In a typical Dutch city of today one can, by walking only a short distance, be transported from the picturesque past to a world of today, if not of tomorrow. Brick, coming from the clay of Holland's many rivers, was used formerly in a highly decorative fashion. Today it serves attractively for the more severe design of modern architecture. Its use adds interesting texture and mellow, subdued coloring to otherwise plain or angular construction.

What strikes most visitors is that there are plants and flowers in the windows of every home. As it rains quite often, the climate is excellent for the growing of flowers, which splash a cheerful note against the gray skies. Whenever possible, the Dutchman surrounds his home with meticulously kept gardens in which hundreds of varieties of flowers, trees and shrubs proclaim his love for growing things—and there is hardly a country in the world where flower shops are as beautiful as in Holland.

Though Holland's climate is inclined to be somewhat wet, when the sun breaks through the massive clouds that vault the sky, the Dutch landscape with its gleaming rivers and green meadows sparkles in a beauty well-known to us from the paintings of the famous Dutch old masters. In winter, when the canals and rivers are frozen over, all Holland turns out on skates, and whole families glide for long trips from town to town. In summer, these same waterways are covered with pleasure boats, both sail and motor, of ev-

PIX

WASTE MATERIAL, in cars hauled by a moving chain, is taken from a Limburg coal pit.

ery description. Holland's national sport is soccer, but swimming, tennis, field hockey and, since the war, baseball are very popular.

As Holland is mostly a flat country, it is made to order for the bicycle and as characteristic as its canals are the endless streams of bicycle riders going to or coming from work or school, riding to the beach for a swim or just taking off for the fun of it. From about the age of six, every child can ride a bike, and at eight most children own one. Every highway has a

THE NORTH SEA knocks at the door of this village on the island of Walcheren off southwestern Holland. Because it lies below sea level, the villagers must rely on great sand dunes for protection from the violence of the sea. Nature furnishes the dunes, but it is up to the people who live behind them to quickly repair them if storm or strong wind lessen their height. The two little girls, in dresses and caps of former days, are sitting amidst the coarse marram grass that grows upon the dunes and serves to bind together the loose, shifting sand.

A WINDING CANAL meanders by tidy, pastel-colored houses in the fishing village of Volendam. The charm of the little village is that of Holland of an earlier day, and it is one of the few places where the traditional Dutch costumes can still be seen.

SOCCER is the outstanding Dutch sport, and the Sunday games are thronged with fans.

special bike path next to its bigger lanes for cars and trucks. In fact, the bicycle paths form possibly the best way to get the real flavor of the country.

In early spring, the bike paths are literally choked with mile upon mile of cyclists making their yearly trip to the bulb district, between the cities of Haarlem and Leiden, and its many flower shows and festivals. The bulb fields themselves are a breath-taking sight. Acres upon acres of daffodils, hyacinths and tulips spread out in a sea of color as far as the eye can range. However, these fields are for the raising of bulbs for export; the flowers themselves are really only a by-product. But they, too, are put to a very picturesque and decorative use. Bushel baskets full of petals are gathered and carefully arranged in tapestries, ranging from simple designs to large, imaginative scenes, on the front lawns of the homes in the bulb section when the season is at its height. Each bicycle rider as well as each automobile is usually completely covered with huge garlands, which are sold along the roadside for a song.

Bulb flowers are only part, however, of the horticulture that the particular combination of Holland's climate and soil produces. Vast areas south of Amsterdam and between The Hague and Rotterdam

are literally covered with glass. In these acres of greenhouses, hothouse flowers and fruits and vegetables thrive. They are an important source of income and are exported to the four corners of the earth.

Charming Scenery, Well-Kept Homes

Bicycling through the meadows and farmlands, one finds that in spite of its pancakelike flatness, Holland's scenery is far from monotonous. The brilliant green of its meadows dotted with black-and-white cows, the glistening canals and rivers teeming with colorful boats of all kinds, the church spires and windmills in the distance, the clusters of shady trees and orchards around the prosperous farmhouses—all give the landscape a unique charm and a look of peace and well-being. Stop at one of the meticulously clean and shining farm homes. By the back door is a neat row of well-used wooden shoes. They keep the feet dry and warm in the soggy fields but are never worn indoors. The farmer and his family may or may not wear the picturesque costume of their area. In any event the farmhouse will be comfortable, every part of it designed for use, and the farm equipment will be of the latest type. The farmer's wife will offer you a glass of milk and a huge slice of bread with butter and cheese. Then you will understand why Holland's dairy products deserve their reputation for excellence.

Industry Thrives Near the Cities

Near the large cities in the west and in most of the more hilly sections in the south and east are Holland's industrial areas. Forty per cent of the Dutch population is employed in industry, which is a high proportion for a country that does not produce a great deal of raw materials. Yet here again the fact that the country is situated at the junction of many waterways connected with the rest of the world is helpful to the Dutch. Raw materials can be imported very cheaply by ship. Then they are processed, and a long and impressive list of finished products is in turn exported to the four quarters of the globe. Holland's few mineral resources consist primarily of coal, which supplies almost the total needs of the country, salt, of which there is more than is needed, and some oil. The oilfield was tapped and developed only after World War II. Early in the 1960's a large reserve of natural gas was discovered, estimated at more than 75,000,000,000 cubic yards. Agriculture and industry combined give impetus to commerce. Shipping is by far the most important business, not only for export and import purposes but for the trade that passes through Holland. For this reason, Rotterdam, the largest port on the European continent, and Amsterdam, only slightly smaller, might be called service harbors of world trade.

There you will find fleets of the famous Dutch Rhine barges. A Rhine barge is a long, flat vessel often painted in gay colors; and the skipper, his family and the inevitable schipperke dog live snugly in their little deck house aft of the hold.

These skipper folks form a respected part of the Dutch population. They are hardworking people who generally live aboard the barges from one generation to the next. As skippers rove, the Dutch educational system includes a chain of special schools for barge children.

Imagine for a moment that you are standing on the bank of one of Holland's wide rivers. A long string of barges is passing. The wife of one of the skippers is hanging out her wash and her husband is at the wheel. In the distance the ancient church spires and the tall, modern buildings of, say, Amsterdam, are outlined against the sky. Straight, narrow drainage canals cut the countryside in a gridiron pattern underneath the towering clouds that drift in from the North Sea. The scene is a typical landscape of this country of peaceful conquest.

By Henriette van Nierop

A PUMPING STATION drains the water from a polder into the former Zuider Zee through a series of canals. Such drainage has reclaimed thousands of acres of fertile farmland.

PHILIPS CO., EINDHOVEN

PRECISION is vital when making electron microscopes. An army of men trained in such work sustains Holland's extensive electronics industry.

LEERDAM GLASS FACTORIES

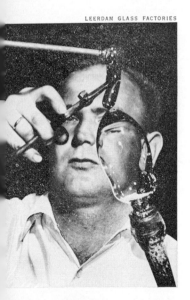

QUALITY is the hallmark of the Dutch glass industry thanks to fifty years' experience and vast deposits of iron-content sand in southwest Holland.

QUANTITY PRODUCTION is ensured by this high-speed Fourdrinier paper maker. Machines like this have made Holland the world's largest exporter of strawboard and turned the paper business from a domestic specialty into a world industry.

J. VAN DIJK, AMSTERDAM

THE NETHERLANDS: facts and figures

Government

CONSTITUTIONAL MONARCHY: monarch head of state; appoints premier, cabinet (real executive power) responsible to bicameral States-General (Parliament); 75-member First Chamber elected for 6 yrs. by the provincial councils; 150-member Second Chamber (more important legislative body) elected for 4 yrs. by popular suffrage

STATUTE OF THE REALM: Netherlands, Surinam and the Netherlands Antilles (West Indies) constitute a single realm under the House of Orange; 3 states have autonomy in domestic affairs; defense, foreign relations (concern of realm as a whole) administered by Council of Realm (ministers appointed by crown, and ministers plenipotentiary appointed by former colonies)

VOTING: universal and compulsory suffrage from age 23

Area

15,765 sq. mi.

BELOW SEA LEVEL: 25%
RECLAIMED FROM SEA: 45%
CULTIVATED: 32.5%
INLAND WATERWAYS: Lake Ijssel (Zuider Zee); Waal, Meuse (Maas), Rhine, Ijssel, Vechte rivers

Climate

TEMPERATURE: Jan. av. 34° F., July av. 63° F
ANNUAL PRECIPITATION: av. 27 in.
WEATHER PATTERN: maritime—cool summers, mild winters; fog, mist frequent

Natural resources

FISHERIES: av. annual catch 220,-000 tons; herring, mussels, plaice, sole, haddock, cod, shrimps, oysters
AGRICULTURE: wheat, rye, oats, barley, flower bulbs, potatoes, sugar beets, flax, linseed, honey, dairy products
LIVESTOCK: 170,000 horses
430,000 sheep
2,800,000 pigs
3,650,000 cattle
MINERALS: natural gas, oil, coal

Population

11,800,000
URBAN: 57%
BIRTHRATE: 20.8 per 1,000
DEATHRATE: 7.6 per 1,000
ANNUAL INCREASE: 1.3%
URBAN CENTERS:
Amsterdam 900,000
(constitutional capital)
The Hague 630,000
(seat of Government)
Rotterdam 800,000
Utrecht 270,000
Haarlem 190,000
Eindhoven 185,000
Groningen 150,000
Tilburg 150,000

Language

OFFICIAL: Dutch
OTHER: Frisian in Friesland; English, French, German 2d language of many

Religion

Complete freedom of worship
Protestant 43%
Roman Catholic 38.5%
Jewish 0.15%
Nonaffiliated 18%

Education and welfare

LITERACY: 99%; education compulsory ages 7–15
SCHOOLS AND PUPILS: 8,000 primary (1,550,000); 1,800 secondary (500,000); 2,000 technical, teacher training (550,000); 12 univ. (45,000)
WELFARE: insurance for illness, accident, unemployment; pensions for old age, disability; allowances for families, children

Commerce

GROSS NATIONAL PRODUCT: $12,000,000,000
GNP PER CAPITA: $1,020
CURRENCY: Guilder (also known as gulden, florin); 3.6 guilders worth $1.00 US
EXPORTS: industrial products of all kinds, dairy products, fish, flower bulbs, eggs, honey
IMPORTS: raw and semifinished materials of all kinds, food
TRADING PARTNERS: BENELUX, Common Market, United States

Transportation

ROADS: 4,200 mi.
PASSENGER CARS: 550,000
TRUCKS AND BUSES: 180,000
MOTORCYCLES: 175,000
MOTOR BICYCLES: 1,200,000
RAILROADS: 1,600 mi., 50% electrified
NAVIGABLE WATERWAYS: 4,200 mi. of rivers and canals; 50% of all goods transported by water
INLAND FLEET: 19,000 vessels, 5,200,000 gross tons
MERCHANT MARINE: 557 ships, 4,342,000 gross tons; Rotterdam main port, some yrs. 2d busiest port in world
AIR SERVICE: Koninklijke Luchtvaart Maatschappij N.V. (KLM)—Royal Dutch Airlines—serves more than 80 countries; most major foreign airlines serve nation

Communications

TELEPHONES: 1,700,000
RADIO AND TELEVISION: 9 radio stations, 3,500,000 radios; 7 TV stations, 1,100,000 TV sets
PRESS: 90 daily papers (circulation 3,600,000); 200 semiweekly papers (1,000,000); 1,250 magazines (16,000,000)
LIBRARIES: 1 national (850,000 volumes); 11 univ. (6,000,000); 400 special (6,000,000); 6,000 science (2,000,000); 3,700 public (6,500,000)
CINEMAS: 600; av. annual per capita attendance 5.7

Membership in international organizations

Aid to India Club
BENELUX Economic Union
Council of Europe
European Atomic Energy Community
European Coal and Steel Community
European Economic Community (Common Market)
European Space Research Organization
North Atlantic Treaty Organization (NATO)
Organization for Economic Cooperation and Development
United Nations and its specialized agencies
Western European Union

For WORLDWIDE FACTS AND FIGURES, refer to Volume 7, pages 390–92

Belgium

...Flemings and Walloons

AT the crossroads of northern European land and water routes, Belgium has been a natural trading area from very early times. Its location, however, has carried not only an asset but a handicap, for it has tempted many conquerors. By turns the land has been under Spanish, French, Austrian and German domination.

The weapons of the atomic age have lessened Belgium's strategic value but it remains pre-eminently a trading country. Lack of natural barriers makes this small nation a gateway to the heart of Europe. By land a network of railways and excellent highways spreads out from Brussels, the capital, into France, Holland and Germany. By water, navigable rivers and an extensive system of canals connect such busy Belgian ports as Antwerp with major industrial centers: south as far as Marseilles, west to St.-Nazaire, east to Frankfort. By air the chief Belgian cities are linked to the rest of Europe not only by conventional planes, propeller and jet but by an ingenious helicopter service.

Along these lifelines flow manufactured goods, raw materials and tourists. Thanks to its trade volume, Belgium has an economic importance out of proportion to its size. It ranks sixth among European nations in world trade; its standard of living and per capita income are both far above the Continent's average. Few countries co-operate so closely and so successfully with their neighbors as Belgium, a "European" country in the fullest sense of the word.

Almost inevitably, therefore, Belgium is an enthusiastic supporter of European federation. In 1922 the Belgians pioneered in this movement by setting up a customs union with Luxembourg. Shortly after World War II, Holland joined them

in another such union. By 1958 this had evolved into the far-reaching Benelux Economic Union. Today goods, capital and people move freely through the three countries. In 1952, meanwhile, Belgium had joined with five other nations—besides Holland and Luxembourg, France, West Germany and Italy—in the European Coal and Steel Community. The ECSC freed trade in coal and steel among the members.

It was at a 1955 meeting of the ECSC that the Benelux group set in motion the most important merger of all. The result, in 1958, was the formation of the European Economic Community (Common Market), with the same six members. The Common Market is gradually eliminating tariff barriers among the six and co-ordinating policies on such matters as social security and wage rates. On the very same day the Common Market came to life, the European Atomic Energy Community (EURATOM) was set up. EURATOM's job is to spur atomic research and peaceful use of atomic energy among the six by pooling scientific talent and raw materials.

One reason why Belgium's role in the swing toward co-operation has been so important is Paul Henri Spaak. Spaak originally rose to fame as a leader in the Belgian Socialist Party before World War II. Beginning in 1936 he served as foreign minister on several occasions. In this position he became one of the leading voices for European unity. At various times he has been chairman of OEEC (Organization for European Economic Cooperation), president of the Consultative Assembly of the Council of Europe and secretary-general of NATO. The crowning glories of his career, however, were the Common Market and EURATOM agreements.

The Socialist Party Spaak had joined in the 1930's went through a gradual but decisive change in the postwar period. Before World War II the Belgian Socialists drew their support largely from the working class. Beginning with 1946, the Socialists were weakened by the gradual decline of the working class. In all the advanced countries of the West the technological revolution of this century has reduced the need for unskilled labor. The party today places much less emphasis on purely economic matters, particularly state planning, than before. When the Socialists formed a coalition cabinet with the Liberals in 1954, for example, they set up the world's first Ministry for the Middle Classes, "to defend the special interests of . . . a quarter of the population."

Postwar Belgian politics have also seen the rise to power of the Social Christian Party, a group that draws its strength from the Catholic vote and is dedicated to mild economic reforms. The Social Christians consistently win more seats than their two strongest rivals—the Socialists and the Liberals. The Social Christians have frequently lost parliamentary control to coalitions however.

The thorniest problem facing Belgium

DOCKSIDE AT ANTWERP, one of the Continent's busiest ports. In a recent year it handled some sixteen thousand cargo and passenger ships from all over the globe.

TIME-MELLOWED WALLS of medieval buildings cast their reflections in one of the many waterways that have earned for Bruges the title "Venice of the North."

UNDER THE AWNINGS of alfresco sidewalk restaurants, the citizens of Bruges, in West Flanders, can dine and relax while they watch the life of their city pass by. Bruges reached the height of its prosperity in the fourteenth century and still retains much of its medieval air.

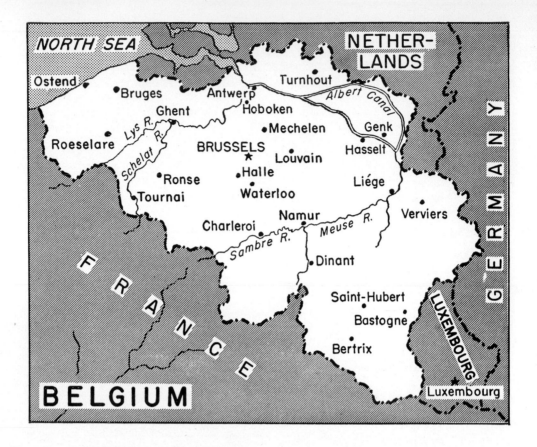

NORTH SEA

NETHER-LANDS

Ostend
Bruges
Ghent
Roeselare
Schelat R.
Lys R.
Antwerp
Hoboken
Mechelen
Turnhout
Albert Canal
Genk
Hasselt
BRUSSELS ★
Louvain
Ronse
Halle
Waterloo
Liége
Tournai
Namur
Charleroi
Sambre R.
Meuse R.
Verviers
Dinant
Saint-Hubert
Bastogne
Bertrix

FRANCE

GERMANY

LUXEMBOURG
Luxembourg ★

BELGIUM

in recent years has been its relation with the Belgian Congo. This great mass of land in the heart of Africa is almost eighty times the size of Belgium. The Congo is the world's leading producer of industrial diamonds and cobalt and is not far behind in production of copper, uranium, tin, manganese and zinc.

Late in the 1950's the fever for freedom coursing through colonies everywhere began to rise in the Congo. There were several outbreaks of violence in 1959. Hastily the Belgian Government decided to grant the Congo independence without further ado. The result was the creation of the Republic of the Congo on June 30, 1960, amid considerable turmoil.

Congolese independence is not likely to have a severe economic impact on Belgium. The Belgians may take some comfort in the experience of the Dutch. Holland has been more prosperous since the loss of its rich colonial empire than before. The Congo was far less important to Belgium than the Indies were to Holland. Congolese production has contributed only a small fraction to the total economy of Belgium; and though Belgium has had the biggest individual share in Congolese trade, independence may not end this.

Regardless of the outcome, Belgium is likely to place even less reliance on Congo trade and production. Many Belgians seem to feel that the future of their country depends on ever closer co-operation with their European neighbors.

Few nations display more sense of national purpose than does Belgium. Its amazing recovery from the ravages of World War II is an example of what a unified people can do. Yet the population of Belgium is made up of not one but two stocks: the Flemings of the north and the Walloons of the south.

Walking through the crowded streets of a Belgian city a visitor would be hard put to separate the passers-by into Walloons and Flemings. While the latter tend to be somewhat fairer and heavier than their co-citizens, it is very hard to find a typical specimen of either folk. Should our visitor decide, however, to stop for refreshment at one of the city's many sidewalk cafés he would experience no such difficulty. From the lively chatter that usually animates these gay places he would be quick to recognize that two languages were being spoken: French by the Walloons; Flemish (a language very similar to Dutch) by the Flemings. Both are recognized as the official languages of the land, and there are even French and Flemish universities.

Arms against a Common Enemy

How then did the Flemings and the Walloons come to think of themselves as Belgians? The answer lies in history. Both peoples have lived side by side in the same area for many centuries. They were already on the spot when Julius Caesar invaded the land in the first century and called it *Gallia Belgica,* the "country of the Belgae," from which the name Belgium is derived. Unfortunately, the Romans were but the first of a long series of invaders. Because of its outlets on the North Sea, its strategic position and its early industries, Belgium was coveted and fought over by stronger powers. Not only did Belgium become the battlefield of Europe, but it came to experience, in turn, French, Spanish and Austrian rule. Through these long periods of trial the Flemings and the Walloons learned to appreciate each other. They worked side by side patiently repairing the damages of repeated wars, thus strengthening their social and economic ties and developing a deep love for the land they shared in common. In Roman Catholicism they also had a common religion. By 1815, when they were incorporated in the newly formed Kingdom of the Netherlands, the Flemings and the Walloons formed one nation in spite of their racial and lingual differences. They rebelled against union with the Netherlands some fifteen years later and in 1831 the independent Kingdom of Belgium took its place among the nations of Europe. The constitution of the new country established a parliamentary monarchy.

In an attempt to protect the new state from aggression, the great powers guaran-

teed the independence and the perpetual neutrality of Belgium. This guarantee was to prove of little value to the Belgians, for the Germans invaded their country at the outset of World War I. The heroic if hopeless resistance of the Belgian Army led by the great King Albert I was to win it the admiration of the world. Years of painstaking reconstruction work went to naught when World War II broke out in September 1939, and Belgium was overrun the following spring. Belgium then endured five long years of German occu-

THE SIGN means that the path is for bicycles only. It runs beside a motor road.

ACROSS THE GRAND' PLACE, the great public square of Brussels, stand the historic Guild Houses of the city's ancient merchants. The squatting lion guards the Town Hall's steps.

CENTER OF BRUSSELS is the Grand' Place, where there was an important market as long ago as the tenth century. On almost every side are masterpieces of Gothic architecture.

OPEN-AIR FLOWER MARKET in Brussels. It is a colorful array of blooms from which to choose; and housewives ponder how this plant or that will look in a room or garden.

THE TOWER of Brussels' Town Hall rises to a height of 360 feet. A sixteen-foot statue of St. Michael stands on top of the spire. The building took three centuries to complete.

THE SANDY COAST and fine surf bathing at Ostend, a seaport in West Flanders, attract vacationists. A wide sea wall (*digue*) of stone and terra cotta makes a spacious boardwalk.

pation. The Belgians did not meet defeat passively. Some of their statesmen refused to accept King Leopold III's surrender and formed a government-in-exile in London. Thousands of their compatriots escaped and swelled the ranks of the Allied armies. At home, the fight was continued through the heroic work of an extensive and well-organized underground resistance group. After VE-Day the Belgian people simply rolled up their sleeves and went to work once again.

In spite of all this, Belgium has had a remarkably peaceful history within its own borders. Its constitution guarantees religious and political freedom for all. While the great bulk of the population is of the Roman Catholic faith, the Government recognizes and supports all faiths on an equal footing. Politically, the country is governed by a constitutional, hereditary monarchy. The executive power is vested in the hands of the king, while the laws of the land are suggested and enacted by a Senate and a Chamber of Representatives elected by universal suffrage—women were given the right to vote in 1948. Belgium is divided into nine provinces for administrative purposes. These and the 2,670 communes of the land enjoy a large measure of self-government in local matters.

The Belgians take their responsibilities as citizens of a free country very seriously. They consider voting a duty rather than a privilege, and fines are imposed upon the absent-minded or the lazy who fail to go to the polls on election days! Realizing that freedom is an empty word for people in want, the Government devoted much of its activities to social legislation from 1918 until 1944 when a wide program of social security was put into effect. As a result democracy has never been seriously challenged in Belgium. Some fascist groups did make their appearance in the troubled 1930's but they were quickly suppressed. In 1953 there were only a handful of communist deputies sitting in Parliament.

The post-World War II scene found Belgium bitterly divided on the question of the role of the monarchy. The pros and cons of the wartime surrender of the Belgian Army by former King Leopold III, and his refusal to lead a government-in-exile, were hotly disputed. Many advocated that the country become a republic. A referendum in 1950 showed a slight majority in favor of the restoration of Leopold. However, there was still so

OLD BUILDINGS fronting on one of Ghent's canals are reminders of medieval days when the city was already a center of north European trade, with a flourishing cloth industry.

SELLING FRESH SHRIMP on the quay at Ostend. Headquarters for the Belgian fishing fleet and a large port city, Ostend is also a popular and fashionable seaside resort.

PHILIP GENDREAU

A LACEMAKER in Bruges works on her fine needle point outside the door of her home.

sea by a series of *digues,* similar to the Dutch dikes. Farther inland, one encounters the River Scheldt lazily meandering through fertile lands dotted with small farms appearing neat and trim with their borders of poplar trees. Continuing to the southeast and after crossing the lively Meuse, queen of Belgian rivers, one reaches a higher and more irregular region that reaches a climax in the beautiful Ardennes forest. There are no grand natural sights in Belgium, but the over-all scenery leaves the visitor with an impression of serenity and moderation.

The climate of Belgium is gentle, and the whole country receives adequate rainfall. The weather is pleasant enough as a whole, although there are many cloudy and drizzly days in the northern and central sections. The atmosphere is clearer and temperatures are more extreme in the Ardennes region where frost occurs on an average of 120 days a year. Snowfalls up to 27 inches a year have been recorded in

much opposition to him that civil war threatened when he attempted to return. In the end, Leopold abdicated in favor of his son, who became King Baudouin I when he reached his twenty-first birthday, on September 7, 1951. Under Baudoin, the monarchy has played a lesser role in politics and government. The King has become more and more a symbol of the Belgian nation. The monarchy was further enhanced with the popular marriage of Baudouin to the Spanish Doña Fabiola de Mora y Aragon in December of 1960.

We have seen that the determination with which the Belgians have met repeated disasters is well explained by their love for the homeland. Let it be said that this love is very understandable, for Belgium is a picturesque, varied and pleasant country. Viewing Belgium from the sea one is first aware of a long expanse of sand dunes and salt marshes. This coastal strip has been reclaimed from and fortified against the

EUROPEAN

A BRUGES SHOP displays lace articles that are exquisite in both design and workmanship.

CANALS divide the port city of Ghent into a number of islands connected by foot bridges. Built on the site of two seventh century monasteries, the city grew up around an old fort.

the high Ardennes. Snow is rare in other parts of the country and its arrival is always a cause of great excitement for Belgian children.

The cities of Belgium are both the object of great pride on the part of the Belgians and the source of considerable pleasure for the traveler. Brussels, the capital and largest city, is a blend of the old and the new. Its wide and handsome boulevards, its smart shops, as well as the bustling activity of its modern business districts and the gaiety of its cafés and places of entertainment have earned Brussels the title of "Little Paris." At the same time, the old quarters have retained their full medieval flavor. The Guildhall overlooking the open flower market on Grand'Place is a sight not soon forgotten. Next in importance is Antwerp whose only rival as the largest seaport of continental Europe is Rotterdam. It is also one of the great historic and artistic cities of the world. A visit to the cathedral of Notre Dame and to the botanical and zoological gardens well rewards the visitor.

Smaller in size but equally interesting are Ghent and Bruges. Ghent is a medieval city par excellence. The second seaport of Belgium, it is also a great textile and educational center—a renowned Flemish university stands within its walls. It is in Ghent that the envoys of the United States and England signed the treaty ending the War of 1812. A pleasant place indeed to carry on diplomatic discussions! Bruges, with fifty bridges crossing its numerous canals, is often called the "Venice of the North." While Bruges has achieved fame as a lace-manufacturing center, it is also well known for architectural wonders, such as the belfry of the Market Hall, with its forty-seven-bell carillon. Hardly less interesting are the old towns of Liége, Namur and Louvain. In 1423, John IV of Brabant founded the university at Liége which is still one of the greatest seats of Catholic learning in the world.

Scenic landscapes and attractive cities, pleasant as they may be, are not enough to assure the prosperity of a nation. Fortunately, the land of Belgium is fertile, while the subsoil contains many of the raw materials necessary to the development of industry. This is a great advantage in another way, for Belgium is the most densely populated country in Europe. It is not surprising that with so many mouths to feed and with so little space available

THE PALAIS DU CINQUANTENAIRE, in Brussels, commemorates the fiftieth anniversary (1880) of Belgium's independence from Holland. In the two vast wings are the Royal Museums

216

of Art and History—among the greatest in Europe—and the Military Museum. The wings are joined by a fine Arc de Triomphe, surmounted by a quadriga (chariot and horses).

217

GILLES, townsmen with yard-high plumes, lead merrymakers at the carnival in Binche.

cheese, sugar, coffee and animal fodder. The Percheron, a native breed of horse, is the most valuable beast of burden on the Belgian farm. These powerful animals are splendid specimens and have been exported the world over to be used as carriage, show or work horses. The use of mechanical farm implements has increased considerably since the end of World War II.

Belgium, however, is primarily an industrial country. Indeed, mining and industry occupy nearly 55 per cent of the working population. In the Walloon country of the south are the coal and iron mines that provide the steel industry with an adequate supply of these basic raw materials. The major output of Belgian steel is exported in the form of crude and semi-manufactured products. The textile industry centered around Ghent is still very important. It is the oldest industry in Belgium, as it was already famous in the Middle Ages. In fact, the Hundred Years' War between France and England was fought, partially at least, for control of the textile industry of Flanders. The Belgian glass industry, considered one of the world's finest, exports 90 per cent of its output. Antwerp competes with Am-

Belgium should be intensively cultivated. The smallest plot of land has been put to the plow. By tradition, industrial workers keep small vegetable gardens in the back of their modest dwellings.

Even in the agricultural districts of central and western Belgium, cultivation still takes place on farms that are small. The work is usually done by the farm family (two-fifths of the cultivated land is worked by owners). Yields are high and varied, and greenhouses are used extensively to increase productivity. As a result, Belgium produces the greater part of her food supply, although it must import 80 per cent of the wheat consumed by its people. Imports also meet the country's needs for

PHOTOS, BELGIAN GOVERNMENT INFORMATION CENTER

A FLEMISH FISHERMAN repairs his net before putting out to sea again in his trawler.

KNOKKE, one of a series of popular shore resorts in the province of West Flanders, faces the North Sea. During spring floods, the sea covers the beach and roars up to the dike.

THE SHIPPING of many nations crowds the harbor of Antwerp, one of the world's great ports. In the background, the tower of the city's famous cathedral dominates the skyline.

BLOWING GLASS in a shop in Boom. It is a delicate art requiring a keen sense of timing. The glass must be shaped rapidly and yet precisely while it is still soft and red-hot.

A MOVABLE BRIDGE SPANS THE DYLE AT MECHELEN IN BELGIUM

Mechelen, or Malines, as the French call it, lies on the bank of the River Dyle. Small tributaries from the Dyle branch out through the circular city, which was once enclosed with a ring of walls. Mechelen is one of the centers of religion in Belgium. Its churches are magnificent, and in them are sculptures and paintings by such famous artists as Reubens.

REAPING A HARVEST OF GOLD

These workmen are busily harvesting a field of flax that will be transformed into the finest of Belgian linen and lace. The quality of the linen from Flanders is world-famous, and the secret lies in the River Lys. Because of some property in its water, it excels all other rivers in rotting flax. Linen thread made from flax that has been so processed is fabulously fine.

ALTHOUGH HER FINGERS may be aged, they are still full of the high skill and artistry that long ago earned Bruges a world-wide reputation as the home of the finest of laces.

sterdam in the diamond-cutting industry, while the guns made in Liége have long been favorites with sportsmen everywhere. Belgian know-how and Marshall Plan aid proved a most happy combination after the war. By 1947, Belgian production had surpassed the prewar level by 15 per cent.

The rapid recovery of Belgian industry was also helped by one of the best transportation systems in Europe. In the 1830's Belgium was the first continental country to adopt the then much-scoffed-at railroad. Today, it has more miles of track per square mile than any other country in the world. The country's many navigable rivers have been supplemented by an extensive network of canals. At the same time, the road system is more than adequate. All this serves to make traveling in Belgium a real pleasure and to assure the swift transfer of goods and raw materials. Belgium's small but efficient merchant fleet provides a link between the homeland and the Belgian Congo, the large and rich African colony that it acquired in 1878. The size of this colony—it is seventy-eight times larger than the mother country—makes Belgium one of the leading colonial powers of the world.

It is not always easy for the visitor to make friends with the Belgians. At first they tend to be a little reserved toward foreigners, perhaps because other nations have interfered in their affairs so often. Once the ice is broken, however, they prove to be friendly and warmhearted. Their new friends, who might have thought that the Belgians were overly serious and did nothing but plow their fields, exploit their mines and run their business enterprises, are in for a big surprise. While the Belgians do have a tremendous

PIX

THE STRATEGIC POSITION of the city of Namur at the junction of the Meuse and Sambre rivers has made it the scene of many battles from the time of the Romans to the present.

capacity for work, there is another side to their nature. The first meal shared with a Belgian family on some festive occasion will be a long-remembered experience. Like their French neighbors, the Belgians are great gourmets and pride themselves on their fine food.

The Belgians are also proud of their cultural heritage. Anxious to add new names to the long list of great artists, scholars and scientists who have brought fame to Belgium, the Government maintains a sound system of primary and secondary schools. Greek and Latin are still required of all students who intend to enter one of the country's four universities. The museums of Brussels, Antwerp and Ghent have splendid collections of the Flemish school of painting. The Belgians are music lovers and every town has its own, well-attended opera house. Too, the people love the music of bells. Belgium is famous for its carillons, sets of fixed bells that are sounded by hammers operated from a keyboard. The world's only school of carillon music was founded in Mechlin by Jef Denyn. Everything points to the fact that the arts are still very much alive and encouraged in Belgium.

One of the outstanding leaders in modern European painting was a Belgian, James Ensor, who died in 1949. The canvases of Paul Delvaux and René Magritte have also won wide acclaim abroad.

For a long time, Belgian architects usually copied the styles of an older day. Early in this century, however, two Belgians, Henry van de Velde and Victor Horta, were among the first European builders to free architectural design from the rules of the past. They believed that design and materials—stone, steel, cement, glass—should go hand in hand.

On the lighter side, the Belgians have developed a great liking for sports. Their soccer teams compete on a par with those of other European countries, and they have no peers in the grueling and popular sport of bicycle racing. The ice-hockey rinks and the basketball courts of the sleek sport palaces are popular gathering places for the youth of the large cities. Track is a great favorite among Belgian girls.

Team sports are not restricted to the schools and the universities. Even the smallest community will field a local eleven, in which it takes considerable pride. In summer the fashionable and numerous beaches of the coast are crowded with bathers. And there are the delightful resorts of the Ardennes for those who prefer quiet.

The favorite pastime of the Belgians, however, is still participation in the great pageants that are held on so many religious and historical occasions. Some, like the procession of the Holy Blood, are of a serious nature. Early in May, thousands of pilgrims and visitors crowd into Bruges to witness this impressive ceremony. Something of the splendor of medieval days is brought back as the city fathers march by, garbed in bright and costly robes and accompanied by church dignitaries and countless banner carriers. Other festivals, like the Carnival of Binche, are the occasion of merrymaking. This fete is held annually and commemorates a visit to the town made by the Spanish King Philip II in the sixteenth century. Grandparents and children alike dress up in costumes of every color and description and join in the fun. The street dancing sometimes goes on late into the night. Even small villages celebrate their patron saint's day.

There may be some truth in the old accusation that the Belgians are the people endowed with great common sense but lacking in vision. Today, however, there are many indications that the Belgians are looking ahead. After the war, they sponsored Benelux, a customs union of Belgium, the Netherlands and Luxembourg; and today they are active partners in such gigantic—and successful—Western European organizations as the Common Market and the European Coal and Steel Community, as well as the international Organization for Economic Cooperation and Development, the UN and NATO. While keeping the traditions that give it its charm, Belgium is adapting itself to the march of time. Belgium is much more important than its size would indicate.

By SAMUEL M. OSGOOD

BELGIUM: facts and figures

Government
CONSTITUTIONAL MONARCHY: king head of state, appoints premier, cabinet (real executive power) responsible to bicameral Parliament elected for 4 yrs.—175-member Senate (106 popularly elected, 46 elected by provincial councilors, 23 elected by Senate itself); 212-member Chamber of Representatives (1 for each 40,000 inhabitants) popularly elected on proportional basis
VOTING: universal compulsory suffrage from age 21

Area
11,779 sq. mi.
CULTIVATED: 60%
INLAND WATERWAYS: Albert Canal; Lys, Scheldt, Meuse, Sambre rivers

Climate
TEMPERATURE: Jan. av. 37° F., July av. 65° F.
ANNUAL PRECIPITATION: av. 35 in.
WEATHER PATTERN: maritime—cool summers, mild winters

Natural resources
AGRICULTURE: wheat, rye, oats, barley, sugar beets, potatoes, dairy products
LIVESTOCK: 70,000 sheep
150,000 horses
1,500,000 pigs
2,500,000 cattle
MINERALS: coal, iron, phosphates, lead, zinc, manganese

Population
9,300,000
URBAN. 83%
BIRTHRATE: 16.9 per 1,000
DEATHRATE: 12.3 per 1,000
ANNUAL INCREASE: 0.6%, among world's lowest rates of increase
URBAN CENTERS:
Brussels (capital) 1,400,000
Antwerp 850,000
Liége 630,000
Charleroi 480,000
Ghent 470,000

Language
OFFICIAL: French, Flemish (related to Dutch)
OTHER: German, English 2d languages of many

Religion
Complete freedom of worship
Roman Catholic 89%
Jewish 0.4%
Protestant 0.3%
Unaffiliated 10.3%

Education and welfare
LITERACY: 99%; education compulsory ages 6–14
SCHOOLS AND PUPILS: 9,100 primary (1,000,000); 3,500 secondary (250,000); 1,350 technical (320,000); 180 teacher training (30,000); Free Univ. of Brussels (5,500); State Univ. of Ghent (3,700); Univ. of Liége (4,600); Catholic Univ. of Louvain (13,300)
WELFARE: insurance for illness, accident, unemployment; pensions for aged and disabled; family and children allowances

Commerce
GROSS NATIONAL PRODUCT: $12,500,000,000
GNP PER CAPITA: $1,300
CURRENCY: Belgian franc; 50 francs worth $1.00 US
EXPORTS: industrial products of all kinds, dairy products
IMPORTS: raw and semifinished materials of all kinds, food
TRADING PARTNERS: BENELUX, Common Market, United States

Transportation
ROADS: 22,000 mi.
PASSENGER CARS: 800,000
TRUCKS AND BUSES: 190,000
RAILROADS: 7,000 mi.
NAVIGABLE WATERWAYS: 1,100 mi. of canals and rivers
INLAND FLEET: 5,000 vessels, 1,900,000 gross tons
MERCHANT MARINE: 83 ships, 680,-000 gross tons; Antwerp major port and one of world's busiest
AIR SERVICE: Societe Anonyme Belge d'Exploitation de la Navigation Aerienne (SABENA), Societe Belge de Transports par air (Sobelair) are the major Belgian lines; country served by the major foreign airlines; SABENA also has helicopter flights to neighboring nations

Communications
TELEPHONES: 1,300,000
RADIO AND TELEVISION: 12 radio stations, 3,000,000 radios; 6 TV stations, 800,000 TV sets
PRESS: 45 daily newspapers (circulation 3,500,000); 3,300 magazines
LIBRARIES: 1 national (1,800,000 volumes); 4 univ. (4,000,000); 2,500 public (11,000,000)
CINEMAS: 1,600; av. annual per capita attendance 11.4

Membership in international organizations
Aid to India Club
Belgium-Luxembourg Economic Union
BENELUX Economic Union Commission for Technical Cooperation in Africa South of Sahara
Council of Europe
European Atomic Energy Community
European Coal and Steel Community
European Economic Community (Common Market)
European Space Research Organization
North Atlantic Treaty Organization (NATO)
Organization for Economic Cooperation and Development
United Nations and its specialized agencies
Western European Union

For WORLDWIDE FACTS AND FIGURES, refer to Volume 7, pages 390–92

France ... *heritage*
and future

THE French are often called the most civilized people on earth. From the days of Louis XIV on, France led the whole Continent toward political and intellectual freedom. Today the country remains a cultural inspiration to the whole world. This sense of national grandeur pervades French thinking, represented most forcefully in the person of Charles de Gaulle, the greatest French statesman this century has produced.

It was De Gaulle who rallied the French to continue resistance after the Germans overran northern France in 1940, who led liberated France in 1944–46 and who returned to head the Government in 1958 and brought forth the Fifth French Republic with a new constitution. The Fourth Republic, plagued by splinter politics, had proved helpless in the face of the crisis provoked by the army revolt in Algeria. One premier after another had been broken on the issue, and the presidency was in the main simply a ceremonial office. De Gaulle returned to power on the promise that he would be free to act and to have a new constitution written. Thus the presidency, to which De Gaulle was elected, was given overriding authority, to the point of rule by decree if neces-

sary. This allowed De Gaulle a free hand in his attempts to solve the difficult problem of Algeria. Once the Algerian situation was settled, De Gaulle applied his energies again toward his goal of making France a first power.

From a longer view there is also the question of how well the constitution will work when De Gaulle inevitably passes from the scene. The presidency in the Fifth Republic was tailored to fit his image.

In any event, De Gaulle has revitalized French self-confidence and made France a force that must be reckoned with in international parleys. Though France is obviously less powerful than either the United States or the Soviet Union, he is determined that France be treated as at least an equal of Great Britain. This underlies his insistence that France participate in all decisions made by NATO. France *is* a vital part of the NATO defense of Western Europe and the Supreme Headquarters of NATO is in Paris. Moreover, Western Europe's political strength hinges largely on the Bonn-Paris axis.

The question of prestige also doubtless played a part in the explosion of the first French atomic devices in the Sahara in 1960 while the other three members of the "atom club"—Britain, the Soviet Union and the United States—had suspended tests informally and were negotiating on banning them. For the record, however, work on the French devices had begun in 1952, while De Gaulle was in retirement.

"National grandeur" also inclines De Gaulle to prefer co-operation between sovereign nations rather than through a supranational body. Yet the economic facts of life seem to be pushing France in the other direction, certainly as far as the Common Market is concerned. The fear that French prices would be too high and French methods too antiquated to meet German competition once tariffs were lowered has proved to be a bogy. Hostility also seems to be dwindling to the admittance of Britain to the Common Market.

The reason for this is that in spite of all the political upsets, colonial strife, and in-

FACE TO FACE in Marseilles: a bust of the artist Daumier (1808–79); twentieth-century apartments; a fifteenth-century house, left, behind the fence.

flation, French industry has been quietly undergoing transformation ever since World War II. Much of it is the result of state planning. Industrial production rose 10 per cent a year between 1953 and 1961. France now has the most efficient coal mines in Europe. French dam constructors have few peers. The Serre Ponçon Dam in the foothills of the French Alps was completed in 1960. It is thus far Western Europe's largest dam and the first to be built of earth. It will provide flood control, billions of gallons of water for irrigation, and eventually will contribute 700,000,000 kilowatt-hours of electricity a year. Many steel, chemical, automotive, aircraft, glass and electronics plants have been modernized. French cars, steel, locomotives, power turbines, airliners are passing textiles and luxury goods as typical French exports.

This expansion of industry and trade has been furthered by bringing order out of the financial snarl that existed before 1958. For the time being at least, inflation was curbed. A major effect was that it changed the French balance of payments from a deficit to a surplus. A new franc went into circulation in 1960, worth one hundred times the value of the old. It was really a bookkeeping change.

Big industry has benefited most. The thousands of small manufacturers, most of them inefficient, seem likely to be forced to merge, accept subcontracting, transform their methods or close down. But the most disaffected group is the farmers. As prices have gone up, their incomes have sunk. Part of the trouble is that most of the farms are small and mechanization is economic only with large areas. In 1959–60 the farmers were clamoring for relief, and they have a strong lever. Representatives of the rural areas are dominant in the National Assembly. Yet the day after a protest meeting a Tours farmer said: "I am a Gaullist; he represents strength and honesty. You can be for a government and against some of its measures."

New housing is needed urgently. Even in Paris the average dwelling is more than a century old. Many farmhouses are still older and have no inside water though gleaming washing machines are beginning to appear in farm kitchens. In 1959 the Government authorized rent increases to spur construction.

With a rising birth rate, France is also faced with the problem of insufficient teachers and schools. The public educational system has been under fire as being too rigorous and conservative. Reforms were initiated in 1959 whereby French children must attend school until the age of 16 but at 13 may go to either the classic *lycées* or take short-term instruction ending at 16. A new system of scholarships was also established to provide more equal opportunities.

The Lovely Land

The fairy godmothers were kind to France at her birth. Although the country is not large in area, it has, in every respect, balance and harmony. Its shape is almost a regular hexagon. While it is in close contact with the rest of Continental Europe, it has easy access to the lands across the seas. In fact, it has windows on four bodies of water—the Mediterranean Sea, the Atlantic Ocean, the English Channel and the North Sea. The surface of France is about half mountain and half plain, and the agricultural and industrial resources are equally well balanced. The climate is mild, with little variation in temperature because France is lapped by water on almost all sides. There is a good

network of waterways, spreading out from four great rivers—the Seine, the Loire, the Garonne and the Rhone.

The country is exceptionally well adapted to man's needs. This explains why so many peoples have attempted to settle there. For hundreds of years a succession of invaders from the east overran the region; and each wave mingled with those who already occupied the land. The unity of the French nation stems from entirely different things: from its history, its will, its culture, its ideals forged and accepted by all who call themselves French.

The settlement of ancient Gaul is lost in the mists of time. Twenty or thirty thousand years before the advent of Christianity, when giant elephants, rhinoceroses and hippopotamuses roamed the banks of the Seine and the Marne, very primitive men were already living in this outpost of Western Europe. Some of their weapons have been found—crude hand axes that scientists call *coups de poing*. After them came men who corresponded more to modern racial groups, some broad-headed and some long-headed. At the beginning of the twentieth century, skeletons thousands of years old were found near Monaco, on the Mediterranean coast.

A series of caves in the Dordogne department, in southwestern France, show one of the most noteworthy stages in the development of man. At Les Eyzies, at Lascaux, at Font-de-Gaume there are remarkable wall paintings of horses, mammoths, bison and even men, showing us how the inhabitants of France lived ten thousand or fifteen thousand years B.C.

In comparatively recent times, that is, in Julius Caesar's day, France was called Gaul. As Caesar tells us in his commentaries, the Gauls were barbarians compared to the Romans. Courageous to the point of recklessness, the Gauls feared but one thing—that the sky would fall upon their heads! But they were also fickle, turbulent and undisciplined. The Roman conquest to which they finally yielded over two thousand years ago brought them many new things: roads, a single language (Latin) and a single government, new ways of clearing and tilling the soil, city life, more refined ways of living —in fact, civilization. Within a few years Gaul became one of the most prosperous of the Roman provinces.

However, the Roman peace did not last and the frontiers of the Empire fell under the advance of the pagan Teutonic tribes, among them, the Franks. During the course of several centuries, their leaders overran the country. One of them, Clovis I, founded the Merovingian dynasty, the first Frankish dynasty in Gaul. He established his rule over a large expanse of land. His wife was a Christian and

eventually he, too, became a Christian. For the second time Rome played a decisive part in the history of the French nation. This time it was no longer the Rome of the emperors but the Rome of the popes. When Clovis was baptized at Rheims in 496, Christianity was established in the west of Europe. Rome not only backed the Frankish kingdom with its worldly power, which was great, but also brought it a new civilization more humane than the Roman had been. The Church opposed slavery, freed men from the yoke of the state and introduced new ideas of brother-

SHAPING A VASE IN THE OLD WAY

Pottery has long been an important French industry; and quaint, charming ceramics are still turned out by skilled artisans using methods handed down from father to son.

hood and justice for all men.

The first two Frankish dynasties, the Merovingian and the Carolingian, did not have an easy time, however. The tribal leaders, or barons, fought hard among themselves and often against the king. For several centuries the Vikings from Norway and Denmark periodically sailed up the rivers of France, devastating the cities along the banks. It was only during the reign of the great Charlemagne, one of the Carolingian rulers, that there was a semblance of order. He established an empire of the West for a few years and was crowned Emperor by the Pope at Rome in the year 800.

Hugh Capet founded the third dynasty, in 987. During his reign, the royal domain was only a narrow strip of land between the Seine and Loire rivers. In 1848, when his last descendant, Louis-Philippe, was overthrown, France had reached the limits that she still has today. For nine hundred years, therefore, the history of France is also that of a family, the family of the kings of France.

The monarchy of the Capets had very humble beginnings. A number of peaceful reigns, succeeding each other without disputes, and alliances through marriage slowly brought about territorial unity. At the same time the kings gathered the reins of authority ever more firmly into their hands. The powerful vassals—the dukes and counts of Brittany, of Anjou, of Aquitaine and of Burgundy, who might have contested the kings' growing control—were kept busy with the Crusades and with the wars with England.

During the fourteenth and fifteenth centuries, England and France wore themselves out in a prolonged struggle. The kings of England, descendants of William the Conqueror, claimed land rights in France and even the crown of France. The strife lasted for a hundred years, and France was put to the fire and the sword. One of the most famous figures of this contest was the Black Prince—the Prince of Wales, son of Edward III of England. Early in the 1400's, Jeanne d'Arc, a humble peasant girl from Lorraine, was inspired to take command of the French army. She won battles, liberated cities besieged by the English, and raised the drooping spirits of the French to carry on the fight to save their country. It was through her efforts that Charles VII, who had not been sure of his rights to the throne of France, was crowned at Reims in 1422. Thanks to Jeanne d'Arc, the English were finally chased from French soil.

Adversity Makes Brotherhood

Throughout the long struggle with the English, when all shared the same anguish and rejoiced in the same victories, the French little by little became aware of their national unity. At the beginning of the sixteenth century, when King Louis XI died—which marks the advent of modern times—it seemed that the French nation had come into its own.

Three of the best-known kings are Louis IX, Henri IV and Louis XIV. Louis IX (1215–70), who was later canonized as Saint Louis, is undoubtedly one of the noblest figures in history. A truly good man, he took care of the sick, built hospitals and dispensed justice himself under

FLYING FINGERS MAKE LACY COBWEBS

Balancing easily on their heads the tall caps that are a feature of the region, these women of
Pont l'Abbé, Brittany, create beautiful hand-made lace. It is sure to find a ready market.

233

BY THE DOCKSIDE, BOULOGNE

Boulogne, on the narrow Strait of Calais, is one of the fishing centers of northern France. Napoleon improved the fine natural harbor, as part of his plan to invade England.

an oak at Vincennes. Every Friday the poor were invited to his table.

Henri IV (1553–1610), a Protestant converted to Catholicism, remains to this day one of the most popular sovereigns in France. It was he who wanted all French-

men to have chicken in the pot every Sunday. Perhaps his greatest achievement was that he put an end to the bitter wars of religion.

One of the most glamorous reigns was that of Louis XIV (1638–1715)—the Grand Monarch. At the beginning of the eighteenth century, the French armies were everywhere victorious. The French navy was as powerful as the English navy, and French navigators were exploring far-away seas. All over France the royal authority was accepted and revered. In the arts and literature, the names of Corneille, Racine, Molière, Pascal, Mansard and Lenôtre are the shining stars of the "great century." But the end of Louis XIV's reign found France impoverished by numerous wars. Moreover, the absence of real individual liberty, the absolute power of the king and the doctrine of rule by divine right had made him almost a despot.

Discontent increased during the reigns of Louis XV and Louis XVI, who were unable to bring about much-needed reforms. The climax came with the Revolution of 1789, and three years later the First Republic was born. A young and gifted general, Napoleon Bonaparte, galvanized the nation and carried its standards to the very limits of Europe. However, with him the ideals of equality and liberty

HARVEST DAY IN THE WHEAT FIELD

The wheat is shocked and piled in a huge stack and covered. Later the threshing machine will come into the field and thresh the golden grain. The scene is at Pontoise, near Paris.

PINNACLES ABOVE THE HILL TOWN OF CHARTRES

At Chartres one of the great Gothic cathedrals crowns a lofty hill. The narrow streets of the old
part of town twist and turn and climb sharply, making driving perilous if not impossible.

CHAMBORD'S CHATEAU WITH ITS FOREST OF TURRETS

There are 440 rooms in the Renaissance Château of Chambord, and thirteen grand staircases. The castle was built for Francis I. It is set in a spacious formal park, enclosed by walls.

BEAUVAIS TAPESTRY IN THE MAKING

In the tapestry factory at Beauvais skillful hands weave colorful and complicated designs. The factory is supported by the Government and its finest products are displayed in museums.

that had arisen in 1789 went into eclipse. In 1804 he became Emperor. When the combined forces of all the sovereigns of Europe finally conquered him at Waterloo, France was left bleeding, ruined and ready to accept the restoration of the monarchy under Louis XVIII. Two more kings followed him to the throne—Charles X and then Louis-Philippe. The last was overthrown by the revolution of 1848, when the Second Republic came into existence.

In spite of everything, the country possessed such resources that it recovered rapidly. In 1851, a nephew of Napoleon I seized power and ruled as Emperor Napoleon III. Twenty years later, the Second Empire crumbled as a result of an unsuccessful war with Prussia. Then the Third Republic was proclaimed. It was more fortunate than its predecessors; it lasted until 1940. After the interval of the German occupation and the Liberation, France again became a republic, the Fourth, in 1946.

One of the foundation stones of France's stability and wealth is her agriculture. Out of 21,000,000 Frenchmen engaged in some occupation, 8,000,000 are employed in agriculture, not counting the village craftsmen and shopkeepers who also live close to the soil. Of this number, 6,000,-000 are their own masters, either as landowners or farmers, and only 2,000,000 work for wages.

French farms in general are small. When one takes a walk in the French countryside or flies over it, he is always astonished to see how the land is divided. In most cases the fields are narrow strips, the color of which changes according to the seasons. This parceling is largely the result of the laws of inheritance enacted at the time of the Revolution. By these laws a landowner must divide his property equally among all his children. This has left him no other choice but to break up his domain if he has more than one child.

The result is a very inefficient means of working the land. Farms have grown smaller and smaller. If a farmer acquires a number of small plots, by inheritance or purchase, they are likely to be widely scattered. This is one reason why the French farmer complains of his lot.

However, since World War II, efforts have been made to remedy the situation. In fact, the life of the French peasant has been undergoing great changes. For one thing, co-operatives of farm equipment have been set up here and there. By 1965 or 1975, it is probable that several sections of the countryside will have been completely electrified and otherwise modernized.

The French farmer gets rich rewards from the soil. He works hard but he fares better than his Bulgarian, German, Italian or Yugoslav counterpart.

No French farm is without domestic animals, and a good part of the farmer's income stems from his livestock. Cereals, beets, potatoes, fruits and vegetables, and

TRANS WORLD AIRLINES

MEDIEVAL CASTLE NEAR CHINON
The castle of Langeais, near Chinon, was built in 990. Its steep roofs, conelike turrets, and small windows show its medieval origin. Here Charles VIII married Anne of Brittany in 1491.

the vine flourish on the rich soil. More rational methods of farming should make the yields even better. As it is, before the war, in 1939, the wheat crop alone had twice the value of the coal and iron ore mined in France in the same year. The wheat crop, however, is just sufficient for home consumption, for the French are great eaters of bread.

The pleasures of the table have always held a high place in France; and French cookery, famous the world over, is both a science and an art. In the tourist guides to the country, some restaurants may have two or three stars, a certain sign of their excellence.

Cassoulet of Toulouse (baked beans with salted goose), sauerkraut of Alsace, bouillabaisse (a sort of fish soup) from Marseilles, foie gras (goose-liver paste) with truffles, chicken with mushrooms, duck à l'orange, lobster à l'armoricaine (Brittany), pike croquettes, ham à la crème, snails à la bourguignonne (Bur-

gundy), not to mention the celebrated châteaubriant (a superlative steak) with French-fried potatoes—these are the favorite dishes of the Frenchman and the delight of the visitor.

A marvelous choice of wines, unique in the world, serves as a worthy accompaniment to the regional dishes. When the Greeks landed at Marseilles several centuries before Christ, they introduced the grapevine into France. It has prospered. For two thousand years, from south of the Loire River to Paris and Alsace, the French peasant has taken the most tender care of his vineyard. In September, gay companies of grape-pickers can be seen, their heads covered with broad straw hats, picking the juicy clusters and placing them in wicker baskets. These are then loaded on carts drawn slowly by horses or oxen. At twilight, the whole company, singing the old songs and the new, takes the road back to the village that is marked by a church spire on the horizon.

STANDARD OIL CO. (N. J.)

RELIGIOUS PROCESSION IN VILLERSEXEL

Villersexel is a small, neat town in Haute (Upper) Saone, not far from the city of Dijon. It was the scene of a battle in the war of 1870-71. Above, a Sunday School procession of children.

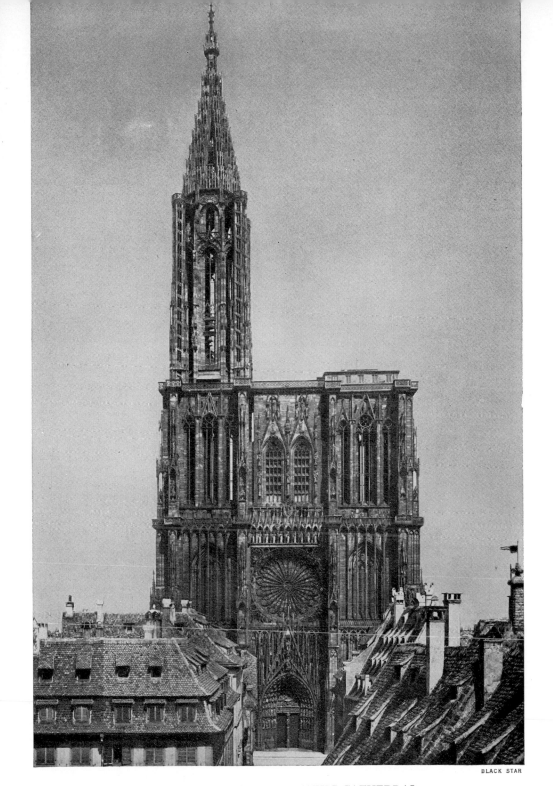

STRASBOURG'S SOARING GOTHIC CATHEDRAL

All the lines point upward in Strasbourg's cathedral, one of the most glorious examples of the Gothic style. Above the arched doorway is a stained-glass rose window forty-two feet wide.

WINTER IS NEVER FAR FROM CHAMONIX

The valley of Chamonix is bordered on the east by the Mont Blanc range, eternally snowclad, with glaciers moving down the slopes. Chamonix is a Mecca for those who love snow sports.

School attendance up to the age of sixteen, the spread of technical education among farmers, the modernization of rural enterprises in the villages and the creation of cultural centers for the French farmers and their families should help to keep them attached to the soil. Young farm people, especially, may be less likely to pine for city life.

Gems of Gothic Architecture

Between the eleventh and fourteenth centuries, a series of unique monuments sprang up all over France—the Gothic cathedrals. They are typical creations of French architectural genius, in a style of artistic expression as characteristic as the Greek temple, the Egyptian pyramid or the American skyscraper. During this late period of the Middle Ages, each city of France tried to perpetuate its name by building a temple to God surpassing in beauty, in lightness of touch and in richness the one of the neighboring town. In Amiens, in Chartres, in Reims, in Bourges, in Rouen, these magnificent

240

TINKLING COWBELLS IN THE ALPS

There is good pasture for the cows in many places high in the French Alps, though the sun glistens on snowy peaks that seem, on a clear day, very near. Most French farms are small.

WHO WILL BUY MY CAULIFLOWERS?

Market day in Nevers. Most French towns have a market day once a week. Farmers bring their produce to sell; and in return buy clothing, household goods, tools and other necessities.

THE DORDOGNE RIVER, before it leaves the Auvergne Mountains, is rapid and wild. Here it flows placidly among grass and trees; later it becomes a busy highway thronged with ships. It runs for three hundred miles through southwest France to unite with the Garonne, thirteen miles from Bordeaux, and form the Gironde, an estuary on the Atlantic coast.

KNOX

LOMBARDY POPLARS border the trim straight roads that are so typical of France, roads as different as can be from the winding, grass-fringed lanes of England. Through the countryside of France the roads dart directly toward their destination past lines of the most regular and erect of trees.

OUTSKIRTS OF SISTERON, SNUGGLED AGAINST THE MOUNTAINS

Sisteron, on the Durance River in southeastern France, hugs its mountain (one of the Maritime Alps). The town was built in the Middle Ages and still keeps something of its medieval character.

244

structures soar to the skies with airy grace. The peaks of the naves reach from 98 to 164 feet high, and the spires from 377 feet (Chartres) to 465 feet (Strasbourg). Delicate openwork in some of the walls belies the actual solidity of the buildings. Inside, a glowing light streams through the stained-glass windows that pierce the large bays.

The stone itself appears to be spiritualized. Pillars, flying buttresses, groined arches, pointed arches—their lines draw the eyes up and up as if the builders had tried to reach the kingdom of heaven itself. Still these temples mysteriously remain linked to man's needs. Under their arches and their jeweled windows one has a sense of peace, of inner security.

Along with the new style in architecture, the construction of the cathedrals also brought about a marvelous rebirth of sculpture. Indeed, in the Middle Ages art was considered a means of education. Few people could read and write, but they could learn from the bas-reliefs and the statues in the cathedrals. Here, in stone, are stories from the Old and New Testaments and the lives of the saints. There

WINE TESTERS, GEVREY-CHAMBERTIN
The wine testers, garbed in red and gold, open the festivities with a procession to church. Silver cups, for tasting the wine, hang round their necks and adorn the leader's staff.

HARVEST IN THE COTE D'OR
The Côte d'Or (Golden Hillside) is a department of France celebrated for its excellent and abundant wines. The prosperous vineyard above is near Beaune, in the heart of this rich region.

245

AN OLD BRIDGE over the Gave de Pau takes us into Orthez, a little town of the Pyrenees whose history reaches far back into the past. In the thirteenth century it had a splendid court. A five-sided tower, at that time the keep of a castle, and some buildings a century older are still standing. In 1569 the town was besieged and taken by Protestant troops, and in 1814, not far from here, the Duke of Wellington with his army won a victory over the French. Orthez stands at an important junction of roads leading over the Pyrenees Mountains and on into Spain.

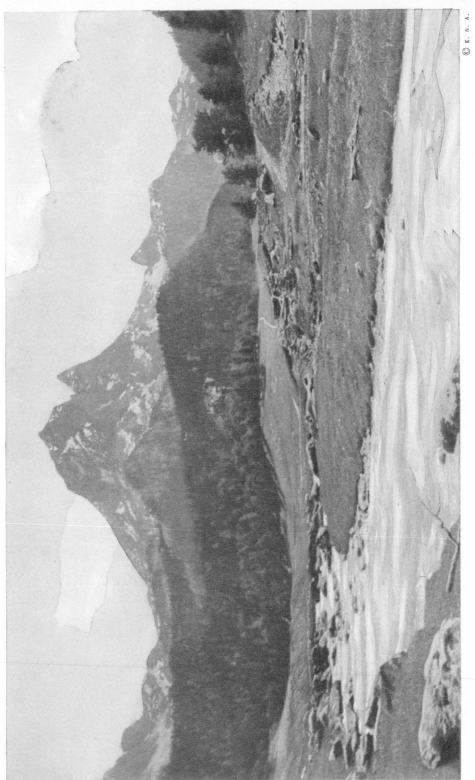

© E. N. A.

IN THE PYRENEES there are few valleys more beautiful than the Vallée d'Ossau which runs northward from the cleft summit of the Pic du Midi d'Ossau, 9,465 feet high. The name means the Valley of the Bears, but no bears are to be found there now, only chamois, and they are becoming fewer and fewer. Once the Vallée was a self-governing commonwealth, and its people are still very independent. The women till the fields and spin with distaff and spindle, and wear quaint red hoods. The men wear clothes of brown wool that are brightened by gay sashes.

are more worldly sculptures, too, that teach man something of the other arts, the sciences and the professions. At Chartres alone there are more than two thousand sculptured figures. It would take more than a lifetime to make a detailed study of all of them. No wonder then that the cathedrals have been called the Bible of the poor.

Besides the great Gothic cathedrals and the earlier Romanesque churches, the wonderful castles of the Renaissance that adorn the banks of the Loire River remind us of the glorious past of this old land.

The French people thus have lived surrounded by masterpieces, in an atmosphere of nobility and beauty. For ten centuries, in spite of military and political reverses, France has been a creator in the realms of thought, of literature and of the arts. Indeed, France still deserves the title "mother of letters and arts" that a poet of the Renaissance bestowed upon her. Always ready to welcome exiles, she has also been open to new ideas. This helps to explain the breadth of her culture.

Among writers and philosophers, there are the names of Pascal, Montaigne, Ra-cine, Descartes, Voltaire, Rousseau, Chateaubriand, Victor Hugo and Balzac. Among her painters are Watteau, Fragonard, Corot, Renoir and Cézanne. World-famous musical composers are Rameau, Debussy and Ravel. Her scientists include Ampère and the Curies. Their work belongs just as much to the heritage of all humanity as to that of France. The vein is not exhausted today. Claudel, Valéry, Péguy, Gide, Langevin, the Duke de Broglie, painters such as Matisse, Rouault, Utrillo, architects such as Auguste Perret or Frantz Jourdain are proof of the vitality of the recent intellectual and artistic life of France.

The average city Frenchman—Monsieur Dupont, as he is usually called—used to be represented as a little man, a bachelor, who sported a mustache, wore a derby, was a great talker, was ignorant of geography and never set foot out of his country. This portrait was never really lifelike.

Today Monsieur Dupont is a married man and a real family man as in the past. In spite of the greater ease that the law of 1945 offers for obtaining a divorce, there

RAPHO-GUILLUMETTE

LYONS TURNS HER FACE TO THE RIVER

Lyons (or Lyon), third largest city of France, is strategically situated on the River Saone, at the point where it joins the Rhone. Lyons is an industrial center and a railroad junction.

are very few. Of the couples who do seek a divorce, most are childless. Since World War II the French population has been increasing. The surplus of births over deaths was 320,000 in 1959 as compared to 35,000 in 1938.

that he can use at once rather than put his savings in a stocking. If he can afford it, Monsieur Dupont has a car. If not, he is contented with a velomotor or a bicycle. The old-time Sunday stroll along the boulevards has given way to a week end in

FUN FOR THE CHILDREN IN PLACE BELLECOUR

Place Bellecour, a spacious open square in the heart of Lyons, in olden days was a stately promenade where fashionable folk gathered. Today it is largely given over to the children.

Monsieur Dupont has, on the average, three children in spite of the fact that his salary is low and his apartment is apt to be small. One of the most distressing problems for young engaged couples is to find a place where they may set up their own household. In cities such as Lyons, Marseilles, Lille, Paris and Bordeaux, apartments are either not to be found or they are extremely expensive.

Monsieur Dupont no longer has a mustache, no longer wears a derby. Nor does he live any longer on a fixed income from land or stocks or bonds. Since 1930 such incomes have melted like snow in the sun. For some years France has been suffering from severe inflation, and Monsieur Dupont has lost much of his old sense of thrift. Today he prefers to buy goods

the forests of Fontainebleau or Compiègne.

Today Monsieur Dupont, the average Frenchman, has also taken up sports. In the winter he takes a ski train to spend a week in a resort in the Alps or the Pyrenees. In the summer he goes camping, or he visits Italy, Austria or England. He is even learning foreign languages.

One of the favorite vacation spots of the French people is Provence on the Côte d'Azur—the French Riviera at the eastern end of the Mediterranean coast. Formerly it was the playground of a privileged few.

The Côte d'Azur is without rival for beauty. It is a land of contrasts, basking in dazzling sunlight. There is contrast in the contours. A few hours from Nice, the peaks of the Alps surge upward to a

THE FAÇADE of Radiant City with its vivid squares of red, yellow, green and white, gives the housing project designed by Le Corbusier for Marseilles the look of a gay checkerboard.

GIANT CASKS in the Byrrh wine-storage cellars at Thuir in the rich vineyard country of the Pyrenees. Wine is aged in wooden vats which, vintners say, permit it to "breathe."

250

CARCASSONNE, with its moat, drawbridge and fifty towers, is one of the best-preserved walled cities of the Middle Ages.

THE SKILLED FINGERS of the lacemakers of Thiers inter-cross and plait the threads to make a lovely edging of pillow lace.

ACRES OF BLOSSOMS NEAR GRASSE

Grasse, in Provence, the southeastern region of France, is the center of the flower industry. Vast fields of fragrant blooms are grown for export, and also to be distilled into perfume.

RICH FABRICS COME FROM LYONS

Textiles from Lyons, especially silks and velvets, are of high quality. There have been times when more than half the citizens depended, directly or indirectly, on the silk industry.

DELIGHTFUL CHAMONIX, one of the best-known and most popular resorts in the French Alps, lies in a narrow valley beneath Europe's loftiest mountain. We do not see Mont Blanc in this picture, though on the left is the foot of the Mer de Glace, its enormous glacier. The cloud-capped peak is the beautiful Aiguille Verte (Green Needle).

MIRRORED in a calm pool amid heavy foliage stands the white Château of Azay-le-Rideau, lovely as the fabled castle of the Sleeping Beauty.

PERCHED on a rock pinnacle beside the gate of Le Puy, the church of Saint Michel d'Aiguille (of the needle) dates back to the tenth century.

CANALS divide the port of Martigues into three quarters. On the Berre inlet of the Mediterranean, the sunny city is the Venice of Provence.

height of six thousand feet, a paradise for skiers until the early months of summer. In this same region are the deep gorges of the Verdon River.

There is contrast along the coast, marked by limestone coves, narrow creeks and wide pebbled beaches lapped by waters of cobalt blue.

Vegetation is just as varied. In a walk of only a few miles, one may pass through scrub, pine woods, forests of hundred-year-old beeches, flowery fields, groves of palm or olive trees and thickets of spiny-leaved agaves or prickly cactus.

There are ancient towns, such as Antibes, Fréjus and Hyères, which date back to the times of the Romans. On high points little villages perch like eagles' nests, a reminder of the days when the inhabitants needed protection from the pirates of the Barbary coast. Only a stone's throw away from these quaint old towns are the modern hotels of summer resorts such as Cannes, Juanles-Pins, Sainte-Mavime and Saint-Raphaël.

The Sun-drenched Côte d'Azur

The Côte d'Azur is well named. Perhaps nowhere else on earth are the blue of the sea and the sky so vivid. Color beguiles the eyes everywhere: the green of the forests, the silver-gray of the olive trees, the red of the porphyritic rock, the white of the limestone. The climate is warm in winter and is freshened in summer by the light breezes from the Mediterranean, whose waters are always cool.

Provence is the center of the flower industry. Alphonse Karr, a writer of the nineteenth century, started it. He settled on the Côte d'Azur during the reign of Napoleon III and was enraptured at the sight of all the flowers growing there. "Leave Paris," he wrote, "plant your cane in my garden, and the next day when you wake up, you will see that roses have grown on it." With the help of a friend, he began to cultivate flowers on a large scale. Then he had the idea of sending bouquets of violets to Paris by mail. This venture turned out to be a huge success.

Nowadays eight thousand horticulturists are engaged in this business, and cut flowers are sent by plane as far as the Scandinavian countries.

At Grasse, Vence, Menton, Vallauris, there are whole fields of violets, mignonettes, jasmine, orange trees, mimosa, carnations and pinks. Anyone who has ever seen these fields in bloom, saturating the air with fragrance, will never forget the experience.

In the region of Grasse the distillation of flowers dates back to the sixteenth century. It was then that Catherine de Médicis had a Florentine specialist in this delicate art settle in Grasse. Today large factories with the most modern equipment extract the perfume-yielding oils from the flowers cultivated in the region. These factories also extract essences from aromatic plants and from fruit, some of it shipped in from outside France.

In one of the most up-to-date methods of distillation, the crushed flowers are placed in contact with a petroleum compound for eight hours. When it has been saturated with perfume, the dissolvent is distilled in a vacuum. The purified residue is then treated with alcohol to produce the essence. Five hundred thousand rose-buds are necessary to yield one quart of rose essence.

Life in the great industrial centers of France is entirely different from life in Provence or in the Basque country of the Pyrenees. The miners in the coal fields of the Nord or of Saint-Etienne, the workers in the big steel mills of Lorraine and Le Creusot work hard. Their poor living conditions have been a cause of concern for many years. Before the second World War, several of the industries had begun to provide better housing for the workers. After the war some of the key industries were nationalized, and this brought about further improvement.

Compulsory Social Security

The Government introduced a general and compulsory social-service system, to which both employers and employees must contribute. Its principle is simple. Each month both employers and employees must pay a certain amount (less for the workers) to a central treasury. Considerable

ENTRANCE TO THE BASILICA, LOURDES

The Basilica at Lourdes is built over the grotto where little Bernadette Soubirous a century ago had a vision of the Virgin Mary. Miraculous cures here are frequently reported.

THE STERN FORTRESS OF CHATEAU D'IF

Francis I had this grim prison built on the tiny rocky isle of If, just outside Marseilles, in the Mediterranean. Here Dumas placed his hero, Edmond Dantès, "The Count of Monte Cristo."

THE PICTURESQUE OLD HARBOR OF MARSEILLES

Marseilles is the greatest commercial seaport of France. There is an Old Harbor, now used mostly by small boats, and a magnificently equipped New Harbor of more than three hundred acres.

CATCHING THE NEWS IN PASSING

Frenchmen are avid readers of newspapers. They will call for a paper to read while sipping coffee
or an aperitif at a café; and the street-corner bulletin board is well scanned.

HAND-FED CAPONS FOR TENDER MEAT

A curious custom is sometimes followed on the farms of southwest France. Capons are kept in cages, so they cannot move about, crammed with corn by hand, to insure fat, tender meat.

TWO-LEVEL TRAFFIC IN ST. RESTITUT

A corner in St. Restitut, in southern France, showing Italian influence in the tiled roof and plastered stones of the building. At the right, a street on a higher level.

sums of money are thus set aside. They are used to pay medical expenses, to help the unemployed, to send tubercular patients to the mountains and to provide pensions for aged workers.

A system of family allowances helps the families with many children and allows mothers to stay at home. Before, many mothers worked outside their homes to eke out the meager family income.

In spite of some flaws, the social-security system represents noteworthy social progress. Eventually, among other results, these measures, including compulsory medical care, will raise the health standards of the French people.

The French generation that came of age during the troubled years of the occupation and after has been schooled in adversity and has found it hard to make its way. That is why some young French men and women have chosen to leave their country. Since the war there has been an emigration movement, similar to that of the seventeenth and eighteenth centuries, toward Canada, South America, Africa and Australia.

After the tragic defeat of 1940 and the years of German occupation, when the life of France almost stood still, the French people realized that only by a tremendous effort could they hold their own in a world dominated by two industrial giants, the United States and the Soviet Union.

FISHERMAN'S LUCK—A DAY ON SHORE AT CANNES

First a health resort, then a winter resort, now a year-round vacation spot, Cannes, on the Riviera, has a charm for all. Its greatest attraction is its sunny, mild weather.

PONT DU GARD NEAR NIMES
There are many remains of Roman occupation at Nîmes, including an amphitheater and temple.
Nearby are some Roman baths and part of an aqueduct, the Pont du Gard, built under Agrippa.

One step in this direction was the Monnet Plan, drawn up in 1947. It called for nothing less than to make French agriculture and industry completely modern. In the years since, considerable advances have been made. Production of tractors and fertilizers as well as coal, steel, cement have all more than doubled. But housing has lagged far behind demand; and many farms remain too small to lend themselves to modern, large-scale methods.

France has great mineral wealth of prime importance to industry, namely, iron ore and bauxite. Following on this comes the need for power and fuel. France has been pushing development of the water-power sites in the Massif Centrale, the Alps, the Rhone Valley. The Génissiat Dam on the upper Rhone, one of the largest dams in Europe, has a capacity of 3,000,000,000 kilowatt-hours. In a recent year, France produced almost 60,000,000,000 kilowatt-hours of electrical energy.

Moreover, in 1959 France became the first nation in western continental Europe to produce electricity generated by atomic power for commercial purposes. It flowed from a reactor at Marcoule, in the Rhone Valley. The main efforts along these lines, however, are at Chinon, in the Loire Valley. According to some estimates, France will be producing at least one quarter of its electricity from atomic energy by 1975.

Production of oil has surged since the discovery, in 1954, of the rich Parentis field, south of Bordeaux.

Though France has plenty of coal, little of it is suitable for industrial use, particularly steelmaking. Coking coal must be imported, and most of it comes from the Ruhr basin and the Saar of West Germany. This situation was one of the motives for the European Coal and Steel Community (ECSC). It was first proposed in 1950, by Robert Schuman, then French foreign minister, and has been in effect since 1953. The ECSC pools the coal and steel resources of France, West Germany, Italy, Belgium, the Netherlands and Luxembourg, creating a free-trade area in these basic products. ECSC's general aims are to decrease costs in the industries that hinge on coal and steel and to allow a better standard of living for the workers.

In 1958 the same six countries joined together in two other organizations: the European Atomic Energy Community (Euratom) and the European Economic Community (Euromarket, or Common

GATEWAY TO TARASCON

On the site of the Roman Tarasco, on the lower Rhone, is the medieval town of Tarascon, surrounded by thick walls. Part of this old gateway has been restored in modern times.

Market). Euratom pools the efforts of the member countries in the development of atomic energy for peaceful purposes. Euromarket links the economies of the member nations, removes such barriers as tariffs among them and, in general, extends the principles of ECSC. The same parliamentary and judicial elements—the European Parliamentary Assembly and the Court of Justice—serve ECSC, Euratom and Euromarket.

Like Great Britain, France long had ties with a vast overseas domain, which after World War II formed the French Union. In the 1950's, however, the bonds began to fray. Former Indochina was lost in 1954; and Morocco and Tunisia became independent in 1956.

Algeria presented the most difficult problem. After negotiations that see-sawed for month after weary month, the French Government and the Algerian leaders agreed to let the Algerian people vote on freedom, on July 1, 1962. Algeria became independent two days later.

By Robert Barrat

BLESSING THE SEA, NEAR BIARRITZ

Mass is celebrated by the water's edge, near Biarritz, at the *Fête de la mer*. This is a tradial yearly blessing of the sea and of those who make their living by the sea.

PHOTOS, FRENCH GOVERNMENT TOURIST OFFICE

THE BEACH AT SAINT JEAN DE LUZ

Among the many popular vacation spots on the Bay of Biscay is Saint Jean de Luz, just south of Biarritz, another famous resort. Hundreds of cabanas (shelters for bathers) dot the sunny beach.

FRANCE : facts and figures

Government

REPUBLIC: consists of metropolitan France (including Corsica), overseas departments, overseas territories, the French Community

PRESIDENT: elected for 7 yrs. by electoral college (members of Parliament and the Assemblies of overseas territories) and elected representatives of municipal councils; president has executive power, appoints and dismisses premier, cabinet (who are also responsible to National Assembly); may dissolve Parliament (calling for new elections), may submit questions of national importance to popular referendum; under national emergency may assume almost dictatorial power

PREMIER: powers similar to president's, limited only by latter's personality and ability

PARLIAMENT: bicameral—273-member Senate (metropolitan France 255, overseas departments 7, territories 5; 6 elected by Senate itself to represent Frenchmen residing abroad) indirectly elected for 9 yrs. (⅓d elected every 3 yrs.), represents local governments rather than the people; 481-member National Assembly (metropolitan France 465, overseas departments 10, territories 6) popularly elected for 5 yrs.

CONSTITUTIONAL COUNCIL: 3 members appointed by president, 3 by Senate president, 3 by National Assembly president for 9 yrs., 3 appointed every 3 yrs.; all former presidents of France life members; Council ensures regularity of all national elections, referendums, rules on constitutionality of all laws

VOTING: universal suffrage from age 21

Area and climate

212,659 sq. mi.

COMPOSITION: metropolitan France, English Channel islands, Corsica

CULTIVATED: 39%

FORESTED: 21%

INLAND WATERWAYS: rivers—Rhone, Seine, Loire, Garonne, Marne, Oise

WEATHER PATTERN: 3 zones—west coast oceanic with cool summers, cool winters, about 55 in. of rain a yr.; south coast Mediterranean with hot summers, cool winters, 22 in. of rain; east, center continental with warm summers, cold winters

with snow, 31 in. of precipitation a yr.

Natural resources

FISHERIES: av. annual catch 570,000 tons; herring, mackerel, cod, sardine, tuna, lobster

AGRICULTURE: wheat, wine grapes, sugar beets, barley, potatoes, corn, oats, fruit, dairy products

LIVESTOCK: 1,700,000 horses
8,700,000 pigs
9,100,000 sheep
19,550,000 cattle

MINERALS: arsenic (3d in world production), gypsum (3d), talc (3d), potash (4th), coal, iron, natural gas, bauxite, lead, zinc

WATERPOWER: 27,000,000,000 kwh; world's 1st tidal-power plant being built on Brittany coast

Population

46,100,000

URBAN: 57%

BIRTHRATE: 17.0 per 1,000

DEATHRATE: 11.4 per 1,000

ANNUAL INCREASE: 0.9%

URBAN CENTERS:

Paris (capital)	3,400,000
Marseilles	700,000
Lyons	680,000
Toulouse	290,000
Bordeaux	270,000
Nice	260,000
Nantes	250,000
Strasbourg	220,000
Lille	200,000

Language and religion

French universal; Breton (Brittany), German (Alsace-Lorraine), Flemish (northeast), Italian (Corsica, southeast), Spanish, Catalan, Basque (southwest) 2d languages; complete freedom of religion

Roman Catholic   80% (practicing 25%)
Protestant   2%
Muslim   1%
Jewish   0.7%

Education and welfare

LITERACY: over 97%, education compulsory ages 6–14

SCHOOLS AND PUPILS: 88,200 primary (7,700,000); 2,550 secondary (1,400,000); 17 state univ. (210,000)

WELFARE: insurance for illness, accident, unemployment; pensions for aged and disabled

Commerce

GROSS NATIONAL PRODUCT: $48,500,000,000

GNP PER CAPITA: $1,100

CURRENCY: franc; 4.9 francs worth $1.00 US

EXPORTS: industrial products of all kinds, dairy products, food

IMPORTS: raw and semifinished products of all kinds; food

TRADING PARTNERS: Common Market, United States, French Community, North Africa, Soviet bloc

Transportation

ROADS: 400,000 mi.

PASSENGER CARS: 5,800,000

TRUCKS AND BUSES: 2,400,000

RAILROADS: 24,600 mi.

NAVIGABLE WATERWAYS: 2,500 mi. of rivers, 3,000 mi. of canals

MERCHANT MARINE: 1,660 ships, 4,900,000 gross tons; Le Havre, Marseilles, Bordeaux main ports

AIR SERVICE: Air France, Compagnie des Transports Aeriens Intercontinentaux (TAI), Union Aeromaritime de Transport (UAT) major French airlines with external, domestic flights; France serviced by the major foreign lines

Communications

TELEPHONES: 4,100,000

RADIO AND TELEVISION: 11,600,000 radios; 2,200,000 TV sets

PRESS: 130 daily papers (circulation 11,000,000); 70 semiweekly papers (1,200,000); 8,900 magazines (118,000,000)

CINEMAS: 9,000, av. annual per capita attendance 8.8

Membership in international organizations

Aid to India-Pakistan Club
Commission for Technical Cooperation in Africa South of Sahara
Council of Europe
European Atomic Energy Community
European Coal and Steel Community
European Economic Community (Common Market)
European Space Research Organization
French Community
North Atlantic Treaty Organization (NATO)
Organization for Economic Cooperation and Development
Southeast Asia Collective Defense Treaty Organization (SEATO)
South Pacific Commission
United Nations and its specialized agencies
Western European Union

For WORLDWIDE FACTS AND FIGURES, refer to Vol. 7, pages 390–92

Normandy and
Brittany ... *the French sea provinces*

CONFLICT marks the long history of Normandy and Brittany: conflict with Paris, with England, with the sea and finally with the Germans. The way of life of the Norman and Breton people has long stood in contrast with the sophistication of Paris and the languor of the Loire Valley. Everywhere there are signs of sturdy resistance: the massive walls of St.-Malo resist the sea; the Breton language resists the encroachment of the French tongue; the dress of the people resists the pressures of uniformity; the Normans and Bretons resist the national habit of wine drinking by quaffing cider. But the struggle has not always been on such a pleasant note. During the German occupation of France in the second World War, Nantes and Rouen were hotbeds of the Resistance.

Then, in the landings that began on D day, June 6, 1944, some 326,000 men swept down on eighty miles of Norman coast to breach the fortress that Hitler had made of Europe. General Bradley smashed through the town of St.-Lô, General Patton through Avranches, and Britain's Montgomery hammered at Caen. In eight weeks the Allies controlled both provinces. But the price of victory was the devastation of one of the fairest regions of France.

Though the Normandy campaign cost the Germans half a million men and the war itself, it cost the French the towns of Caen, Vire, Lisieux, Falaise, Mortain,

THREE HAY HARVESTS a year repay the efforts of Normandy's farmers, and new oil refineries (like this one at Quevilly, near Rouen) the talent of its growing number of industrialists.

Tilly-sur-Seulles, Avranches, St.-Malo and Fougères. It cost them their factories, their railroads, their crops, their livestock, their people. It cost them the near annihilation of Brest and St.-Nazaire. In the midst of Rouen, the cathedral stood a gutted wreck.

Undismayed by the shambles, the French rebuilt their land. By the end of the war half a million buildings had been destroyed and three times that number damaged; ports were ruined and idle; road, rail and water communications disrupted. In the Caen area the fields had been sown with 100,000 mines. Thousands of people were homeless amid the heaps of rubble that had once been towns. The recovery of the towns in Normandy and Brittany, the most war-torn area of France, proclaims the success of the mighty over-all effort in reconstruction and expansion. Today Rouen and Nantes stand fifth and third among the nation's ports and handle a merchant fleet that has grown fivefold since 1946. Throughout France some million new houses and a magnificent railroad, air and highway system complement a booming economy. Through the 1950's industry expanded 10 per cent a year; trade thrived; productivity increased; living standards rose. Le Havre emerged from its ashes an ultramodern city. Caen has been almost totally rebuilt. Nantes enjoys dock and commerce facilities far better than those of 1938. The harbor has been deepened. Coal, sugar, phosphates and peanuts pour into some warehouses, while others disgorge iron ore, grain, superphosphates, preserves and chemicals into the waiting ships. In Rouen the carillon of the restored cathedral again rings out across the city.

The Sea and the River Seine

Until the French Revolution, France was divided into provinces for administrative purposes. Since then it has been divided into departments. But the old provincial names, of which Normandy and Brittany are two, linger on. The departments, which are much smaller than most of the provinces, are usually named after rivers. For France is a land of rivers and to a Frenchman each of the major rivers has a character of its own. The two most important rivers, the Seine and the Loire, flow to the sea through Normandy and Brittany, the first reaching it in the departments of Seine Inférieure and Eure and the second in Loire Inférieure.

The ports that lie near their mouths, Rouen and Nantes, were once capitals of the two provinces and their trade was vital to provincial prosperity. Though Nantes is the greater port, the Loire, which flows through it, is less important than the Seine, which alone among the major rivers is easily navigable far inland.

Standing on one of the chalk bluffs that command the lower Seine Valley one sees numbers of barges making their cumbrous way to Rouen. They have been to Paris or beyond with coal, petroleum, phosphates and timber. Now they return with ships' stores, textiles, leather goods, perfumes and some of the raw materials needed by Rouen's industries. The barges glide down river past rows of poplars standing in lush meadows, past the old town of Mantes, past Rosny, birthplace of some zealous royal servant four centuries ago, past Gaillon, graceful château of the archbishops of Rouen, round the bend that curves under the walls of the Château Gaillard, round two more bends to sleepy little Pont-de-l'Arche, and thence through Bon-Port to Rouen.

This city of cranes and spires has a wide variety of industries, some fourteen miles of docks and a few beautiful old buildings. Its industries range from shipbuilding and large-scale petroleum refining to the production of flour and candied apples. While the war destroyed much of the harbor and the city center, it left the old church of St. Ouen and the Grosse Horloge clock tower intact. The damage to the other ancient monuments

267

has been made good and to the casual visitor the cobbled streets of the city seem little changed.

If no scars remain on the towns and fields of Normandy and Brittany it is a tribute to the spirit of the people. Over the centuries they have shown a dogged refusal to admit defeat. St.-Lô, for example, pillaged by Norsemen (889), Geoffrey Plantagenet (1141), Edward III of England (1346) and by Huguenots in the 1500's, has always emerged again as a bustling little road center and market town. Then as now its people had little to count on in the hard road back to prosperity but their own skill and effort.

Perhaps Norman vigor is connected with viking ancestry. A far more outgoing people than the Bretons, the Normans have a long history of expansion behind them. Today the expansion is economic rather than territorial. Where a Norman baron once extracted favorable terms from a French king, today a Norman industrialist wrests a good bargain from a Paris tycoon.

In ancient times the land of the Normans was inhabited by wild Gallic tribes. Later it became part of a Roman province, and Christian missionaries reached it at an early date. Then, as a feudal duchy of the bishopric of Rouen, it was conquered by King Clovis I, in the sixth century. When Rollo (Hrolf) of Norway seized Rouen he forced Charles the Simple (King Charles III), whose sister, Gisela, Rollo married, to make him Duke of Normandy. But when Rollo's proxy had to perform the rite of allegiance by kissing the King's foot, that ruddy viking stood erect, lifted the royal foot to his mouth and toppled the King over backward, at which Rollo's men shouted with laughter.

Thus from Rollo sprang the dukes of Normandy. One of them was William I of England, known as William the Conqueror. So adaptable were the Northmen that they soon became more Gallic than the more civilized Gauls themselves, and zealously restored the very monasteries they had destroyed. William the Conqueror himself was present when the rebuilt church at Jumièges, west of Rouen,

was consecrated in 1065. William was the son of Robert the Devil and a maid of Falaise, and a famous tapestry at Bayeux depicts his conquest of England. United with England for a time, Normandy then broke away. It was saved from English invaders by Joan of Arc, burned at the stake in Rouen in 1431.

Throughout Normandy one still sees examples of the ponderous Norman architecture, as in the chapel of Mont-St.-Michel, a granite structure (just across from St.-Malo) where abbey and fortress were once combined on this rocky island laved by a forty-eight-foot tide. Fortresses like that of Château Gaillard at Les Andelys once enabled the dukes of Normandy to hold back the kings of France. Normandy impresses the visitor as a land of chalk cliffs and half-timbered villages, of emerald fields and fragrant apple orchards reaching inland along the valley of the Seine. Cider is not unnaturally the favorite beverage of the countryside. Le Havre (The Haven) owes its fame as a port to the fact that it stands where the Seine, the water route from Paris, widens to six miles before blending with the English Channel. Cherbourg, on the peninsula of Cotentin, is a renowned seaport with a vast breakwater. Dieppe, to the northward, was aptly named for the deeps beneath its cliffs.

Faith and the Sea

Brittany is a rugged promontory swept by salt winds and Atlantic storms. Celtic rather than French, its people are mainly dependent upon the sea. The men have the strength and simplicity of the sailor and the faith of those constantly in peril. Strangely enough, though the priest is a great power in every community, communist unions thrive. Piety and trade unionism go hand in hand to counter the dreadful insecurity of the fishermen, their families and dependents. In time of storm one can see wives, even employers, devoutly carrying candles to the great parish church while in the background the bell buoys toll, emergency sirens wail and the surf crashes endlessly.

The truly Breton towns are on the coast

TAKING ADVANTAGE OF A CLEAR AND BREEZY DAY IN NANTES

An enterprising housewife calmly hangs out her wet clothes as the town hums with action on the other side of the canal. The well-worn cobblestone streets and sharp-gabled roofs show plainly that Nantes is an old and historic French city, where automobiles now travel on the streets once meant for carriages and saddle horses. Nantes is a port on the Loire River.

not the barren uplands. The old walled town of St. Malo, the gateway to Brittany, has a harbor protected by many islets, including Grand Bey where Châteaubriand lies in his grave. In this region and as far westward as Cape Fréhel there are bays in which the sea leaves wide expanses of sand at low tide; but for the most part the coast is wildly picturesque. Around Ploumanach there is as weird a stretch of wilderness as can well be imagined. The actual "land's end" presents to the Atlantic dangerous reefs, bold capes and rocky desolation. And yet Brest roadstead is accounted the finest natural harbor in Europe; for within its bottle-neck entrance, illuminated by five lighthouses, lies a harbor fourteen miles long by half as wide. Just beyond, in the bay of Douarnenez there is something every tourist ought to visit—the grottoes of Morgat, the largest of which can be visited only by boat with the passengers lying flat at the cave mouth. Here the waves have

hollowed a cavern 150 feet long into which the blue light enters through the sea, and in the middle of this grotto stands a huge block of red granite, the "altar" The sight is impressive.

Where the coast bends sharply southeastward, it is protected by a chain of islands and becomes less rugged until it ends in sand dunes at the mouth of the Loire. It is here that relics of the Bronze Age and Neolithic remains are most numerous. The first people in Brittany to leave records behind them were the Armoricans, as they were called by the Romans. These Druidical people erected strange monuments to which the Bretons even to-day make journeys, superstitiously taking their cattle to be blessed. These monuments were of three kinds, dolmens, menhirs and cromlechs. The dolmen was a cairn rudely constructed of upright stones and roofed over by a capstone, and it is thought that in some prehistoric age it was used as a repository for the bones of the dead. Menhirs are single upright stones, possibly used to mark boundaries, more likely placed to do honor to those buried in the dolmens. At Carnac fully twelve hundred of these stones stand ranged in eleven rows, and at Erdeven near by are similar alinements. It is also believed that the tribesmen of those pagan times used to dance down these aisles, leading their victims to stones called cromlechs where the priests stood ready to make the sacrifices. At any rate, the place names in this region are largely derived from funeral ceremonies: Plouharnel means "the bone houses," Kerlescan, "the place of ashes" and Kermario, "the place of the dead." The Armoricans were vanquished in the fifth century by the invading Celts from Britain; but in the "pardons" of which we shall presently tell, there is more than a suggestion of a Druidical religion marked by an elaborate cult of the dead. The Bretons, living isolated from the rest of France and daily faced by the hazards of the sea, although a Christian people, cling superstitiously to certain pagan customs. To a

mutilated Roman statue of a horseman at St. Marcel, for instance, the sick are brought on horseback.

The Breton is peculiarly religious. He has the cemetery in the middle of the town in order that the dead may hear the church services; and the great days of the year are the "pardons" when he believes his sins will all be forgiven and his bodily ills cured by the particular saint whose day it is. He therefore spends the early part of the day in pilgrimage and prayer. Penitents will kiss the stones and on their bended knees make their painful way to the spot where they believe the saint to be buried, and afterward will drink of the fountain that rises nearest his grave. But in the evening there is merry-making and the erstwhile devotee dances to the shrill music of the "biniou," the Breton bagpipe, or the concertina.

There is the Pardon of Rumengol, remarkable for the number of people who attend it and for their costumes. At Rumengol is a celebrated statue of the Virgin which the Bretons believe has the power to cure the ills of body or soul. This

PHILIP GENDREAU

PAYING A FRIENDLY VISIT IN THE TOWN OF QUIMPER, BRITTANY

On the Breton peninsula, where life in the small towns moves at a dignified pace and ladies still wear snow-white caps, the two-wheeled carriage is a practical method of travel.

A VILLAGE IN THE HEART OF BRITTANY, DOZING IN THE SUN
The stone houses sit close together, presenting an unbroken front. Almost everywhere in France, farming families live in hamlets, with their fields some distance away.

PHILIP GENDREAU

A WOOD-CARVER OF BRITTANY CHISELS OUT A NEW FIGURE

His neighbors and friends may have served as models for some of these scowling, smiling or saintly faces. With skill and experience he captures their changing moods and expressions.

AN IMMACULATE COIF SETS OFF A GENTLE BRETON FACE

The becoming coif is a fashion that has come down from medieval times. This one is typical of
Brittany. Many old ways survive here, even the language of the Bretons' Celtic ancestors.

FLOUR for delicious loaves of crusty French bread is still ground in old stone windmills in the tradition-loving country regions of the province of Brittany.

SCULPTURED over the centuries by the pounding waves of the Atlantic Ocean, the craggy coast of Brittany assumes weird shapes at Belle-Isle-en-Mer.

CROWNING A ROCKY ISLET, the fortress-abbey of Mont St. Michel is a marvel of Gothic architecture. A little medieval village hugs two sides of the rock. The island is connected to the mainland (about a mile away) by a causeway.

FEW BRETON FESTIVALS, weddings or other celebrations would be complete without a blue-and-gold-clad piper puffing away on his bagpipes or, as they are called in Brittany, *binious*. The women wear traditional Sunday-best costumes with winged lace collars and starched caps.

A LITTLE CHURCH NEAR QUIMPER

The Crucifixion is portrayed above the entrance. Quimper is at the west tip of Brittany.

The Pardon of the Sea, which is the Fête of Sainte Anne de la Palude, is the greatest of all. Then the procession includes widows with extinguished candles, and survivors of wrecks with a small ship's model. Ste. Anne is the saint of all who lie beneath the sea or make their living in deep waters. Her story is full of that mystical meaning which the Breton loves. Ste. Anne, when young, was a much-beloved duchess in Brittany, and married a king of France. When the king found she was likely to become a mother, he drove her from home and she came down to the sea in great distress. But a "ship of glory" was provided for her, and the helmsman was an angel. He guided her to the Holy Land, where she gave birth to the Virgin Mary—or, some say, the Lord himself. When Anne was growing old, she longed for her Breton people and begged to be taken back, so the "ship of glory" came back, with the angel still at the helm, and her own people assembled

is also called the Pardon of the Singers, and it obtained its name from a very old legend. It is said that a king of ancient Brittany, Gralon by name, threw his lovely daughter, Ahes, into the sea that he himself might escape from drowning. She became a siren, luring fishermen and mariners to their doom by her wonderful singing. Gralon heard it and was sorrowful, and on his deathbed asked the Virgin to deprive Ahes of her voice. This the Virgin said she could not do; but she promised that a race of sweet singers should come to the earth and that every year they should sing at the Pardon of Rumengol.

On the night of the twenty-third of June the Pardon of Fire is celebrated. On a hillside at St. Jean du Doigt, or St. John of the Finger, will be built a great bonfire. The peasants gather around it, excitedly getting scorched in their efforts to seize brands to carry away as charms—"Joy and good health from the blessed St. John!"

PHOTOS, FRENCH EMBASSY PRESS AND INFO. DIV.

ALONG A QUAY AT DIEPPE

Fishing smacks and a Channel steamer hug their anchors in front of shops and warehouses.

A SHRINE AT ROUEN—TO JOAN OF ARC, THE MAID OF ORLEANS

This statue of Joan stands near the place of her execution in Rouen. She led the French legions to victory over the English at Orléans and died at the stake, falsely accused of sorcery. The statue immortalizes the tragic moment when flames leaped up to destroy her, and shows the dignity and courage of the heroine who continues to inspire the land she loved.

THE SHINING WHITE BASILICA of Saint Theresa at Lisieux has sixteen chapels, each donated by a different nation. Lisieux is a place of pilgrimage.

NORMANDY has many fine old timbered houses with overhanging roofs and decorative beams. This manor house is outside Deauville, a fashionable resort.

QUIMPER, in Brittany, is famous for its china factories where gay figurines of Breton beaux and belles in festival costume, correct in every detail, are made.

THE TUNNY and sardine catches are in; the fishermen have gone home and the usually lively quay of the Breton fishing port of Concarneau is deserted.

AT OMAHA BEACH, A LANDING CRAFT AND BAREFOOT CHILDREN

On the Normandy beach where the Allied invasion of Europe began, June 6, 1944, French children turn the hull of a landing boat into a perch from which to view the now peaceful horizon.

on the shore to give her a welcome as their queen. But St. Anne would have none of this. "I give all my goods to the poor!" she cried; and she was as good as her word, ending her life in poverty.

There is a wonderful legend about the City of Is, so beautiful a city that when the people of France were seeking a name for their capital they could find nothing better to call it than Par-is—*the like of Is*—an ingenious but untrue derivation.

A City Under the Sea

The City of Is was below sea level, but it was protected from inundation by walls and dykes with doors that could be opened for the water to flow out or in. The Princess Dahut carried the silver keys that unlocked those doors suspended from her neck. One night a stranger made his appearance and captivated the princess by his beauty and masterfulness. As soon as he got an opportunity, he snatched the keys from her neck, or (one version has it) she gave them to him; at any rate he made away with them and opened the floodgates. The sea streamed in; the waves mounting higher and higher, swamped the streets, houses and palaces, until finally there was left only the wide surface that to-day makes the Bay of Douarnenez.

For years the clergy used to embark on fishing-boats every year to say Mass over the drowned city, and it is still said that when the sea is calm and the weather is clear, the remains of a great town may be seen at the bottom of the bay, and the ringing of its church-bells can be heard.

Legend of St. Galonnek

The feast of St. Galonnek is held every first of April, when "the time of the singing of the birds is come." St. Galonnek was a native of Ireland, a disciple of St. Patrick, and his heart was said to be "like a fresh spring of water, ever bubbling-up with blessing," hence the name Galonnek, which means open-hearted. At the age of eighteen, Galonnek crossed over to Brittany, and after many adventures came to a place where he seated himself on the doorstep of a house and waited for an invitation to enter; but its owner bade him go away. He went from house to house, always meeting with the same injunction to "Get up and begone," which in Breton is expressed by the word "zevel." Ever afterward that village bore the name of Plouzevel. In a neighboring village there was a poor widow who received Galonnek as if he had been her own son. To reward her he dug for water on her land and a fountain sprang up. Her land became rich meadow and cattle came to feed there. When the villagers saw this, they begged Galonnek to take up his abode with them and he did so. Living in a hut, he persuaded them to abandon their custom of lighting fires on the rocks to lure ships to destruction.

Later, when Galonnek was made Bishop of Cornouailles, he had many a struggle with the nobles on behalf of the serfs. His body lies buried in the Cathedral of St. Pol where its resting-place is covered by a granite slab. On that slab the Breton mothers lay their baby boys, praying: "St. Galonnek bestow on my child two hearts— the heart of a lion, strong in well-doing and the heart of a turtle-dove, full of brotherly love."

In Lace Cap and Velvet Apron

We see the Bretonne at her best at a wedding. In some districts she wears a butterfly cap of fine lace, a velvet bodice and an apron of brilliant flowered velvet. First there is a civil ceremony at the mayor's office, then a church ceremony, where the bridal couple occupy two chairs at the altar rail with candles placed in front of them. If the wedding is a country one, there follows a feast in a meadow which everyone attends, especially the beggars. When old and young, rich and poor have feasted, the oldest woman may recite a litany for the dead. After that there may be several days of merry-making.

There is a considerable nomadic population in the province, including "sabotiers," the makers of wooden shoes, who go in groups to the woods to get their material, then divide into small bands to go through the villages and sell their

GRAY COTTAGES of weather-beaten stone with thatched roofs seem to blend into the landscape at the pleasant little market town of Locminé in Brittany.

A CHÂTEAU near the city of Rouen displays the circular towers and steep roof that distinguish French country houses built in fairy-tale Gothic style.

DOMINATING the town of Le Petit Andely in Normandy are the ruins of the Château Gaillard, the castle built by Richard the Lion-Hearted in 1196.

THE PICTURESQUE HARBORS of Brittany, with their water as blue as the Mediterranean Sea, have long been favorite subjects for artists.

A THOUSAND BAGPIPES skirling in unison is one of the highlights of the Breton festival of the Queens of Cornouaille held every year at Quimper.

WHERE THE RIVER RANCE MEANDERS THROUGH ANCIENT DINAN

A story-book town, Dinan dates back to medieval times, when the Dukes of Brittany were all-powerful. They fortified it, and the castle and parts of the walls they built still stand. Today it is a trading and manufacturing town. At Dinan the Rance River widens out into a thirteen-mile-long estuary. It finally empties into the English Channel at Saint-Malo.

A TRIO OF LIGHTSHIPS BACK IN HARBOR TO BE REFITTED

Le Havre, at the mouth of the Seine, is one of the world's great harbors. A huge breakwater forms a great outer basin that supplements the natural inner harbor. There are docks, warehouses and modern service installations on a grand scale. The entire harbor area suffered tremendous damage from bombardment in World War II, but was rebuilt after liberation.

BUSY CORNER IN ONE OF THE OLDER SECTIONS OF LE HAVRE

Transatlantic travelers seldom see much of Le Havre, for the express train is waiting at the dock when the ships come in, ready to carry the passengers to Paris. The city is well worth a visit, however. It has been important since the days of Francis I, who fortified it. There are fine, modern residential streets as well as business and industrial centers.

A GOOD MAN with an ax! With steady hand the cobbler of Huelgoat carefully carves Breton wooden shoes, or sabots, from a wood block. Sabots are still worn in remote areas.

D. FORBERT

LOBSTER FISHERMEN line their lobster pots along the quay at Belle-Ile in Brittany. The region is a fishing center and a delightful resort.

THE MUSEUM at the Benedictine distillery at Fécamp houses the library, statues and other works of art from the old Benedictine abbey where the liqueur was first distilled.

TWO BRETON BOYS sit on the curbstone in front of a *charcuterie* (pork shop) at Le Faou. *Charcuteries* are town fixtures, where hams, sausages and pork products of every kind are sold.

PHILIP GENDREAU

A SHAGGY ROOF SHELTERS AN OLD FARMHOUSE IN NORMANDY

The steep roof overhangs the building so that rain and snow will drip off away from the walls. Farmhouses like this are still in use among the hedgerows and apple orchards of Normandy.

wares. There are charcoal-burners, weavers of linen and wool, thatchers, rag-merchants, all leading a kind of gipsy life.

Tourists ought to see the great châteaux at Nantes and at Josselin, go boating on the silver Rance and go driving past the apple orchards, where perhaps they will hear the evening notes of the Angelus coming from some village church tower. The motorist will find both roads and inns surprisingly good; and there is a regular passenger service between Southampton and St. Malo.

It is related of that ancient seaport that in the sixth century a holy man called Malo (Maclow, Maclou, Machut or Maclovius) came sailing over from Wales in a stone dugout, and with a resident hermit named Aaron as audience, held religious services on the back of a whale. He then built a hut of the native granite and started to perform miracles. Druid competition in time drove him out, but by 680 he had been canonized; and though Charlemagne's warriors destroyed the city in 811, Charlemagne restored it. It

was a warlike Bishop, Châtillon, who (in 1155) started the seaward-facing ramparts that remain to-day; and in time the church rubbed elbows with merchant-corsairs who cut cellars into the rock to hide their booty from the tax-collectors. The island city had to grow skyward since it could not expand far otherwise. In the days before it built its inner harbor, the receding tides left wide stretches of sandy beach exposed, and a dozen ferocious watchdogs were kept on guard at night. When the Bastion of Holland was built to overlook the sea and receive William of Orange, these dogs were put in a bomb-proof room which may still be seen.

In all, the corsair city took toll of English shipping to the number of 4,500 merchantmen and between 300 and 400 warships, and it took England and Holland together to subdue the rocky isle. Its flag saw Madras and Rio de Janeiro, and it was a son of St. Malo that gave Canada to France. But "my blood tints the banner of France," Châteaubriand the writer reminds us from over the doorway of

288

his father's dwelling—now become part of a big hotel. Among the names in blue and white enamel that mark most of the streets and public squares we find that of Cartier, discoverer of the St. Lawrence; De Gournay, France's first industrialist; and Thévenard, her first cannon-founder.

St. Thomas's Gate was named for the Breton sailor's favorite patron and the gate was endowed with a shrine by a crew that declared the Saint had answered their prayer and saved them from an octopus that had clutched their boat. Another landmark is the palace of Anne of Brittany, who married King Louis XII of France in 1499 and thereby brought Brittany to the crown of France.

The old piratical days of St. Malo have long been past. The island city now broods, in its towering aerie overlooking the sea, amid the many souvenirs of its romantic past.

The Bay of Morbihan is said to contain as many islands as there are days in the year. When we look across the water from Tregastel we see the Isle of Avalon, to which King Arthur was carried to be healed of his grievous wound and where he is supposed to have died. But the Bretons say he is not dead, but only held a prisoner in an underground palace, from which he comes out occasionally in the form of a raven. Certain it is that there are ravens occasionally to be seen.

RAPHO-GUILLUMETTE

RIVER FRONT OF HONFLEUR ON THE NORMANDY COAST
Seaport and fishing town, Honfleur looks across the mouth of the Seine at its famous and much bigger rival, Le Havre, only seven miles away. Honfleur is on the river's southern bank.

Paris ...the City of Light

EVERY man, it has often been said, has two countries—his own and Paris. Almost everywhere you go, you find someone who has fixed a map of Paris to his walls, even though he may never have been there. Paris is more than the capital of France. Many people consider it the capital of Western culture. It has been called the City of Light, more for the brilliance of its spirit than for its nightly illuminations, spectacular as they are. In Paris the fine arts of poetry, painting and music are joined with the practical arts of cooking, conversation and architecture to form the supreme art of civilized living.

Today, many visitors catch their first sight of Paris from the air. There, just as they imagined it, is the Seine River. Flowing in from the southeast, it forks at the center of the city around two islands, the Ile St. Louis and the Ile de la Cité, then curves gracefully to the southwest. Looking downstream to the left, is the Left Bank and to the right, the Right Bank —two distinct and different worlds. The Right Bank, the largest part, is the area best known to tourists. The Left Bank, however, is just as important to the city's everyday life.

West and north of the Seine the air traveler can clearly see modern Right Bank Paris with its long avenues and boulevards. Three of these—the Champs Elysées, the Rue de Rivoli and the Rue St. Antoine—form an almost straight line just north of the Seine between the Place de l'Etoile and the Place de la Bastille. From north to south there is another straight line formed by the Boulevards de Strasbourg and de Sébastopol (Right Bank), the Boulevard du Palais (crossing the Ile de la Cité) and the Boulevard St. Michel (Left Bank).

On the Right Bank twelve wide avenues, including the Champs Elysées, radiate from the Place de l'Etoile (*étoile* means "star"), with the Arc de Triomphe de l'Etoile in the center. The celebrated Grands Boulevards swing north in a shallow semicircle between the Place de la Concorde and the Place de la Bastille. South of the Seine there is a similar but shorter semicircle of boulevards, chiefly the Boulevard St. Germain.

Compared with London or New York, Paris is small. It covers only about eight square miles. Some three million people live within this area. Until the early years of this century the city proper was still bounded by fortifications, with gates (*portes*) whose names remain in use. Today the line of ramparts has been built over and Greater Paris is expanding rapidly beyond them. About four million Parisians live in the suburbs, and blocks of apartment houses are going up there constantly. Such a development may mean the end, at least at its old location, of the picturesque Flea Market some time in the 1960's. It is a mad jumble of second-hand articles and dubious "antiques" of every description around the Porte de Clignancourt, in the north. If the market is moved, the city planners hope to tidy it up, though some of its color will probably be lost in the process.

Rive Gauche, Rive Droite—Left Bank, Right Bank. Together, they explain why Paris is all things to all men. On the Left Bank are the famous *quartiers*, including Montparnasse, St. Germain des Prés and the Latin Quarter. Living on this Bank are artists, students, writers, editors, little shopkeepers, office workers and just plain workers. On the Right Bank are the theaters, fashion houses and luxury establishments of stylish Paris. You'll also find little shops and ordinary people as well, though they tend to be overwhelmed by their modish neighbors, particularly along the Champs Elysées and the Rue de Rivoli.

High on the Right Bank is the hill of Montmartre. Sitting on the butte is the white, romantic and Moorish-looking church of Sacré Coeur (Sacred Heart). Montmartre was the artists' quarter before World War I and spiritually belongs on the Left Bank. But then the Eiffel Tower, lifting its strong lacework of iron into the sky, belongs to the Right Bank, though it happens to be on the Left.

Exploration of Paris should begin on that island in the middle of the Seine where it all began—the Ile de la Cité, the Island of the City. At its eastern end loom the towers of the Cathedral of Notre Dame. The view from the tower is godlike, yet intimate and human. From here

291

you can gaze for hours at the spectacle of Paris and its monuments rising in the soft, fugitive-gray light that Monet, Renoir and other impressionist painters caught so delicately on canvas.

The view also invites you to descend and stroll within it, which is part of the charm of Paris. So many large cities, built on a giant scale, inspire cold inspiration from a distance. Paris has the peace and serenity of a smaller, more human scale. Almost all buildings are low, and they are kept low by law. In general no one is allowed to build above a certain uniform height in each quarter. Thus far there are few soaring structures either to block the sky or to reduce the city's human beings to insignificance, spiritual as well as physical.

It is hardly surprising, therefore, that two recent exceptions to the beloved low skyline have aroused controversy. (An earlier exception, the Eiffel Tower, also annoyed the Parisians when it was finished in 1890.) One is the headquarters of UNESCO (United Nations Educational, Scientific and Cultural Organization), built in the 1950's. The central office building, a Y-shaped, concrete-and-glass structure raised on stilts, is ninety-five feet high, top limit allowed in the city building code. The design is the work of three famous architects: Bernard Zehrfuss, of France; Pier Luigi Nervi, of Italy; and Marcel Breuer, of the United States. Two outdoor walls are splashed with the gay colors of huge ceramic murals designed and baked by the celebrated artist Juan Miro. The result is emphatically modern, stark and dramatic, and in violent contrast to the beautiful eighteenth-century building it faces, the Ecole Militaire. The site is on the Left Bank behind the Eiffel Tower and the Champ de Mars.

The other controversial structure—really a group of buildings—will be completed some time in the 1960's. It too is on the Left Bank, replacing the old Gare Montparnasse (railroad station). The center building will be a fifty-five story skyscraper hotel, more than half the height of the Eiffel Tower. A shopping center,

office and apartment buildings (lower but still high) and the like will be grouped around the skyscraper. The plans also include a park, a garden and an underground garage.

The Ile de la Cité

The Ile de la Cité was the birthplace of Paris. It was the home of the Gallic tribe of Parisii, who would withdraw to the security of their island (actually three islands at that time) whenever an enemy threatened. Nevertheless, like the rest of Gaul, they eventually succumbed to the Romans, who unkindly called their island home Lutetia, from the Latin word *lutum,* or mud.

However, the Parisii outlasted the Romans and Lutetia became Paris. Thirteen centuries after Caesar's conquest the Temple of Jupiter was long forgotten and the Cathedral of Notre Dame already stood on the same site. By then Paris extended to both banks. Each century thereafter the city spread out in circles like widening ripples in a pool. Walls were built around each circle only to be pulled down to permit the city to expand.

Even so, the city proper has remained conveniently small. You can easily walk from one end to the other in a morning or afternoon. If there were less traffic—quite unlikely—you could bicycle to the gentle countryside just outside the city in an effortless hour or so. And that is exactly what you see the Parisians doing every week end of pleasant weather—one by one or in family groups of father, mother, baby, dog, often on a bicycle.

The Ile de la Cité is still the center of Greater Paris, if not of France. All distances in France are measured from a marker embedded in the pavement before Notre Dame. On the island stand the Prefecture of Police; a large hospital; golden-spired Sainte Chapelle, a small, exquisite jewel of Gothic architecture; and the gloomy fortress of the Conciergerie. The Conciergerie is where Marie Antoinette, Danton and a thousand others spent their last nights before being guillotined in the French Revolution. The crowning glory of the Ile de la Cité is, of course, the

PARIS AND ENVIRONS

English Channel

AMIENS •

• CHERBOURG
LE HAVRE •   • ROUEN
                      • BEAUVAIS
        • CAEN
SAINT LÔ •   PARIS •

SCALE OF MILES
0   25   50   100   CHARTRES •

METROPOLITAN PARIS

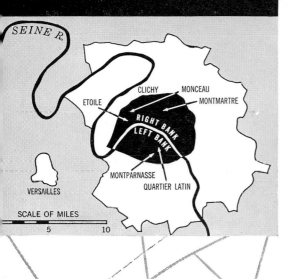

SEINE R.

CLICHY   MONCEAU
ETOILE   MONTMARTRE

RIGHT BANK
LEFT BANK

MONTPARNASSE
VERSAILLES   QUARTIER LATIN

SCALE OF MILES
5   10

great cathedral of Notre Dame, largely completed by 1235.

The loveliest view of Notre Dame is from the Left Bank. The cathedral rises noble and serene from its island site, its reflection shimmering in the water. From the gardens in the rear you can best see the famous flying buttresses, strong arms of stone holding up walls that have been weakened by the many full-length windows of stained glass. The western façade (the front) of Notre Dame is a glory of French Gothic architecture. The twin towers rise more than two hundred feet from the square in front. Beneath the towers the great portals and striking statue columns are remarkably composed and harmonized. As Victor Hugo wrote so eloquently in *Notre Dame,* all the intricate elements move "upward before the eye without disorder, their innumerable details of statuary, sculpture and carving united powerfully with the tranquil grandeur of the ensemble—a vast symphony in stone."

N

BUILDINGS AND MONUMENTS

1. Arc de Triomphe
2. Arc de Triomphe du Carrousel
3. Basilica de Sacre-Coeur
4. Bibliothèque Nationale
5. Bourse
6. Cathédrale Notre Dame
7. Chambre des Députés
8. Comédie Française
9. Conciergerie
10. Ecole Militaire
11. Eiffel Tower
12. Foreign Ministry
13. French Academy
14. Grand et Petit-Palais
15. Hôtel des Invalides
16. Hôtel de Ville
17. La Madeleine
18. Louvre
19. Opéra
20. Palais de Chaillot
21. Palais de Justice
22. Palais de l'Elysée
23. Palais de Luxembourg Senat
24. Palais Royal
25. Panthéon
26. Sorbonne
27. Sainte-Chapelle
28. UNESCO headquarters

PLACE PIGALLE

PLACE DE L'ETOILE

CHAMPS-ELYSEES

PLACE DE L'OPERA

PLACE DE LA REPUBLIQUE

RUE ROYALE
ROND POINT
RUE DE RIVOLI
PLACE VENDOME
PLACE DE LA CONCORDE

SEINE RIVER

PONT NEUF

BOULEVARD DE SEBASTOPOL

PLACE DES VOSGES

RUE ST-ANTOINE

BOULEVARD SAINT-GERMAIN

ILE ST-LOUIS

PLACE DE LA BASTILLE

BOULEVARD RASPAIL

BOULEVARD SAINT-MICHEL

ILE DE LA CITE

PARKS AND GARDENS

A. Bois de Boulogne   C. Jardin des Tuileries
B. Bois de Vincennes   D. Jardins du Luxembourg
        E. Parc Monceau

SCALE OF MILES
0   1   2

THE GRAND STAIRCASE of the Opéra, an appropriate setting for feminine elegance.

The broad gamut
of Parisian life

MODELING a figure for the Grevin waxworks museum.

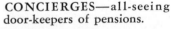

NO PARISIAN is more worldly-wise than a waiter.

CONCIERGES—all-seeing door-keepers of pensions.

»

WORKROOM of a *grand couturier,* one of the high-fashion dress-making establishments that set international styles.

294

DALE WHITNEY

HURRYING TO WORK along the Rue de Richelieu side of the National Library. An *agent de police* stands by.

A ROULETTE WHEEL attracts customers to the stall of a peanut vendor.

IN MONTMARTRE a clove of garlic and a grape are offered to a newborn baby. The ceremony is in honor of the district's patron saint, Glinglin.

Inside, the visitor experiences the soaring exaltation that perhaps only Gothic architecture can inspire. The massive pillars thrust upward to the pointed arches of the vaults one hundred feet overhead. The long aisles between the pillars lead the eye toward the distant altar and to the colorful rose windows, more than forty feet in diameter. The religious stories pictured in the stained glass explain why cathedrals were once, when few people could read, called the Bibles of the Poor.

The Left Bank

From the Ile de la Cité it is only a short step across, say, the Pont Neuf (the most painted bridge of Paris) to the Left Bank. There Parisians and visitors alike browse through the book stalls along the quays. A bit east of the Pont Neuf is the Place St. Michel, where the Boulevard St. Michel (the beloved Boul' Mich' of students) comes down to meet the Seine.

The Boul' Mich' is usually crowded with students in earnest discussion, some of them dark-skinned youths from Africa, busy sidewalk cafés, pushcarts of fruit and little shooting galleries along the curb. It is close to the Sorbonne (part of the University of Paris) and in the heart of the Latin Quarter.

Why Latin? Because the only language the professors and students who congregated there from all over Europe during the Middle Ages had in common was Latin. Woe to the man who wandered into the quarter and could not speak it. He risked being stoned. That danger has passed, but there still lingers in the Latin Quarter a scorn for the *bourgeoisie* —dull people with no love of learning.

Off the Boul' Mich' is the Luxembourg Garden, the city's only Renaissance garden. In the summer you can sit there in the shade of old trees, among flowers and classic statues. Or you may rest on a bench on the terrace, overlooking the huge stone basin where children are sailing toy boats. Other children are watching a Punch and Judy show with excited shouts or openmouthed wonder. Older boys and girls are sitting and reading or talking near the Médicis Fountain. Not far away is

the handsome palace built by Marie de Médicis, the second wife of King Henry IV, in nostalgic memory of her native Tuscany, in Italy. Formerly a royal residence, the Luxembourg Palace today houses the Senate of the French Republic.

Opposite the Luxembourg Garden is the domed Panthéon. There rest many of France's most illustrious dead—Voltaire, Victor Hugo and Emile Zola among them.

Farther south on the Left Bank is Montparnasse (the Hill of Parnassus—in Greek myth the mountain sacred to Apollo and the Muses). This is where Ernest Hemingway and a number of other American writers, famous later, lived during the 1920's. Gertrude Stein called them the "lost generation" of post-World War I. In this quarter, painters and sculptors, such as Matisse, Modigliani, Marinetti, Foujita and others, led the revolution in art that is known as "modern."

In the neighborhood where Boulevard Raspail meets Boulevard Montparnasse, the scenes have changed hardly at all since Hemingway described them in his youthful works. Such sidewalk cafés as the Dome and the Rotonde are still patronized by Parisians and tourists. However, most of the artists and writers have since moved down from Montparnasse to Saint Germain des Prés, their Left Bank gathering place today. Saint Germain des Prés itself is one of the oldest churches in Paris. Ironically, the quarter is better known for the "literary" cafés opposite the church— the Deux Magots and the Café de Flore— than for its twelfth-century tower.

The Romanesque interior of St. Germain des Prés is in striking contrast to the Gothic style of Notre Dame. In comparison with the soaring heights of Notre Dame, St. Germain seems earth-bound. Its vaulted ceilings are lower and more barrel-like. Romanesque architects could not be so daring with windows as were the later Gothic builders. St. Germain's windows are hardly more than slits in the massive walls. Little daylight enters and the interior is usually dim. To step from St. Germain des Prés out into the brightness of the day is to make a swift and exciting transition from the twelfth to the twentieth century. It is such contrasts that make Paris so lively and stimulating for the creative person, as well as for anyone alert to the drama of its streets.

The St. Germain des Prés quarter draws a fascinating mixture of people. Many are simply visitors from America, North and South, from Scandinavia, from Great Britain, from the Far East. Many more are students, young intellectuals, would-be poets and painters, permanently or temporarily in Paris. It is in this setting that the declarations are written advocating surrealism, cubism, dadaism, futurism, existentialism and other extreme views on art and life. Each ism flares up with a momentary popularity and appeal, and then as suddenly it dies down to make way for another.

What is it about the Left Bank that specially encourages brave new ventures in the arts and literature? The answer explains the appeal of Paris to artists and writers from all over the world. To them Paris offers two priceless gifts: privacy and beauty. Such was the case of the Scottish writer Robert Louis Stevenson. In Paris, his biographer Clayton Hamilton has written, Stevenson "lived more freely, more fully and more happily than in any country. . . . In Paris, the city of the free, he recovered his mental sanity."

The visitor to the Left Bank may be taken somewhat aback by the careless dress, the untidy young beards, the occasional showing-off. He should recall, however, that in this setting of freedom much of the greatest art, literature and music of the twentieth century has been created.

Picasso, Stravinsky, Joyce, Stein and Proust—some were French and some were foreigners, but all were residents of Paris when they made their great contributions to the culture of the world.

Let us cross another of the many bridges that span the Seine, to the Right Bank. The focus of interest there is the Place de l'Etoile. As we said earlier, twelve avenues radiate out from it. Beneath the imposing Arc de Triomphe at the center, erected by Napoleon to commemorate his victories, is the tomb of the French Unknown Soldier. An eternal flame burns before it.

Standing under (or, even better, on top) the 164-foot-high memorial, you can look down the length of the most famous of all the twelve avenues—the Champs Elysées —to the Place de la Concorde, a mile away. Ideal for a parade, the Champs Elysées is more often enjoyed as a promenade, especially on a sunny Sunday afternoon. Then all Paris takes its ease along the elegant avenue, which is lined with chestnut trees.

The first part of the avenue from the Place de l'Etoile displays smart shops, first-run cinemas, a variety of sidewalk cafés and covered arcades. About halfway down is the Rond Point, where six avenues meet. Flower beds surround the fountains in the center of the Point. Beyond it is a park—a quarter mile wide—of trees, shrubs, lawns, gardens and restaurants. On one side children ride in carriages drawn by solemn goats or else amuse themselves at another of Paris's many Punch and Judy shows. On the other side are the Grand and the Petit Palais. Both were erected for the exhibition in 1900 and are still used for the same purpose. Their halls display everything, from paintings and automobiles to household gadgets. A bit to the north is the Palais de l'Elysées, official residence of the president of the Republic.

The Place de la Concorde is vast, beautiful and in perfect balance. Each side of the square is 750 feet long. From the middle of it rises a seventy-five-foot-high Egyptian obelisk, flanked by splendid fountains and statuary. The parklike Champs Elysées on the square's west side is balanced by the lovely gardens of the Tuileries on the east. In the corners of the square are eight eighteenth-century pavilions, placed in pairs, that support statues representing important French cities. Along the north side run two handsome palaces with colonnades. The palaces are separated by the short stretch of the Rue Royale so that the classic columns of the Madeleine, the famous church at the other end of the Rue Royale, can be seen from the square. The Seine forms the south

STANDARD OIL CO. (N. J.)

AT NIGHT the river glitters with light reflected from the city's many bridges—here the Pont Royal.

A REGATTA draws a crowd of boat lovers to the pleasure-craft dock within sight of the Eiffel Tower.

ROMANCE on the bank. Lost in dreams the sweethearts are oblivious of passers-by—and cameras.

RUSSELL MELCHER, PIX

DALE WHITNEY

Dividing line of the city— the Seine River

ARTISTS PAINT the Seine constantly. Fishermen, no less persistent, rarely seem to get a nibble.

«

THE FLYING BUTTRESSES of the apse of Notre Dame Cathedral appear to float above the trees and shrubbery at the east end of the Ile de la Cité.

side of the Place de la Concorde. Thus the columns of the Madeleine are mirrored by the columns of the Chamber of Deputies, across the river, on the Left Bank. At the end of each of the long vistas to west and east loom the great arches of triumph—the one in the Place de l'Etoile and the other the Arc de Triomphe du Carrousel, topped by sculptured horses, at the far end of the Tuileries.

The square was first laid out under Louis XV and named for him. During the Revolution, Marie Antoinette and many other notables were guillotined there. When the Reign of Terror ended in 1794 the square was renamed the Place de la Concorde, symbolizing peace among the French people.

On holidays and on summer week ends the fountains, statuary, palaces and monuments are imaginatively floodlighted. Every evening the square is glamorous with gaslights that glow brighter and brighter as night falls. It is truly a place of concord these days. Only memory reminds us that it once was the Place de la Révolution, where executioners became the executed as the wheel of history turned, bringing them to the guillotine to suffer the same fate as their victims.

Garden of the Tuileries

The Garden of the Tuileries, designed by the landscape architect Le Nôtre, is an outstanding model of a classic French garden, where order and symmetry reign. It is the favorite playground of Right Bank Parisians, who have much to enjoy there: almost sixty-two acres of lawns, paths, two pools and trees. The trees are kept clipped in beautifully tailored shapes, like giant hedges. Against this background of foliage gleam marble statues of gods, nymphs and horses. This statuary stays in place all year although in cold weather it is covered with sacking.

An even finer collection graces the museums within the Tuileries: the Jeu de Paume with its Manets, Degas, Renoirs, Cézannes; the Orangerie with its changing shows of important paintings; the Museum of Decorative Arts with its rooms of period furniture. Above all, extending from the garden's western end, is the enormous structure of the Louvre.

The Louvre contains the world's greatest art gallery. Its treasures, pictured thousands of times, are known everywhere: the winged Victory of Samothrace, the armless Venus of Milo, Da Vinci's *Mona Lisa* with her enigmatic smile, Whistler's study of his mother.

The Palais du Louvre is as great a work of art as any object it contains, and its architecture has been the model for many of the important buildings of Paris. Centuries of architects have slowly transformed it from a fortress constructed during the Crusades to the superb U-shaped palace we know today, one wing of which is used for the famous museum.

To appreciate the architecture of the Louvre in the order in which it was built, you should walk first along the side on the Seine. The façade that faces the river is pure French Renaissance of the sixteenth century. The spacing of the windows has a rhythmic regularity and all the details are in fine proportion.

Turn the far corner to the left and you are looking at the seventeenth-century wing built under Louis XIV. (Across the street is St. Germain L'Auxerrois, a charming church of flamboyant, or late, Gothic.) Turn left again around the next far corner to the north side and you discover the nineteenth-century wing of the Louvre.

You are also now on the Rue de Rivoli. It is a singularly distinguished and well-ordered street. The north side, lined with shops, hotels and apartments, has covered arcades. The columns that support the arcades give somewhat the same impression of regularity and rhythm as the Louvre.

Besides the Place de la Concorde, Paris has a number of other fascinating squares. The Place des Vosges is so hidden away, northwest of the Louvre, that it is hard for the visitor to find without help. In shape, it is indeed a perfect square, and is surrounded on all sides by early seventeenth-century buildings. Their arcades give the square the look of a cloister. For a time, Victor Hugo lived in one of the houses. Calm and serene, a pool of quiet in a noisy, working-class district of Paris, the Place des Vosges is one of the most interesting but least known of all the *places* of Paris.

Far more familiar is the six-sided Place Vendôme, just off the Rue de Rivoli and the Tuileries Gardens. This *place* is the very heart of the most fashionable part of the Right Bank. World-famous dressmakers, jewelers and perfumers are installed there. In the center rears the graceful Vendôme Column with a small figure of Napoleon at the top. The column is of bronze, made from cannon that Napoleon captured in 1805–07.

Between the Place Vendôme and the Place de l'Opéra runs the short Rue de la Paix. On the Place de l'Opéra it is the Opéra that first catches the eye. Huge and ornate, it was designed and decorated in extravagant nineteenth-century style to be the largest and most luxurious theater in the world. Its wide grand stairway of marble and onyx is the height of splendor. Nevertheless—or because of the setting—hearing grand opera in the red and gold auditorium, then strolling at intermission in the gallery among the beautifully gowned Parisiennes are unforgettable experiences.

On the Place de l'Opéra is the renowned Café de la Paix, sometimes called the crossroads of the world. At least it is at the crossroads of Paris, where the boulevards come together and *tout le monde* (all the world) seems to meet by appointment late every afternoon. You do have the feeling, as you sit on the terrace, that the whole world is sauntering by—at a leisurely pace.

The Grands Boulevards were largely the work of Baron Haussmann, Napoleon III's prefect for the Seine department. He laid them out between 1853 and 1870. His main purpose was to make street riots easier to control. That the boulevards also provided magnificent vistas was secondary. Machine guns and cavalry could maneuver more effectively on those avenues and thus discourage the kind of rioting that occurred in 1789 and 1848.

Those revolutionary times are brought back to mind by a long walk down the Grands Boulevards from the Place de l'Opéra to the Place de la Bastille by way of the Place de la République. Gradually the fashionable world of the Right Bank is left behind and you enter the district of the large laboring population. One area is as important as the other for one who would know Paris as a whole.

The Place de la Bastille is large but not particularly beautiful. However, it has profound meaning for the French. It was there that the six hundred rioters stormed the fortress (then used as a prison) of the Bastille on July 14, 1789. Shortly thereafter it was torn down as a symbol of royal tyranny. On July 14, 1790, and every 14th of July since then, except during war, the people of Paris have danced in the Place de la Bastille—and in many other squares and streets—in celebration of the people's victory. Bastille Day is the gayest holiday of the year for all Paris.

Paris "villages"

Near the Place de la Bastille is legendary Ile St. Louis, the island at the rear of Notre Dame. An iron footbridge joins it to the Ile de la Cité, as if it were being towed down the Seine. The entire Ile St. Louis is a national historical monument, preserving its seventeenth-century character. No part of Paris is more highly regarded by the Parisian. No quarter is more sought after for residence. Its villagelike streets and shops, its noble mansions with their handsome courtyards and stately staircases—all are a delight.

There is also a villagelike atmosphere in the older parts of Montmartre, that famous haunt of the artists of yesterday, only a mile from the Place de l'Opéra. There is even a tiny vineyard there which produces a yearly wine. To find it, however, you must climb steep stairways and narrow streets.

Easier to reach are the art galleries, the studios of amateur painters, the restaurants where one dines under trees. The original Moulin Rouge (Red Mill), the cabaret that was the haunt of Toulouse-Lautrec, no longer exists. Yet one can still sense the presence of the extraor-

ON JULY 14 the Place de la Concorde is jammed with merrymakers, Parisians and visitors alike.

Bastille Day—

THE TRICOLOR—blue, white and red—is traced in the sky over the Champs Elysées by zooming planes.

»

SPAHIS, the dashing Algerian cavalrymen, swing down the Champs Elysées, keeping their superb white horses in perfect formation.

302

DANCING IN THE STREETS may last until dawn in Montmartre. Young and old are tireless that night.

the city's gayest fete

SKYROCKETS BURST into flaming colors over the Obelisk in the Place de la Concorde. "RF" stands for Republique Français (French Republic).

dinary artist in the crowded dance halls that have replaced it. Along the boulevards of Montmartre are street fairs and a permanent, one-ringed circus of the intimate kind he loved to paint. Sometimes a woman passes who might have stepped out of his posters.

A stone's throw from the Place du Tertre, one of Montmartre's most charming nooks, is the Basilica of Sacré Coeur. Begun in the last quarter of the nineteenth century, it is the most modern of Paris' important churches. Its stark white cupolas and dome, its 336-foot bell tower, its site crowning the heights of Montmartre, make it an outstanding landmark. From the terrace in front of it there is a breath-taking view of the whole city, and Sacré Coeur is visible from virtually everywhere in Paris.

Even more visible is that unique phenomenon in metal that spells Paris to the rest of the world—the Eiffel Tower. It is at the other end of the city from Montmartre, a mile south of the Place de l'Etoile, just across the Seine from the Place du Trocadéro. The Tower was built for the World's Fair of 1889 under the direction of Gustave Eiffel, a bridge engineer. It then was the world's tallest structure, 984 feet high (New York City's Empire State Building is about 490 feet higher). There are platforms at three levels which visitors can reach by elevator. The top platform is at 902 feet and offers another thrilling bird's eye view of Paris. Today there is a powerful television transmitting station at the top of the tower.

Not far from the Tower, on the Left Bank, is the Hôtel des Invalides, originally a home for disabled soldiers. Under its dome, in a sunken crypt, is the tomb of Napoleon I. Also on the Left Bank, but much farther to the east, is the Jardin des Plantes, covering sixty acres. Within the grounds are a beautiful botanical garden, a well-stocked zoo and a remarkable natural-history museum.

The parks are called "the lungs of Paris." The Bois de Boulogne is the most familiar of them, boasting two large lakes, two race courses, thousands of trees, miles of roads, avenues, footwalks and lanes. Somewhat outside Paris on the east is the Bois de Vincennes with its interesting old château. Inside Paris are some smaller parks, among them elegant Monceau in the fashionable neighborhood on the northwest.

As one might expect, Parisians love the theater. The Comédie Française (or Théatre Français) has been famous since the days of the playwright Molière, in the 1600's. His witty satires are as popular today as then. Both the Comédie Française and the Théatre National Populaire are supported by the Government. The latter tours the provinces and brings plays to students, working people and the like at prices they can afford.

Paris has as gifted a touch with practical matters as with artistic. Its subway system—the Métropolitain (Métro, for short)—is the easiest in the world for even the visitor to use. The station signs giving directions are clear, perhaps because the French language is so precise.

One of the unique experiences Paris offers is an early morning visit to Les Halles, the vast market to the northwest of the Louvre. The stalls are mouthwatering mounds of fruit, vegetables, meat, poultry, dairy products, just in from the country. The French everywhere are sticklers for freshness. To complete the experience the visitor should join the husky market porters in a nearby restaurant for a hearty bowl of onion soup. Les Halles, however, have been aggravating the city's traffic problem. Produce is brought in on trucks, blocking thoroughfares. A fire there in 1959 forced the decision to set up most of the markets, eventually, on the city's outskirts.

All this is the sunnier side of Paris. There are some depressing poverty-stricken districts, such as Ménilmontant on the northeast. Yet Paris and the Parisians, no matter in what neighborhood they live, have something in common: a sense of style and respect for the individual. "Style" in this sense means much more than simply fashion. It is a flair for grace in living that gives a touch of elegance to the most commonplace activity.

BY JOSEPH A. BARRY

Spain ...the country
of the unexpected

THE Iberian Peninsula was known to the ancient world as *finis terrae*—the end of the earth. Even today it still strikes the visitor as remote and strange. Many books have been written about Spain, and there are almost as many different opinions. At one extreme is the picture of a poor backward land hardly touched by European civilization. At the other extreme is passionate enthusiasm for the rich variety of its landscapes and art treasures, for the dignity of the Spanish man, the fiery grace of the Spanish woman, for the mystic and quixotic spirituality of the Spanish soul.

Spain shares in European history, especially in that of its Latin sisters France and Italy. Yet to the non-Spaniard the image of the country seldom fits the familiar European pattern. Spain sometimes seems more Oriental or African. Thus the phrase "Africa begins in the Pyrenees" is often repeated thoughtlessly. Even several Spanish intellectuals, at the end of the nineteenth century, adopted the slogan "Europeanize Spain."

Spain covers about four fifths of the Iberian Peninsula, which was known to the Greeks as Iberia, to the Romans as Hispania. It is one of the three large peninsulas at the southern rim of Europe. Like the other two, Greece and, later, Italy, Iberia was both a frontier and a

«

SPANISH GAIETY in Barcelona. Every Sunday young and old join in the regional (or folk) dances performed in the historic square back of the cathedral.

305

PETER SCHMID FROM SHOSTAL

THE FACE of Spain itself. There is pride as well as beauty in the features of this woman of Salamanca Province. Her costume is that of the village of La Alberca.

TRANQUIL LOVELINESS —a courtyard in the Alcazaba, an ancient citadel in Malaga, beautified by the Moors. They loved such retreats as this.

W. L. CONDIT FROM SHOSTAL

A NARROW BYWAY in Cordoba, shadowed by graceful arches. On no other Spanish city did the Moors leave a greater impress. It was a center of Islam in the 900's.

LONG AGO, sentries kept watch from this tower over Malaga Bay. The tower and walls are part of the Gibralfaro, a citadel. It is said that the Phoenicians and Romans built it first. Later it became a Moorish fort.

link with the Asiatic and African worlds. At the same time, Iberia stood on the edge of the unknown Atlantic. So legend placed the Pillars of Hercules (guarding the Strait of Gibraltar), beyond which no one ventured, at Iberia's southernmost tip.

Like Italy, Spain is separated from the rest of the Continent by a high barrier of mountains. The Italian Alps, however, were easily overcome and have never been a real barrier to trade and communication with the rest of Europe. The Pyrenees have often been more of an obstacle. The barrier also lent strength to the desire of some rulers to keep Spain apart. Yet even in medieval times the mountains did not stop pilgrimages to St. James of Compostela, in Galicia. Centuries later, Napoleon's armies swept through the passes.

On the other hand, the great length of the Iberian coast encouraged invasion by sea. Later, Iberia's position on the Atlantic opened the way not only to western and southern Africa but also to the New

REGIONS

1 Andalusia	5 New Castile	10 Leon
2 Aragon	6 Old Castile	11 Murcia
3 Asturias	7 Catalonia	12 Navarre
4 Basque Provinces	8 Estremadura	13 Valencia
	9 Galicia	

World and to unexplored oceans. Spain and Portugal discovered, conquered and colonized these places before any other European countries. What had once been the outer gate of the known world became an advanced post on the road to America.

No matter how the traveler reaches Spain—from north or south, from east or west, by land, air or sea—his first impression is likely to be one of roughness. This is unexpected if he has a romantic idea of Spain as a southern land of gardens and orange groves bathed in Mediterranean light. Though the idea has some truth. The light in most of Spain has a glowing quality. Beautiful gardens and orchards are not uncommon although they are small in area and far apart. The visitor soon realizes that he is in one of the highest countries in Europe (only Switzerland is loftier). Spain is crossed from east to west by four abrupt ranges of mountains. High sierras (ridges) rim most of the coast, the deep valleys between them dropping to the sea. So that no matter what direction the traveler takes, every hundred miles or so he must go through a mountain pass or cross wide moors and paramos (high uplands).

On the extreme northwest the mountain mass is broken by the Galician rias (inlets). The heart of the Iberian massif is formed by a central tableland, or *meseta central*. The vast plateau has an average altitude of two thousand feet and is hemmed in on all sides by mountains:

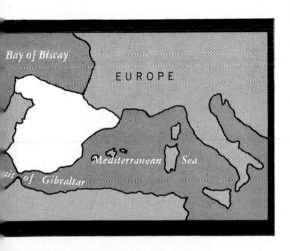

the Cantabrian range to the north; the Iberian range in the northeast; the Sierra Nevada and Sierra Morena to the south; and the terraces of Galicia and Portugal in the west. The Iberian range slopes down to the Ebro Valley in Aragon. The Guadalquivir Valley, in Andalusia, opens below the southern sierras. The central plateau itself has two levels with a slight difference in altitude. One level takes in Old Castile, an austere steppe where the River Duero runs. The other level is in New Castile, cut by the valley of the Tagus River. To the southeast are the endless plains of the Mancha, the land of Don Quixote. Between Old Castile and New Castile, in the very center of the peninsula, lie the ranges of the Somosierra, Guadarrama and Gredos. The Pyrenees, really a continuation of the Cantabrian system, hem Spain in on the northeast. Along the country's southern rim runs the Penibetica range. This is a continuation of the Moroccan Rif cut by the Strait of Gibraltar.

Along the Cantabrian coast

The Cantabrian (Bay of Biscay) coast offers an impressive variety of scenery: surging sea, high-walled passes, and cliffs; beautiful bays and fashionable beaches such as those of San Sebastian; busy fishing and commercial harbors, including Bilbao, Gijon and Santander. Inland, contrast continues: pastoral stretches close to rich industrial zones, in the Basque country; the imposing summits of the Picos de Europa, in the province of Santander; green valleys surrounding the important mining towns of Asturias.

Around the Galician capes the Cantabrian Sea blends with the Atlantic Ocean. South, toward the Portuguese boundary, the coast breaks, forming the great port and bay of Vigo, one of the largest in Europe. From the mouth of the Guadiana River, on the Portuguese border, to the bay of Cadiz and on down to Gibraltar and Algeciras, the coast is more uniform. Extensive dunes of claylike mud form natural canals, the *narismas*. There the Guadalquivir River breaks up into meandering arms before it finds its way to the

RING-ROUND-A-ROSY IN RONDA! Ronda is really two towns, an old one that may have been founded by the ancient Romans, on the south hill, and a new town on the north hill. A single road leads to the Andalusian town.

IN THE CAVES of the white chalk cliffs of the Sacro Monte section of Granada are the homes of Andalusian gypsies. They are known the world over for their mastery of the guitar and for their fiery flamenco dances.

PETER SCHMID FROM SHOSTAL

CHARLES J. BELDEN

GRAND ENTRANCE of the elaborately costumed toreros into Seville's bull ring. Though it has brutal aspects, bullfighting is partly a gorgeous spectacle.

310

CHARLES J. BELDEN

J. BARNELL

IBERIA AIRLINES OF SPAIN

THE ALCAZAR stands on a lofty precipice in Segovia. Its foundations may be Moorish,

GREMIGNANI, BLACK STAR

THE GRAN VIA is one of Madrid's main thoroughfares. Open-air restaurants extend out onto the side- walks, where it is pleasant to sip coffee and watch the passing show. The street is in the city's old quarter.

sea. The soil of this coast is salty and sterile. Yet vineyards have been made to thrive in it, near Jerez, Sanlucar and other towns. From these vineyards comes Spain's most famous product, sherry wine.

The Mediterranean part of Spain's coast stretches between the Strait of Gibraltar and the French border, at the eastern end of the Pyrenees. Along these shores lies the loveliest part of Spain, lapped in crystal-clear blue water, bathed in bright sunshine and with an ideal temperate climate. From the map you can see that the general outline of this coast is a series of four unequal curves: from Gibraltar to Cape Gata; from Cape Gata to Cape Palos; from Cape Palos to Cape Nao; and from Cape Nao to the French border. From around Cape Gata on up to Cape Palos (the provinces of Almeria and Murcia), the land is sun-parched, almost a desert. A year can pass with hardly a drop of rain falling. Beyond Cape Palos come the fertile palm and orange groves of Alicante and Valencia.

The section from Cape Nao to upper Catalonia is the Spanish "levantine" (Oriental) coast. Here the Ebro River forms a wide delta. Farther north is the spectacular Costa Brava (rugged coast), which today is a sort of Spanish *riviera*. Off the coast between Valencia and Barcelona are Mallorca and the other Balearic islands, long a delight for tourists and artists.

A traveler has called Spain the "country of the unexpected," for even within each natural region the contrasts are striking. The only possible exception could be the monotonous treeless plain of La Mancha. Yet even here, fertile vineyards, olive groves and wheat fields alternate with arid stretches where there is hardly a sign of vegetation.

In spite of the vast tracts of bare and unproductive land, Spain has about eight thousand plant species, more than in any other country on the Continent. Of these, 60 per cent are common to Europe; 20 per cent are common to North Africa; and the rest are found only on the peninsula.

Spain has other curious features, such as the caves of Antequera, Arta (in Mallorca) and Santillana. Besides impressive mountain passes there are *tajos,* or giant gorges. Most famous of the *tajos* is the one above which Ronda perches, in Malaga. The "enchanted city" of Cuenca (northwest of Madrid) is a fantastic mass of rocks that look like the palaces and houses of a real city.

Yet all these rich contrasts provided by nature have created difficult problems for the population. Richly fertile soil is limited to fairly small sections. The courses of many rivers—the Ebro, Duero, Tagus, Guadiana, Guadalquivir—are broken by falls or rapids at lower levels. At times they run almost dry. In fact, at one place the Guadiana is swallowed up by the earth, to reappear leagues away. Deep gullies have been cut and there is serious soil erosion. Only one river, the Guadalquivir, is navigable for any appreciable distance within Spanish territory. The Duero and Tagus are navigable only in Portugal, in their lower courses as they flow toward the Atlantic Ocean.

A climate of extremes

Rainfall is irregular. On the northern coast it rains perhaps three hundred days a year. But in some central and southern sections, rain is almost an oddity. The climate runs to other extremes. Winters are long and cold, with an average temperature of 41° F., and summers are hot with an average temperature of 68° F. Nearness to water, of course, moderates the coastal climate.

Strabo, an ancient Greek geographer, described the Iberian Peninsula as lying like a stretched bull's skin at the extreme of the known world. It seems to have been destined to become the meeting place of northern and southern peoples, of European and African. Little is known of the earliest inhabitants. Yet Spain is rich in prehistoric remains, especially Stone Age cave paintings. Those in the cave of Altamira, near Santillana, are world famous. Altamira is sometimes called the Sistine Chapel of prehistoric art. With the beginning of written his-

DURYEE, MONKMEYER

TOURISTS' HAVEN—a Madrid newsstand that sells postcards and foreign magazines.

tory the people known to us as Iberians appeared. They probably came from Africa. Closely related to them were the people of the near legendary kingdom of Tartessus, on the Atlantic coast of present-day Andalusia. It was no doubt the reputed wealth of this kingdom that attracted the Phoenicians to the eastern coast of the peninsula.

Later, Celts entered from the north and mixed with the primitive Iberians to form, at least in central Spain, the group known as Celtiberians. Greeks and Carthaginians followed the Phoenicians in founding colonies and commercial out-

AVENIDA JOSE ANTONIO is a fashionable business street in the heart of Madrid.

EMIL BRUNNER, PIX

FISHING PORT near San Sebastian, which is in the Basque country on the Bay of Biscay. Four- and five-story houses, in sun-bleached reds and browns, cluster close to the edge of the water.

BASQUE DANCERS go through traditional paces atop Mount Urgull, across the lovely little Bay of Concha from the seaside resort of San Sebastian.

THE COURT OF THE LIONS of the Alhambra, the magnificent Moorish fortress-palace in Granada. The fountain in the center is supported by twelve lions, all in gleaming marble.

RAMPARTS and towers of the fortress part of the Alhambra, which is on a high promontory overlooking the city. The citadel was built around 1250, other buildings about a century later.

THE MESS ROOM of Franco's Moorish Guard had the handsome furnishings of a wealthy Moroccan home.

After Spain gave up its portion of Morocco, Franco was forced to disband the Moorish Guard.

posts along the Mediterranean coast. During the rivalry between Carthage and Rome, the Romans came to the peninsula. They conquered it totally after a series of wars lasting almost two hundred years.

During the next five centuries (19 B.C.–A.D. 476), the peninsula became thoroughly Romanized. As Hispania it was one of the important provinces of the Empire. There were flourishing cities: Corduba, Hispalis (Seville), Caesarea Augusta (Zaragoza), Merida, Tarraco (Tarragona) and many others, with imposing monuments and buildings. A splendid network of roads, some of which are still in use, was built. Wheat, olives, vineyards and fruit trees were cultivated. Spain adopted the Latin language, the base of modern Castilian and of such tongues as Galician and Catalonian. Spain gave to Roman literature some of its most distinguished writers, among them Seneca, Martial, Lucan and Quin-

tilian. There were also several emperors of Spanish stock: Trajan, Hadrian, Marcus Aurelius and Theodosius I.

When the Roman Empire broke up, the barbarians entered Spain. Two kingdoms

MOORISH LANDMARK in Toledo—the medieval Gate of the Sun, with city crest.

316

were formed, those of the Suevi and of the Visigoths. Later they were unified under Visigothic rule. For two or three centuries, especially after the Visigoths were converted to Christianity, learning and the arts flourished in Spain. Thus Spain was one of the few areas in Europe where Latin culture lived on, to reappear in medieval Christian forms. The country was united still more strongly with Toledo as the nominal capital of the kingdom and the central seat of the Church.

In 711 the event occurred that was to set Spain off from the rest of Europe. That year the Moors, or Saracens, burst into the peninsula, bringing with them their Islamic faith. Their conquest was swift. From then on, Muslim culture was influential in Spain in varying degrees until the end of the fifteenth century. Spain was then the frontier of the West. Here the West faced the powerful Arab culture that, until the eleventh century, was far more advanced than any in Europe.

Though the Moors overran the peninsula in a few years, it took eight centuries to force them out. This was the long period of *Reconquista,* or Christian Reconquest. Resistance began as early as 718, among Asturians and other small groups of northern Christians. As resistance slowly spread southward, what had been a relatively united country under Roman and Visigoth rule was broken up. Small Christian kingdoms and do-

INNER COURT of the Alcazar, the Moorish castle in Seville built in the 1100's.

TWA

ANDERSON, ROME

DETAIL of the interior of the Mosque of Cordoba—Moorish architecture at peak.

mains were set up, vaguely like the feudal states elsewhere in Europe: Asturias, Galicia, Leon, Navarre, Aragon, Catalonia and, finally, Castile, the land of castles. Castile eventually emerged as the leader. In each of these realms, Latin, already becoming a modern Romance language under the Visigoths, developed into five different dialects.

By the eleventh century the Christians had the upper hand. It was then that Rodrigo, the Cid (lord), who is the great Spanish epic hero, conquered Valencia; and Alfonso VI, king of Castile, entered Toledo, the old capital. Now Moorish power declined, and Castile gradually became dominant. However, Castile could not prevent Portugal, with French help, from forming a separate kingdom.

From the eleventh to the thirteenth centuries, when the Christians took Seville, the pace of the Reconquest quickened. And from the thirteenth century up to 1492, when Granada, the last refuge of the Moors, fell, Muslim power was reduced to some little city-kingdoms in southern Andalusia. There some of the most exquisite examples of Arabic art were created as the last sparks of a dying civilization.

As Arabic power declined, Aragon as well as Castile became powerful, and the

A MEDIEVAL FORT overlooks Tossa, a sunny resort on the Costa Brava (rugged coast). This stretches along the Mediterranean Sea, north of Barcelona.

A FISHERMAN'S WORK is never done. Yet mending nets is a pleasant task on the beach at San Feliu de Guixols, active Costa Brava port since the tenth century.

ANDALUSIAN GYP-SIES who live in the caves of Sacro Monte, just outside Granada. The caves have running water and electricity.

THE ESCORIAL, part palace and part monastery, dominates the plain twenty-seven miles northwest of Madrid. Spanish kings are buried there and it has a priceless collection of art treasures. Augustinian monks live there today.

319

A WINDMILL on La Mancha calls up visions of the mad adventures of Cervantes' Don Quixote.

two absorbed the other Spanish kingdoms. They also strengthened their relations with western Europe, particularly France. In this way, medieval Spain counteracted the Arabic influences. Art, institutions, manners and court life were increasingly shaped by French models. There were many contacts: French pilgrimages to the shrine of St. James (Santiago) of Compostela, in Galicia; an influx of the monks of Cluny and other French religious orders; frequent visits of troubadours and jongleurs. Romanesque and Gothic architecture and literary forms spread into Spain, as well as the exquisite arts of miniature and altar painting. Arabic culture was not wiped out, however, but blended with European. The result was a peculiar hybrid style. It is described by such words as *mozarabe* (applied primarily to the Christian living among Moors) and *mudejar* (the Muslim living among Christians). Both terms are used in connection with architecture, other arts, and cultural patterns.

In order to grasp the roots of Spanish characteristics, nothing is more important than an understanding of the long period of the Reconquest. Moorish and Christian institutions—religious, cultural and social—existed side by side. There was also a large Jewish population which had been living in the peninsula since ancient Roman times. During the Middle Ages, Jewish culture in Spain reached a peak second only to that attained in Biblical and Alexandrian times. Protected first by Moorish caliphs and kings and, later, by Christians, the Jews excelled, as did the Arabs, in science, poetry and philosophy. At the same time they acquired wealth and power. The synagogue in a Spanish city stood close by the mosque or the Gothic cathedral. In the court of Alfonso X, the Learned (1226?–84), works of science, history and philosophy were translated for the first time into a modern European language, under Arabic, Hebrew and Castilian scholars. At the same time, Oriental models influenced Spanish poetry and prose; and Castilian borrowed a considerable number of words from Arabic.

Many splendid monuments of Moorish Spain still stand. Among them are the alcazar and the Giralda tower in Seville; the Mosque of Cordoba, today a cathedral, with its forest of colored marble columns; the magnificent Alhambra and the lovely gardens of the Generalife in Granada.

Contact with Semitic cultures also had more subtle effects, on character, habits, food. The Arabs introduced such important agricultural products as rice,

sugar cane, and cotton. Their system of irrigation is still in use in such regions as Valencia, Aragon and Andalusia.

A modern historian, Professor Americo Castro, in a study of "the historical reality of Spain" between the tenth and fifteenth centuries, adopted as a subtitle for his book "Christians, Moors and Jews." The accent should be on the Christian element. Muslim remains cannot match the enormous wealth of Christian art and architecture inherited from medieval Spain. Romanesque and Gothic churches and cathedrals, monasteries, palaces, castles, cloisters, paintings and sculpture— these are the glory of such cities and towns as Santiago de Compostela, Oviedo, Leon, Burgos, Salamanca, Toledo, Avila and Segovia.

Yet during the Middle Ages—for more than seven centuries—Spanish life centered on war. There was the struggle with the Moors as well as conflict between the Christian kingdoms. The latter were torn by contradictory impulses. They needed unity in the face of the Moorish conqueror. Yet each wanted to stay completely independent. In the common zeal against the Moors, a crusading spirit was created. Religion became all-absorbing. Even today it is still perhaps the strongest force modeling Spanish life and character.

These are the main factors lying behind the policy of the Catholic Kings—as

DON QUIXOTE still rides forth on his steed Rosinante, followed by the faithful Sancho Panza on a donkey. The statue of the characters graces a plaza in Madrid.

Ferdinand and Isabella are called—and their minister, Francisco (later Cardinal) Jimenez de Cisneros. They strove for national unity and for expansion with a strong religious tone. On these grounds they built the first modern European nation and empire and at the same time kept internal conflict in hand.

Through the marriage of Ferdinand and Isabella, the two medieval kingdoms of Castile and Aragon, which had absorbed other smaller units, were fused. Then, by conquering Granada, in 1492, they brought an end to Moorish domination. After the territorial unity was accomplished, political and spiritual unity

321

CORNER BALCONIES add to the attractions of a modern apartment building in Madrid. The style of the structure is seen in many European cities.

CHARM AND GRACE to the sound of clicking castanets. The dancer is a girl of Majorca, one of the Balearic Islands. Relieving her somber black dress are a striped apron, a gay straw hat and an exquisite kerchief of snowy white lace.

RICHLY DECORATED ARCHES open one beyond another from a courtyard in the Alcazar, the old Moorish palace in Seville. Marble floors, the murmur of a little fountain, the long vista—all make for an impression of coolness and serenity.

»

COAL pours from an open gondola into a cargo vessel docked at Gijon. The town is the main seaport of Asturias, province on the Bay of Biscay.

A TALGO TRAIN gets a thorough cleaning in a station. Low-slung and swift, the Talgo is one of the most modern trains in all Europe.

had to be established. There were several steps. The feudal lords were forced to accept the authority of the crown. Castilian became the official language of all Spaniards, although Galician, Catalan and Basque tongues survived. Religious unity was imposed. Muslims and Jews were obliged to accept Catholicism or else be considered heretics and forced to leave Spain. To root out heresy, the Inquisition was established. It became a tool of political as well as religious unity. Years later, after the rise of Protestantism, the Inquisition served to watch over the purity of the faith. Thus the Spanish land that in the Middle Ages was often a model of tolerance became, according to some critical historians, the symbol of intolerance.

Circumstances combined to open many roads to the religious fervor, zeal for expansion and adventurous mood of fifteenth-century Spain. Queen Isabella and Jimenez carried the spirit of religious crusade into North Africa. King Ferdinand married his children into the most powerful ruling families of Europe. To crown all this, in 1492, the same year that Granada was recovered, Columbus sailed from Palos (on the coast of Andalusia) under the Spanish flag, in Spanish ships and with Spanish crews, to find new routes to the Far East.

The result was that Spanish power rose at a pace and with an absorbing force that the world had not known since the time of Julius Caesar. By the middle of the sixteenth century, all the oceans had been opened by Spanish and Portuguese navigators. A large part of the New World had been discovered, conquered, explored and colonized. Many important cities in Mexico, the West Indies, Central and South America were built, with schools, convents, universities, printing presses and imposing palaces. The half-Flemish, half-Spanish grandson of Ferdinand became Holy Roman Emperor as Charles V. (His other grandfather was a Hapsburg.) He defied and defeated France and came to rule over much of America, several territories on the African coast, the Low Countries, half the Italian peninsula and part of northern and southern France. The Castilian and Aragonese ruling families now had been replaced by the Hapsburgs. Charles, however, was completely Hispanized and made Spain the center of world power and policy.

Then the Protestant Reformation dawned. In the beginning Charles V was willing to compromise. Later, when compromise became impossible, Spain assumed the leadership of the Catholic Counter Reformation. A Spaniard, Ignatius of Loyola, founded the Society of Jesus; and Philip II, son of Charles, made the core of his policy the defense of Catholicism. Philip fought the Turks in the Mediterranean, the rebellious Dutch in the Netherlands, and the rising power of England.

At last Spanish domination was checked, especially by the defeat of the Spanish Armada off the coast of England in 1588. Spain's power began to slip,

THE FIRST OIL REFINERY to be built in Spain is at Cartagena. Crude oil must be imported.

SHOSTAL

J. BARNELL

MOORISH PALACE gardens of the Alhambra in Granada. The beautiful scene has been preserved much as it was in the days of the Arab caliphs.

AVILA, capital of Old Castile, is truly a museum of medieval architecture. Its well-preserved granite walls date from the eleventh century.

TALAVERA DE LA REINA, a trading and industrial center of west-central Spain, is known all over the world for its artistic ceramic products.

TWO PRETTY SEÑORITAS of Valencia dressed for a festival. Their costumes harmonize with the colorful tile domes and walls of the old city.

though during the seventeenth century the successors of Philip II kept most of the Spanish territories and a semblance of greatness. In 1700, however, Philip V, a grandson of Louis XIV of France, came to the throne. Spain and her empire now became, to an extent, pawns of the French Bourbons in the game of world politics.

To go back a bit, during the 1500's the vast empire, its military and naval strength, and the gold flowing in from America formed the foundation for a period of splendor and creative imagination known as the Golden Century. Renaissance and baroque architecture and sculpture flourished in cities and towns, where the new palaces and churches sprang up, rivaling in grandeur those of the Middle Ages. Philip II, at the height of his power, moved the court to Madrid. In commemoration of the defeat of the French in the Battle of St. Quentin, he built the imposing and severe monastery of the Escorial, near the capital. He intended it to be a monument to his power, a place of retirement and the pantheon of Spanish kings.

FOR NIGHT FISHING, small boats carry lamps—at Algeciras, near Gibraltar.

Spanish genius in arts and letters

In this period dawned the great school of Spanish painting, second only to that of the Italian Renaissance. El Greco was the first Spanish master, followed over the next hundred years or so by Velasquez, Murillo, Zurbaran, Ribera. Their canvases can be seen in the leading art galleries of Europe and America. Above all, with the works of Goya, from a later period, they are the main attraction of the Prado, in Madrid, one of the world's most magnificent museums. Lesser arts, such as the working of steel and precious metals, ceramics, embroidery and furniture making, also reached a high degree of perfection.

For almost two centuries—to the death of Calderon in 1681—Spanish literature held a commanding place. There was a series of gifted writers. Modern forms such as the novel appeared. Picaresque (in which the "hero" is a rogue) and Moorish fiction were born. Finally, Cervantes (as a playwright), Lope de Vega, Tirso de Molina (creator of Don Juan) and Calderon de la Barca created the Spanish drama. Moreover, the traditional *romancero* (originally a folk ballad) was spreading, enriched by well-known poets.

In religious literature the period is also the time of great mystics such as Luis de Leon, St. Theresa and St. John of the Cross. Distinguished lyric poets came to the fore: Garcilaso de la Vega, Herrera, Lope de Vega, Gongora and Quevedo, the last also a master of Spanish prose. All of them had considerable influence on other European literatures.

Perhaps the most characteristic trait of Spanish literature is its extremes, going from coarse realism to lofty idealism. The picaresque novel is contemporary with the mystic spirituality of the writing of St. John of the Cross. Gongora, a sophisticated poet, excels in poetic language and, at the same time, writes popular, brazen poems. Quevedo, a stern moralist, stoic and religious thinker, produces the most shameless satires. And Cervantes creates in Don Quixote and Sancho the immortal couple—the ideal and the earthy made inseparable. The same can be said of Spanish painting. Velasquez, for instance, paints both portraits of royalty and of the dregs of humanity—its dwarfs, buffoons and idiots. Murillo unites in his canvases the religious and the familiar.

The universities of Salamanca and Alcala were at this time among the best in Europe. Even in speculative thought and in science—somewhat alien to Spanish genius—a few Spaniards attained some prominence. The philosopher Luis Vives was a friend of Erasmus, the famous Dutch scholar, and lectured at Oxford. Father Vitoria preceded Grotius in the formulation of international law. Somewhat later appeared Father Suarez, the last of the great scholastic philosophers.

But for all the splendor in arts, letters and courtly life, the economy stood still. Spain wasted in wars and luxury the resources of the mother country and the gold coming from the Indies (America). War and religion were the chief interests. Work and material well-being did not matter; and agriculture, commerce and some budding medieval industries declined. The outcome was a paradox: the most powerful country in the world growing poor and decreasing in population. By the end of the seventeenth century, though Spain still held most of her empire, she

THE BULLFIGHTING RING in Malaga is near the water front and breakwaters.

SILBERSTEIN, MONKMEYER

had become a land of grandees, lazy and impoverished hidalgos (petty noblemen), monks, beggars, and a dwindling rural population working hopelessly on unproductive land. The most ambitious men still took the road to America.

Steps toward a modern state

From this low point, Spain began a long, steep climb toward a modern social organization. There were three giant steps: checking the decline; breaking the country's isolation; and adopting new economic and political ideas and institutions. For almost one hundred years the Bourbon monarchs, helped by able ministers, worked to break the impasse. They opened Spain, to a moderate degree, to the liberating ideas stirring in France, England and Italy. However, the efforts were hindered by alarm over the triumph of the French Revolution and by constant wars. Spain, trying to save the remnant of her empire, played alternately into the hands of England and France, the rivals for European supremacy. From the point of view of culture, only one Spanish name has universal significance during this period: that of the painter Francisco Goya.

The nineteenth century opened with invasion by Napoleon. The aroused Spanish people struggled heroically for freedom, aided by their ally England, during the Peninsular War. The invader was vanquished. Yet almost until the present day the country has seemed to be hopelessly divided. On the one hand have been the liberals, trying to push Spain into new ways, at times with little respect for custom. On the other have been the traditionalists, anxious to keep ancient privileges. Though compromises were attempted, the history of the last 150 years has been largely a series of frustrated revolutions, pronunciamentos (barrack uprisings) and civil wars. The strife reached a climax in the Civil War of 1936–39, which brought about the downfall of the Second Spanish Republic (1931–36). It was not simply an affair of totalitarians fighting liberals and a new republic, nor of fascism fighting communism, nor of a new Spain represented by

BROKEN TILES form a gay mosaic in the Park Güell playground in Barcelona. The park was built in 1910–14 by Antonio Gaudi, a Catalan architect who delighted in playful and sometimes bizarre effects.

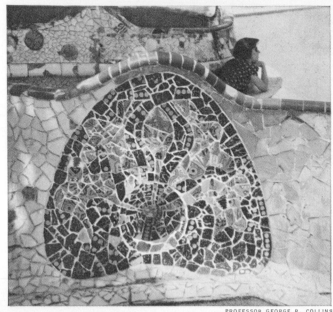

RUG MAKING in Granada. The colors blaze in a bewildering variety of designs. Granada artisans have been making such rugs by hand for centuries.

LAGARTERA GIRLS in traditional costumes, heavy with embroidery. Lagartera, a town in Toledo Province, is celebrated for keeping up the region's old customs.

SIGNAL FLAGS are hoisted in a drill at the naval school at Marin, in Galicia. In the northwest corner of Spain, Galicia has a wild coast, pounded by the Atlantic.

WATER-BARREL SHOP in Betanzos, a city on the coast of Galicia. The barrels are made of wood and banded with metal. In Spain, drinking water is a precious commodity.

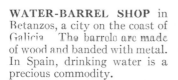

FISHING FLEET off Galicia, the "sardine coast" of Europe. The waters teem with herring and other fish, and shellfish in delicious variety are caught in the wickerwork traps.

331

ART-LOVERS' MECCA—the Prado, Madrid, home of a superb collection of masters.

the Republican Government defending itself from the forces of reaction. It was all this and much more, including an urge in such outlying regions as Catalonia, Galicia and the Basque Provinces for more self-government. The issues were further confused by the intervention of foreign powers, fascist Italy and Nazi Germany on one side, and communist Russia on the other.

With the defeat of the Republic Government the regime of General Francisco Franco was established. It combines totalitarian features with traditional Spanish ideas and institutions. Its main supports are the Army, the Catholic Church and the Falange, the only legal political party. As a result of Franco's open partiality for Germany and Italy during World War II, Spain was isolated for some years thereafter. In the 1950's, however, Spain allowed the United States to build military and naval bases on Spanish soil in return for economic help. In 1955 Spain was admitted to the UN and various other international organizations.

Officially, since a referendum of 1947, the Spanish nation has been a monarchy —but without a king. General Franco's title is chief of state. Nominally he acts as regent, until such time as, according to the Law of Succession, one of the descendants of the last king, Alfonso XIII, ascends the throne.

The administrative system of the country has been only slightly altered since the beginning of the 1800's. It is patterned on the Napoleonic Code of France. The country is divided into fifty provinces, including the Balearic and Canary islands. Each province has a civil governor. Provincial affairs are handled by a *diputacion,* or provincial council. The fifty provinces are loosely grouped into eleven regions: Asturias, Galicia, Catalonia, Navarre, Leon, Aragon, the Basque Provinces, Old Castile, New Castile, Estremadura and Andalusia. Most of the regions correspond to old medieval kingdoms. The chief city in each region is usually the seat of a university and of a regional court of appeals as well as the residence of an archbishop and a captain general. But all authority—political, economic, military, educational, juridical—stems directly from the central Government, in Madrid. What was once a powerful empire has dwindled to a few unimportant territories and possessions on the western coast of Africa (Ifni, Spanish West Africa and Spanish Guinea) and to two cities— Ceuta and Melilla—remaining under Spanish sovereignty since the independence of Morocco.

The "generation of '98"

In spite of two centuries of turmoil, Spain did make progress, intellectually and economically. The pace was slow and often interrupted but at times remarkable. However, it was a blow—the defeat of Spain by the United States in 1898—that brought about the real awakening. From that event issued a spiritual and intellectual movement of lasting consequence. It was led by a group of writers known as the "generation of '98." From then until the outbreak of the Civil War, Spanish letters and Spanish culture in general compare favorably with any other in Europe. There were many writers of great distinction. Best known of the "generation of '98" outside of Spain are Miguel de Unamuno, philosopher,

EL GRECO'S PORTRAIT of a beruffed gentleman is a treasure of the Prado.

poet and scholar, and Jacinto Benavente, Nobel Prize dramatist. Those who came later include the philosopher Ortega y Gasset (author of *The Revolt of the Masses*), the poets Antonio Machado and Juan Ramon Jimenez (who was awarded the Nobel Prize for literature in 1956), and the poet-dramatist Federico Garcia Lorca (who died tragically during the Civil War).

Side by side with the literary revival there was progress in science and education. Public opinion became an important factor in the life of the nation. On the economic front, agriculture, manufacturing, banking and transportation all advanced. By the time World War I broke out, neutral Spain was able to provide the belligerents with many essential products. Seaports and such industrial cities as Barcelona and Bilbao became prosperous as never before; and the wealth gained was applied to further economic development. However, this encouraging trend was broken by the severe, world-wide depression that began late in the 1920's. Moreover, political strife

flared up, which resulted in the fall of the monarchy and, five years later, in the Civil War. Spain was left very nearly in ruins. Only since the late 1940's has the national economy begun to recover.

Spain continues to be a country of striking contrasts. Such cities as Madrid, Barcelona, Bilbao, Seville and Valencia offer comforts and facilities equal to those of the most advanced cities anywhere. While preserving many of the art treasures of the past, they also have numerous modern buildings, luxurious hotels, wide avenues and lovely parks. Yet at the edge of the cities—and even more often in the countryside—are villages little changed since the Middle Ages. And over the hills roam shepherds with flocks of sheep and goats, bringing to mind Biblical scenes.

Spain has the most modern train in Europe—the low-slung Talgo—and some that are practically falling apart. There are a number of excellent highways. Yet among the high-powered trucks, buses and private cars roaring by, country folk amble along on burros, and plodding oxen pull *carretas* (primitive two-wheeled carts). Close to a beautiful medieval monastery or an impressive modern factory may stand small huts of straw and adobe (sun-dried brick). It is precisely this mixture of ancient and new, of wealth and poverty, of fertile land and barren that makes Spain so fascinating.

Many farmers; limited land

In general, agriculture is the main occupation and source of income. Of Spain's 125,000,000 acres, about 110,000,000 are in use; about half of this area is cultivated, the rest being pasture and woodland. Some 15,000,000 acres are entirely unproductive. Because of the irregular rainfall, a great proportion of the land, especially in the central plateau and surrounding valleys, is dry-farmed and sowed to cereals and leguminous plants. A third of the tilled land is left to lie fallow every two years. Some sections yield rich harvests; but on the whole the average production is insufficient. Spain usually must import wheat in order to feed its increasing population. Though the ir-

333

PHOTOS, MAX TATCH FROM SHOSTAL

THE GRACEFUL SPAN is one of several little bridges that cross a semicircular pool in front of the Palace of Justice, in Seville.

"GOD GIVES a house in Seville to those He loves" says an old proverb. White walls and wrought-iron work are part of the charm.

TAILOR FOR BULLFIGHTERS. A matador prides himself on his elegance as well as his grace and courage.

RUFFLED SKIRTS meant to swirl. No dancers have greater speed and lightness than the girls of Seville.

rigated areas are extremely fertile and yield generously, they are relatively small. In spite of this, Spain provides many foreign markets with onions, tomatoes, oranges and other fruits. Olive oil and wine are also produced abundantly and are exported in large quantities. Other Spanish crops worth mentioning are rice, cotton and saffron.

Spain was once important for livestock, as attested by the fame of its Merino sheep and Andalusian horses. Spain's wealth in livestock fell sharply for several centuries, and there were even more serious losses during the Civil War. Today livestock raising is perhaps on the increase, though only in sheep and hogs has it reached much importance. The production of dairy products and beef is limited largely to the green, rainy regions of the north: Galicia, the Cantabric coast and the Pyrenees. There are also extensive *dehesas,* or pasture lands, in Andalusia.

GYPSY CAVE DWELLINGS in a hill near Granada. There the visitor may hear and see the fiery Andalusian-gypsy flamenco.

KARL BISSINGER

But here, as in small sections of central Spain, the breeding of bulls for bullfights predominates.

Forest resources and problems

The forests also suffered during the centuries of war and decline. Today most of the country below the northern sierras and valleys is a vast dry plain, its baked soil cracked and barren. Even the surrounding mountains and hills are bare. Yet there were once extensive zones of woodland there. War, neglect and overcutting were not the only enemies of the forests. The worst was that land really unsuited to cultivation was broken to the plow. Wind and weather then eroded the soil, which could no longer hold any rain that fell.

Nevertheless there are still some valuable though limited forest resources. These include groves of pines in the Iberian range of the northeast; extensive plantations of cork trees in Estremadura, Andalusia and Catalonia; scattered woods of oak, ash, chestnut, poplar and beech. Cork and pine resin are important Spanish exports. Otherwise there is barely enough lumber to meet home needs for flooring and paneling, charcoal and furniture. Wooden houses are rare.

As a sort of by-product of the woods, there is a growing perfume industry. The perfume is made from such fragrant plants as thyme, lavender and rosemary, which thrive in underbrush and thickets.

The need for reforestation has long been recognized. Only since the 1950's, however, has a real effort been made to tackle the problem. Now groves of pine saplings, poplars and eucalyptus are beginning to cover the nakedness of the Spanish landscape. Eventually they may remedy some of the ills of land use.

Mining is perhaps the oldest industry in the peninsula. Mineral wealth was one of Iberia's attractions for the ancient colonizers. Even today Spain is surpassed only by the United States in the production of such ores as copper, lead and mercury. Spain is also rich in coal, iron and, to a lesser degree, wolfram, tin, zinc, silver and manganese. As happened with every other activity, the development of mineral resources also was held back by Spain's decline, this just as the industrial era was dawning. Lack of initiative and capital, difficulties in transportation, and government indifference account for the fact that until the 1920's more than half of the mining industry was in the hands of foreign companies, especially British ones. A considerable drawback in Spain's modern economy is the scarcity of oil, though many geological factors point to its existence in the peninsula. Thus far, repeated drillings have failed to find it.

Industries and crafts

Only by virtue of the wool and cotton textiles of Catalonia, and of some kinds of metal production—around Bilbao, Santander, Zaragoza and Valencia—does Spain have much claim to being industrialized. Though chemical industries are on the increase, their output is below that to be expected of a country rich in salts and other chemical raw materials.

In contrast to manufacturing is the high quality of many craft products. Here the artistic genius of the Spaniards asserts itself: in pottery, ceramics and glassware; gold, silver and other metal articles; finely tempered and engraved arms; laces, brocades and embroidery. All express an inborn sense of beauty, which even the most average Spaniard seems to possess. Moreover the crafts provide considerable income.

Fishing, both as an occupation and another source of national income, is naturally important in a country that has one of the longest coast lines of Europe.

In general the nation's economic life is improving though it lags behind that of European and American leaders. Spain has the handicaps of an unfavorable trade balance; lack of enough modern transportation, including shipping; and low income for most of its people. The average yearly income per person is less than $300. There are, nevertheless, some encouraging factors. In recent years, miles of modern roads have been built; and power output has been doubled, especially by the harnessing of hydroelectric resources. Some of these activities are under the Government. Foreign capital has been welcomed cautiously.

The most hopeful sign, however, may well be the growing demand for the material comforts of life, a desire felt by Spaniards of all classes. One result is that new working habits are appearing, not only in the increasing middle class but even in the aristocracy. Not so many years ago the aristocrats led a life of leisure or subsisted on the income provided by an overgrown and inefficient bureaucracy. The state was the great provider. Thus the new attitude toward work is slowly bringing about a transformation in the structure of Spanish society, a change similar to the one that occurred elsewhere after the Industrial Revolution. Yet some of the causes of Spain's economic difficulties have hardly been touched. Perhaps most basic of these is the unequal distribution of wealth. Great fortunes and enormous latifundia (vast estates) still exist.

The many types of Spaniards

Geography and history have combined to give Spain great variety. Nor is there uniformity in customs or the bearing and temperament of people. Not all Spaniards are dark in complexion, as many foreigners believe; many are fair and blue-eyed. From province to province a visitor meets many different human types: the strong, self-possessed fisherman and sailor of the busy Cantabrian and Galician ports; the determined, class-conscious industrial worker of Bilbao or Barcelona; the hardened Asturian miner; the solemn-looking, dignified and wiry peasant of the Castilian plateau; the robust Aragonese; the graceful Andalusian herdsman of brave bulls; the Moorish-looking *huertano* (orchardman) of the Valencian citrus groves. Each dresses, walks, looks, speaks in a different way.

This is at least partly the result, of course, of the mixture of stocks that came to the peninsula in ancient and medieval times. Spain's social structure has also contributed. A sharp division still exists between lower and upper classes and be-

DRUM BEATS announce a *corrida* (bullfight) in Sanlucar de Barrameda.

Bullfights and colorful processions

A MATADOR swirls his cape, slowly turning the bull. It is a test of the matador's courage and skill, watched tensely.

« AT PAMPLONA, in Navarre, spectators scurry for safety as the bulls are run through the city streets to the ring. The running of the bulls is one of the dangerous thrills of Pamplona festivals.

»

A MONSTRANCE passes through the streets, part of a Corpus Christi procession.

PAUL PIETZSCH, BLACK STAR

CANOPIED WAGONS, drawn by oxen and gaily decorated, on a pilgrimage.

tween country and city people. Diversity is further intensified by extreme individualism. The Spaniard, no matter what region he comes from or what class he belongs to, has a strong sense of his own personality. This is clearly shown, for instance, in the pride of Spanish beggars and the dignified faces of Spanish peasants, which many visitors have noticed with admiration. Though twentieth-century communications and transportation are making people more alike everywhere, in Spain the process is slow. The Spaniard will not give up his personal habits easily, even for the sake of more comfort and easier living conditions.

In spite of all this the Spanish people do have an unmistakable national character, which goes beyond all political, regional and linguistic differences. That character shows itself most plainly in the individualism we have mentioned, common to all Spaniards of whatever region. Moreover, they all share an extremely high respect for courage and personal dignity; place moral, artistic and religious ´values above intellectual values; judge a person for what he is rather than for what he owns or has accomplished. Finally, in a truly democratic feeling, not political but human, and in spite of social and economic inequalities, Spaniards believe that no man is superior to any other, for all are creatures of God.

Individualism in moral attitudes

Much of the turmoil of the last 150 years can be traced to these individualistic traits. Spaniards are born with a mistrust of authority; hence their social sense is weak. No Spaniard likes to delegate to others what he considers to be his personal rights and moral responsibilities. The story is told of a Spaniard who was called as a witness in a criminal trial. He testified not to what he knew to be the facts but to what he thought would have the defendant acquitted, because he considered the defendant morally innocent. This is typical. A moral attitude as deeply rooted as this can be explained only by the strong influence of religion on Spanish character.

The dryness of more than half of the

ROMANESQUE ARCHITECTURE—the twelfth-century church in Santillana.

country, the ruggedness of the mountains and coasts, the uneven climate, the fact that the country is only now slowly emerging from a long period of economic stalemate—all this has made life difficult for a great majority of the people, especially in rural Spain. Unthinking foreigners have sometimes called the Spanish lazy. Actually the Spanish peasants are among the hardest-working people to be found anywhere. Even the supposedly indolent, guitar-playing Andalusian has to struggle hard for a living. Much of the Spanish soil yields only a bare subsistence after long hours of labor. Endurance and frugality are therefore the outstanding qualities of a large part of the people. The toiler in the fields works from dawn to dusk, sustained only by bread, with a piece of bacon and an onion or tomato, or by a dish of boiled potatoes.

Nevertheless, living standards *are* improving in the rural sections. And city people, under the pressure of new desires, are modifying their old habits. This is true even among the upper middle class and the aristocracy—the so-called *señoritos,* who for centuries considered work of any kind beneath their dignity. Yet in the cities the visitor notices large groups who seem to have all the time in the world. They stroll leisurely up and down the

A MODERN BUS, for tourists, waits in Santillana, striking contrast to the old church.

main street or talk for hours around the table of a café or casino. The *paseo,* or daily promenade, and the *tertulia,* or gathering for conversation, usually in a public place, remain strong habits in Spanish social life. Discussion of everything and everybody remains the great pastime and passion of the Spaniard.

The homes of Spanish grandees are often pictured as symbols of formal magnificence. In general, however, the homes of most Spaniards reflect the limited resources of the land. There is no one type. The farmhouse of the north has wooden balconies, with a silo and a stable nearby. In Valencia the gay-looking *barraca* is surrounded with flowers. The dwelling of a Castilian peasant is of adobe or stone. Immaculate in fresh whitewash, the Andalusian house has patios and terraces. No matter how run-down and deserted a Spanish village may look, somewhere in it or nearby stands an old palace, a castle or a manorial house, romantic though probably in ruins and abandoned.

Modern conveniences are slowly appearing, while the construction of new buildings is thriving all over Spain. In the traditional Spanish home the most treasured furnishings are likely to be holdovers from the past, though many of the lovely old things are in the hands of collectors today. Yet even in rural dwellings one may still come across high, comfortable old beds, with fine upholstery; pieces of exquisite brocade and lace; lovely pottery; handsome painted and gilded desks, chests and sets of chairs, and other furniture of the purest sixteenth- and seventeeth-cen-

tury styles. Almost always, especially in southern Spain, and no matter how poor the people may be, there is some ornamental detail or a few plants and flowers that show an innate artistic temperament.

From a blend of traditional spirit, artistic sense and love of color springs the wealth of festivals and popular customs. Some, such as Holy Week in Seville, and Corpus Christi in Granada, Toledo and Cordoba, are world famous. Every town and city has celebrations of its own, to mark the day of a patron saint or other date on the church calendar. Some of the observances are extremely solemn. Usually they are followed by fiestas, *ferias* (fairs) or *romerias* (pilgrimages), in which it is hard to separate the sacred from the profane.

During many of the fiestas and fairs, performances are given whose origins go back to medieval times. Grotesque, masked figures called *gigantes y cabezudos* (giants and big-headed dwarfs) march in procession. A joust between "Moors" and "Christians" may be acted out in dance and pantomime. The town of Elche, in the province of Alicante, presents a particularly famous mystery (a kind of medieval religious play) every year.

Dances and popular music

The fiestas are usually the best times to see and hear, in their traditional settings and rich regional variety, the dances and popular music of Spain. Among them are the Andalusian flamenco, of gypsy origin, which may be a wailing song or a fiery, incredibly fast-stepping dance; the stately *sardana* of Catalonia; the *danzaprima* of Asturias; the energetic jota, accompanied by clicking castanets, of Aragon, Castile and Valencia; the gay Galician *muñeira;* and the quaint *aurrescu* of the Basque country. Various combinations of guitars, bagpipes, flageolets, drums and tambourines provide the music. Each dance, as each region, has its distinctive costume.

A fiesta is also a good time to sample Spanish food. Like everything else in Spain the cuisine varies from region to region. In general it is highly seasoned; hot peppers are a favorite ingredient. Much

WENDY HILTY, MONKMEYER

A WINERY WORKMAN of Jerez.
His basket is laden with grapes.

Earning a living takes many forms

IN MADRID—a cheerful young
helper in a restaurant.

SPANISH TOURIST OFFICE

FASHIONING PLATES in a
pottery at Manises.

GOAT HERDER and his flock on a rocky hillside in Malaga.

ANY POTS AND PANS to mend?—a tinker in a market in Barcelona.

A BUNDLE of esparto-grass
fiber is weighed.

A FLOWER SELLER hawks a fragrant, many-hued armful.

rice and olive oil are used as a rule.

The best-known Spanish amusement is, of course, bullfighting. As a public pastime it has now been competing for years with *futbol* (soccer) and other foreign sports which Spanish youths are adopting with increasing enthusiasm. As an age-old spectacle, almost a rite, however, bullfighting will not be displaced easily. It is, furthermore, the one spectacle that unites all Spaniards: poor and rich, from Galicians to Andalusians. Bullfights are held everywhere during the season, between Easter and early fall, in the great plazas of Madrid, Seville, Barcelona and Valencia and in improvised arenas in the public squares of the most humble hamlets. In little towns it is the most courageous neighborhood youths who perform, instead of professional matadors. To some foreigners and even to some Spanish intellectuals, bullfighting is a survival of cruel and barbarous times. Even so, bullfights represent something deeply rooted in the Spanish temperament. They combine tragedy and beauty, emotional force and the thrill of combat. Spaniards are at one in their admiration for the person who faces danger and the possibility of death with grace, dignity and a sense of play. These are the qualities expected of a bullfighter. In his performance, fatalism (what will be, will be—a viewpoint that is probably of Moorish origin) is balanced by artistic skill and personal courage.

In such attitudes, as in many other matters, Spain clings to the past. Yet it should not be forgotten that for almost two centuries, Spain has been making determined, if interrupted, efforts to overcome the results of earlier neglect. Though Spain may never again be the leader it once was, its history and the creative originality of its people make it worthy of an important place among the world's nations.   By ANGEL DEL RIO

SPAIN: FACTS AND FIGURES

THE COUNTRY

Bounded north by Bay of Biscay, France and Andorra, east by the Mediterranean, south by the Mediterranean and the Strait of Gibraltar, southwest by the Atlantic and west by Portugal and the Atlantic. Area of continental Spain, 189,392 square miles; including island provinces in the Canaries and Balearics, 194,232 square miles; population, 30,000,000.

GOVERNMENT

Spain, which had been a constitutional monarchy since 1876, was proclaimed a Republic in 1931. In 1936, a revolt broke out against the Republican Government and developed into a civil war; a Nationalist Government, headed by General Franco, was proclaimed. In 1939 the supporters of the Republic were defeated and Franco became dictator of Spain. On his death the monarchy may be restored.

COMMERCE AND INDUSTRIES

Eighty-four per cent of the land is in pasture, fallow or under cultivation. Leading crops are wheat, barley, corn, rye, rice, oranges, olives, potatoes and tobacco. Livestock, 33,000,000 head, including 16,344,000 sheep. Leading minerals are hard and soft coal, lignite, iron ore, lead, iron pyrites, potash, zinc, tin, wolfram and copper. Leading manufactures are cotton, woolen and rayon goods, paper and cement. Fisheries are important; leading catches are sardine, tuna and cod. Leading exports: tin, iron and wolfram ores, cork, hides, salt, fish, vegetables, citrus fruits, wines, potash, olive oil and mercury. Imports: cotton, cereals, potatoes, sugar, coffee, tobacco, wood products, nitrates, machinery, automobiles, petroleum, coal. Monetary unit, the peseta.

COMMUNICATIONS

Railways, about 12,000 mi.; highways, about 75,000 mi.; some 233,000 motor cars and 122,000 motorcycles; 1,100,000 telephones; radio and television stations in Madrid area; international and domestic air service; merchant marine, about 1,385,000 gross tons.

RELIGION AND EDUCATION

Roman Catholicism is the established religion; there are about 26,000 Protestants. Primary education free and compulsory; 61,000 public elementary schools, 119 national secondary schools, 12 universities and 106 teacher-training institutions.

CHIEF CITIES

Madrid, capital, 1,768,000; Barcelona, 1,362,-000; Valencia, 543,000; Seville, 405,000; Malaga, 288,000; Zaragoza, 281,000; Bilbao, 253,-000; Murcia, 235,000; Cordoba, 182,000; Palmas (Las), 165,000; Vigo, 156,000; Coruña (La), 155,000; Granada, 155,000.

LANDMARK for mariners, the Tower of Belem. It stands in the Tagus River near Lisbon. In the elaborate Portuguese version of Gothic called Manueline, the structure is adorned with many nautical devices such as the "ropes" that encircle the turrets.

Portugal ... *a corporative republic*

BY law no one may go barefoot on the streets of Lisbon. The purpose of this odd edict seems to be an attempt to conceal the poverty of most Portuguese from visitors. Actually most city men do wear shoes, but many of the women shuffle along in cheap, flimsy scuffs. Even the scuffs are likely to be carried until a policeman comes in sight.

Continuing poverty is the most glaring blot on the record of the "corporative republic," which came into existence under the constitution of 1933. The average annual income is only $200, one of the lowest figures in Europe. Between 1910 (when the monarchy was overthrown) and 1932, Portugal had no stable government. Violent revolts were frequent and

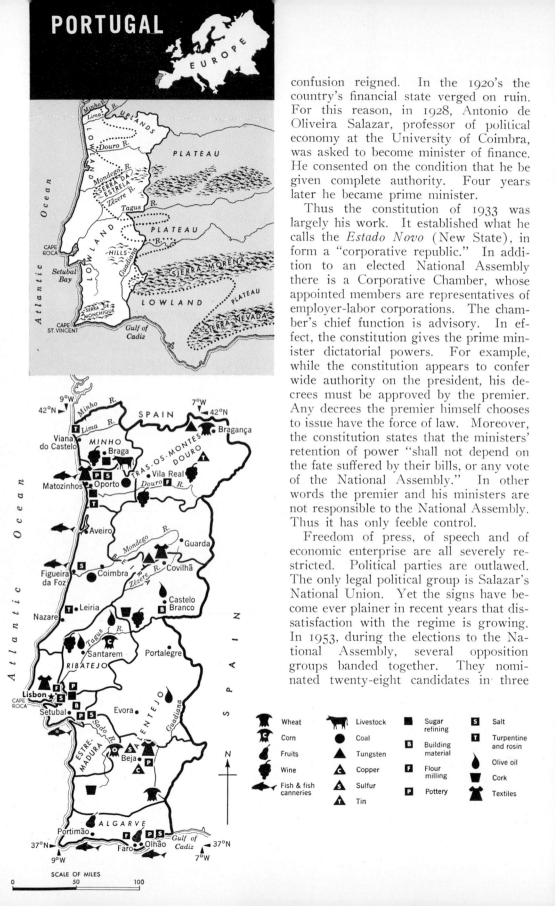

PORTUGAL

EUROPE

confusion reigned. In the 1920's the country's financial state verged on ruin. For this reason, in 1928, Antonio de Oliveira Salazar, professor of political economy at the University of Coimbra, was asked to become minister of finance. He consented on the condition that he be given complete authority. Four years later he became prime minister.

Thus the constitution of 1933 was largely his work. It established what he calls the *Estado Novo* (New State), in form a "corporative republic." In addition to an elected National Assembly there is a Corporative Chamber, whose appointed members are representatives of employer-labor corporations. The chamber's chief function is advisory. In effect, the constitution gives the prime minister dictatorial powers. For example, while the constitution appears to confer wide authority on the president, his decrees must be approved by the premier. Any decrees the premier himself chooses to issue have the force of law. Moreover, the constitution states that the ministers' retention of power "shall not depend on the fate suffered by their bills, or any vote of the National Assembly." In other words the premier and his ministers are not responsible to the National Assembly. Thus it has only feeble control.

Freedom of press, of speech and of economic enterprise are all severely restricted. Political parties are outlawed. The only legal political group is Salazar's National Union. Yet the signs have become ever plainer in recent years that dissatisfaction with the regime is growing. In 1953, during the elections to the National Assembly, several opposition groups banded together. They nominated twenty-eight candidates in three

SCALE OF MILES

0   50   100

districts and managed to win a sixth of the votes cast. In the 1958 presidential election there was an even stronger contest. (Nominally, the president appoints the premier. Thus an opposition president could—and undoubtedly would—appoint someone other than Salazar as premier.) Salazar's candidate won, of course, but the opposition's candidate garnered almost a quarter of the vote.

On the other hand, after living in a political backwater for so many years, the Portuguese in general were finding it hard to understand the reverses suffered by their country in the early 1960's. First was the seizure by India of the Portuguese territories, including Goa, on India's coast. While India's action was not exactly condoned, the Western powers gave Portugal no help to get the territories back.

Even more serious, there has been violent unrest in Angola since 1961, provoking worldwide criticism of Portugal's handling of its African territories. One of the mildest terms used to describe Portuguese rule is "repressive." The matter was brought before the United Nations and there disputed bitterly—to the point that late in 1962 Portugal was threatening to leave the UN. In any case, Portugal was continuing to refuse permission for a UN investigating committee to visit Angola. This while the agitation was spreading to Mozambique. Portugal announced some reforms in the administration of the African territories but at the same time was increasing its military forces there. It was believed that some thirty thousand Portuguese troops were already stationed in Angola.

At home, economic conditions have been improving gradually. The gross national product increased 23 per cent between 1953 and 1958. In 1961 a huge steel mill was opened at Seixal, and a hydroelectric power dam (with a yearly capacity of 810,000,000 kw) at Miranda do Douro. These projects were completed under the first Six-year Development Plan (1953–58) and a second (1959–64) has been introduced.

The sea-washed land

Far in the west of Europe, Portugal looks out over the vast expanse of the Atlantic. One of the smallest European nations, its territory is somewhat less than Indiana's; among Canada's provinces only Nova Scotia and Prince Edward Island are smaller than Portugal. Yet for all its limited size, Portugal built the first colonial empire of any modern European country. Even today its flag flies over territories spread across Europe, Africa and Asia.

Portugal faces the Atlantic and throughout their history the Portuguese have been fishermen and sailors. Once they were empire builders across the seas. Nevertheless, the great majority of the Portuguese people stay on their land, as farmers, herdsmen, artisans. The history of Portugal and the present character of the country are defined by these two themes, the sea and the homeland. Portugal lies next to Spain and had to defend its independence more than once against its much larger neighbor. At the same time it sought its fortunes on the unlimited waters of the ocean.

Modern Portugal has retained, in a large measure, not only the monuments of its past glory but a way of life that has not as yet caught up with the faster rhythm of industrialized nations. More than half of its people live in small towns and villages. Tall chimneys of factories, throngs of workmen on their way to vast industrial plants are almost unknown. The great majority of Portuguese are small farmers, or workers on great estates; fishermen sailing their own small craft or working on large fishing trawlers or cutters; artisans making pottery, leatherware or gold filigree jewelry in small shops.

From rainy valleys to semideserts

Portugal has the shape of a rectangle. In the north and east it borders on Spain, in the west and south it faces the Atlantic. Much of the northern and northeastern part of the country is mountainous, the rest is either rolling plain or low hills. In spite of its small size, Portugal shows amazing variety in its landscape, in its climate, in its vegetation. The north of the country is rainy, and large sections are in lush pasture. In the northeast, the upper valley of the Douro, one of Portugal's principal rivers, is warm, dry and sunny, the home of the country's most famous wine, port. The central and southern portions remain very dry throughout the spring and summer. These are Portugal's chief farm districts, where wheat and corn are grown; and carts, piled high with cork, the bark of cork oak gathered from large groves of trees, go creaking on their way to railroad stations. Southernmost Portugal is almost a desert. There only scrub covers the steep mountainsides looking out toward the Atlantic. There rows of whitewashed, cube-shaped houses stand near tiny beaches, with nets drying on the sand.

Minho and Tras-os-Montes

Minho is Portugal's northernmost province, adjacent to the Spanish region of Galicia. It is a cool, moist region of green meadows, small vineyards and small farms. There are fishing villages along the Atlantic, sleepy market towns in the interior. Braga has long been Portugal's religious capital and the goal of popular pilgrimages.

The name of the province of Tras-os-Montes (over the mountains) reveals the mountainous character of the region. This, the remote northeast corner of Portugal, was the home of Portugal's last royal house, the House of Braganza. It is rugged, inhospitable and barren for the most part. The only fertile part of Tras-os-Montes is the *Pais do Vinho,* the port-wine country of the upper Douro River valley.

Beira

South of the Douro River are the three provinces of Beira: Beira Alta (Upper), Beira Baixa (Lower) and Beira Litoral (Coastal). There is a great deal of variation among these three, for they represent a true cross section of Portugal, from the coastal plains of the Atlantic to the high, desolate uplands near the Spanish frontier. The coast is low and includes the strange lagoon of Aveiro, the town sometimes called Portugal's Venice. Fishermen there reach their nets by poling flat-bottomed boats through the salt marshes. Farther inland the land rises gradually to the *serras,* which are the westernmost extension of the ranges of Spain, mountains now slowly developing as centers of hydroelectric power. The eastern districts of Beira are known chiefly for their grazing grounds, used by herds of sheep and goats. These mountain districts have long been the guardians of one of the main routes from Spain to Portugal, and the town of Guarda perpetuates in its name their ancient role.

Estremadura and Ribatejo

The political, industrial and commercial core of Portugal is the province of Estremadura, which extends along the coast north and south of the Tagus River. Except for the low Serra de Sintra most of Estremadura is flat or gently rolling. Here is Lisbon, Portugal's capital and greatest port; here are Portugal's most famous seaside resorts. For centuries this region has been the main gateway to the heart of the country.

Inland from Estremadura lies the province of Ribatejo, the fertile middle valley of the Tagus, noted for its corn and wheat, for its herds of cattle and picturesque cowboys, for charming and sleepy river towns. Beyond Ribatejo, the two provinces of Upper (Alto) Alentejo and Lower (Baixo) Alentejo occupy most of southern Portugal. Entirely agricultural, these regions are noted for their herds, their cork, their special dishes, especially a delicious preparation of chicken. Some of their cities bear names famous in Portuguese history. Best known is Evora, a fascinating combination of Roman ruins and medieval atmosphere.

Algarve

The southernmost province, Algarve, derives its name from the Arabic. *Al Gharb,* "the West," is where the Arabs held out for more than a century after they lost their hold over the rest of Portugal. It is here that Moorish influences—in architecture, in folk dress, in the Arabic words of the local dialect—remain stronger than anywhere else in Portugal.

The sea provides the livelihood of a sizable number of Portuguese. Some fish near the coast, catching tuna, anchovies, sardines. Portuguese canned sardines and anchovies are known the world over. Others sail larger ships in search of fish to the waters of the Atlantic off western Africa. Many Portuguese fishermen go clear across the North Atlantic every year to fish for cod off the shores of Newfoundland. *Bacalhau* is the Portuguese word for cod, and "Codfishland" (Terra do Bacalhaus) was the name given to Labrador on the first European maps showing that part of Canada, maps drawn more than four centuries ago.

Source of the world's cork

Of all Portuguese forest products cork is the best known. There are large groves of cork-oak trees throughout the southern third of the country, and Portugal is the world's largest producer of cork. The thick bark, surprisingly light, is stripped off the trunks of cork oaks once every nine years. The bare tree, with its red-colored trunk, looks almost as if it were bleeding until the bark starts growing again. For many kinds of bottles, nothing else is as good as cork for stoppers, the chief use of the bark. Fine wines are always corked.

Naval stores—turpentine and resin—are another important product, obtained from the millions of Portuguese pines. In value of production, however, grapes (wine), olive oil, and fruit are Portugal's leading crops.

Two kinds of wines are produced in Portugal. Local wines are consumed almost entirely within the country. Port wine is symbolic of Portugal's close relations with its oldest ally, England, which remains the wine's principal market. The trade began in the seventeenth century and was given further impetus by the Methuen Treaty, in 1703, by which England gave Portuguese wines preferential treatment over French ones.

The making of port wine

The vineyards of the warm, dry upper Douro Valley, in northern Portugal, yield a heavy red grape. In the fall, barefooted villagers tread the ripe clusters in shallow tanks or troughs from which the sweet juice gushes into oak casks. There the juice is allowed to ferment for a time and then brandy is added. New wines are carried by oxcart from the vineyards to the banks of the Douro and thence on narrow, flatboats with high prows to Oporto. Vintage port, the best port wine, is bottled early and allowed to mature in the bottle. If kept long enough, with care, it acquires a tawny color. Ruby port, matured in the wood, is of lesser quality.

Olives, which grow almost everywhere in Portugal, and almonds, grown in the south, are other export products. But the farms do not produce enough food for Portugal's population. Quantities of wheat and corn, Portuguese staples, must be imported to satisfy the country's needs.

Factories and mines

There is comparatively little large-scale manufacturing so that only a small number of Portuguese work in factories. Textiles make up the largest single industry, the mills relying largely on imported cotton and wool. Food industries, such as flour milling and fish canning, are second in importance. Portugal is seriously handicapped by a lack of fuels. Very little coal is produced within the country, and there are few streams that could be harnessed to produce electricity. The day atomic energy is within reach of all nations will most likely have profound effects on Portugal's economy. With its large man power but few opportunities for industrial work, Portugal and its people should profit as the power necessary for industrial progress becomes available.

Minerals are produced, although the variety of products is greater than the quantity. Tin and tungsten, cement and kaolin, copper and sulfur are among the

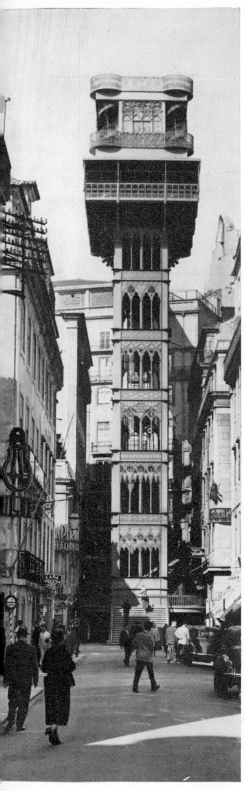

LOOKING TOWARD the Tagus River over the peaked roofs of Lisbon's Alfama section. Just above Lisbon the river widens into Lisbon Bay.

A STREET ELEVATOR is one of Lisbon's most famous structures. It carries pedestrians between levels of the city, built on several hills.

«

Lisbon—tradition

CLOTHING SHOPS on the Praçada Figuira in Lisbon. The *camisaria* sells shirts; the *gravataria*, neckties; *las-algodoes*, cotton goods.

NATIONAL SYMBOL— ravens guiding St. Vincent's ship—in a mosaic sidewalk.

THE TOWERS and the dome of the Estrela (Star) Basilica may be seen from all over the city. The church was modeled on St. Peter's in Rome. »

and commerce

OUTDOOR LIBRARY in the Estrela Basilica park. Periodicals as well as books are stocked, to be read on the benches nearby.

most important. Yet most of the ores have to be sent abroad, for Portugal has few facilities for smelting and refining.

Products of skilled artisans

Because industrialization has made only limited headway in Portugal, everyday objects—the earthenware dishes on the table, the carved yoke of a pair of oxen harnessed to a cart—are handsome as well as useful. Loving handwork has been expended on them. Small workshops employing a few men and women working in their own homes are the backbone of Portuguese handicrafts. Delicate gold filigree jewelry, using thin gold wire, is made in and around Lisbon. Portuguese pottery and glazed tiles, mostly in blue and white, are among the loveliest made in Europe. Excellent homespun woolens, colorful embroidery and beautiful lace comes from the artisans, and the table linens made in the Madeira Islands, Portuguese possessions about six hundred miles southwest of the mainland, are prized the world over.

Time-dimmed splendor

Looking at Portuguese industry, mining or agriculture today we find a small nation of hard-working people but not one of the Great Powers. Yet Portugal's past includes glory as well as greatness, and the land is dotted with monuments that recall its days of splendor.

Three abbeys, among the greatest and most beautiful of Christendom, stand today like milestones of Portugal's golden age: the Abbey of Alcobaça, the Abbey of Batalha, or Battle Abbey, and the Abbey of the Friars of St. Jerome, or *Os Jeronimos*. Built between the twelfth and sixteenth centuries, they commemorate Portugal's battles against the Moors, which led to the founding of the nation; Portugal's long struggle with Spain to gain independence; and Portugal's great overseas adventure of empire building.

Alcobaça Abbey stands in a small, pleasant valley, only a little more than an hour by car from Lisbon and only a short distance from the Atlantic Ocean. It was founded by King Alfonso I (in Portu-

guese, Afonso Henriques) in the twelfth century, at a time when Portugal, a tiny nation then only recently independent of Spain, was fighting the Moors. Alfonso I was the son of a French knight. During his long reign he succeeded in driving the Moors from the greater part of the country and made Lisbon a Christian city and his capital. To celebrate his victories he built Alcobaça Abbey. The abbot who governed this monastery was second only to the King in wealth and power in Portugal. The kitchen of the monastery was so huge that a water supply was provided by diverting the waters of a nearby stream through it. In the church of Alcobaça were laid to rest the kings of Portugal's first royal house, the House of Burgundy. These were the men who drove the Moors from Portuguese territory, established the boundaries of Portugal where they are now, built its leading cities and made the name of Portugal famous throughout Europe.

Batalha—Battle—Abbey

Ten miles from Alcobaça stands Batalha, or Battle Abbey, built near the spot where, in 1385, the troops of King John I won a resounding victory over Spain and thus secured Portuguese independence. King John I came to the throne after the death of the last scion of the House of Burgundy and founded the Portuguese royal House of Aviz. He married Philippa of Lancaster and thus began what is the oldest alliance in the world, that between Portugal and England, nearly six centuries ago. King John and Queen Philippa are buried in Battle Abbey, and surrounding them are the tombs of their sons, the men known in Portuguese history as the Great Princes. Valiant in battle for the defense of Christendom, the sons of King John strengthened Portuguese armed might at home. One became a world figure, Prince Henry the Navigator.

Prince Henry the Navigator

Five and a half centuries ago the world known to Europeans ended only a short distance south and west of Portugal.

Few ships ventured forth on the mysterious waters of the Atlantic, and the shores of Africa seemed forbidding deserts. The easiest route the Europeans knew to the riches of the Indies—the gold, gems, spices—was through lands held by the infidel Muslims, Egypt and Arabia. Prince Henry the Navigator devoted his life to finding a way to the Indies by sea. He assembled sea captains, astronomers and map makers in his modest castle in southern Portugal. He outfitted ships and sent them along the west coast of Africa. Perhaps somewhere the coast turned so that ships could sail around Africa and thence to the Far East. Year after year these vessels went out, and within Prince Henry's lifetime they pushed past the desert shores of the Sahara to the "Green Cape" (Cape Verde), where there were trees, grass and water, and on to Guinea and its gold. In 1488, some years after Prince Henry's death, a Portuguese vessel reached the southernmost tip of Africa and found that the coast did indeed turn northeast there. After this ship returned to Portugal the King named that southernmost tip of Africa the Cape of Good Hope, the hope of final success in finding the way to the fabulous riches of the Indies.

An abbey once a seamen's hostel

The Abbey of the Friars of St. Jerome, *Os Jeronimos,* stands a couple of hundred yards from the banks of the Tagus River, which leads to the open sea, in Belem, a suburb of Lisbon. There was once a seamen's hostel on the site of the abbey, and it was in the tiny chapel of that hostel that one of Portugal's heroes, Vasco da Gama, spent a whole night in prayer, before sailing in search of the sea route to India, in 1497. Da Gama's ships accomplished the great feat. In a few years after he and his men landed in India, in 1498, Portugal had become one of the richest countries in Europe. King Emanuel, "the Fortunate" (known also as Manuel I), built the Abbey of St. Jerome as a monument to Portugal's success and glory overseas.

The last years of the fifteenth and the first half of the sixteenth century saw Portugal establish an empire that reached from Brazil, in the west, to the shores of China, in the east. Spices, then worth their weight in gold, as well as the precious metal itself and fabulous gems poured into Lisbon. Portugal shared with Spain the wealth of the Indies and of America while Portuguese ships plowed the seven seas and Portuguese priests and friars spread Christianity throughout the world. In the Abbey of St. Jerome, near Lisbon, rest two of the great figures of that golden age: Vasco da Gama, the daring navigator who laid the foundations of Portugal's Indian empire; and Luiz Vaz de Camões, Portugal's greatest poet. Camões' *Lusiads* (published in 1572; the title comes from the ancient name of Portugal—Lusitania) sings of the deeds of Da Gama and made Da Gama and his adventurous contemporaries immortal.

The Tower of Belem

A stone's throw from the Abbey of St. Jerome, on the banks of the Tagus River, stands one of Portugal's most famous monuments, the Tower of Belem (Portuguese for Bethlehem). It was built under Emanuel during the period of Portugal's great empire building, at the beginning of the sixteenth century. Ever since, the white tower has been a landmark for sailors returning to Lisbon from long voyages. It is in a style of architecture called Manueline, or Manuelino (for King Emanuel). An elaboration of flamboyant Gothic style, Manueline is characterized by masses of intricate ornament covering almost every available space. On the tower the decoration is nautical in theme: carvings in stone of ropes, seashells, anchors, symbols of Portugal's mastery of the sea. There is also the perfect, symmetrical cross of the Order of Christ. This knightly order, founded in the fourteenth century, possessed vast wealth, and its grand masters were the kings and princes of Portugal. Prince Henry the Navigator used the revenues of the Order of Christ to support the voyages of exploration he organ-

ON A HILLSIDE near Nazare a farmer leads his yoked oxen, drawing an old-fashioned harrow in their wake.

TURNING THE SAILS of a windmill, to catch the breeze, takes strong muscles. Windmills are still in use in cool Minho, Portugal's northernmost province.

SPRAYING A VINEYARD near Evora. The work is done by migrant laborers dubbed "little mice." They are so called because they eat very little in order to save money to tide them over when the season's work runs out.

The yearly cycle of the good earth

A GOAT AND SHEEP amble along a pleasant road on the outskirts of Celorico da Beira. There is good pasture in the mountainous section of the Beira provinces.

«

CHARLES MAY

IRRIGATED FIELDS near Nazare. To get well water the farmer hauls on the rope to lower the bucket. Then it is drawn up by the weighted pole.

HARVESTING GRAIN in Tras-os-Montes: the mowers, with scythes, march ahead of the binders.

ized, and the cross of the Order was long part of Portugal's coat of arms.

Lisbon, the hilly capital

It is only a brief ride by streetcar or bus from Belem to the heart of Lisbon, yet in that short distance, one leaps from the sixteenth to the twentieth century. Lisbon, one of Europe's oldest cities, owes its foundation to the Phoenicians. Its undisputed leadership in Portugal, on the other hand, is due largely to the magnificent natural harbor formed by the mouth of the Tagus River. The way to see Lisbon at its best is to view it from the river, that is, to arrive by ferry from the opposite bank, from the suburb of Barreiro.

Pombal's checkerboard plan

The traveler arriving in Lisbon by water first sets foot on Praça do Comercio (Commerce Square, nicknamed Black Horse Square by the English). It is one of the most beautiful squares in Europe. Arcaded buildings, in perfect harmony, face it on three sides, and the fourth side is open to the Tagus. After much of Lisbon was destroyed by an earthquake, fire and tidal wave in 1755, the Marquês de Pombal, prime minister at about this time, partly rebuilt the city according to a master plan. The section of Lisbon lying immediately back of the river and of Commerce Square follows this plan. There the streets are at right angles. Many of their names—Street of the Silversmiths, Street of Goldsmiths—reflect the fact that they were once set aside for certain artisans. Nearly all buildings are in the same, late eighteenth-century, style. However, as Lisbon is situated largely on hills, Pombal's master plan affected only a small part of the city. So quite a few picturesque, cluttered old quarters remain.

Contrasts abound in Lisbon. From one aspect it is a city of broad avenues and spacious squares, strikingly modern buildings, sports fields and handsome new apartment houses. Yet elsewhere it is a maze of narrow streets with whitewashed, small houses, the window sills

bedecked with pots of flowers. There life goes on much as it has for centuries, in tiny patios invisible from the street. To walk about the Alfama, one of Lisbon's oldest sections—there to climb to the castle of St. George, a Moorish fortress; to visit the cathedral built on the site of an Arab mosque; to browse in tiny shops where African masks, Indonesian batik, Chinese ivories stand on the shelves—is to feel far away from twentieth-century bustle.

Among Lisbon's most unusual features are the handsome pavements made of mosaics, still found on many streets. They were introduced less than a century ago and quickly became popular. Such sidewalks are also found in the great overseas city that still shows so many traces of Portuguese influence—Rio de Janeiro, in Brazil.

Gay resorts around Estoril

Between Lisbon and the Atlantic the hills of Sintra act as a windscreen, protecting the north shore of the mouth of the Tagus from chill ocean winds. There a small and elegant group of resorts, centered about the town of Estoril, has become very fashionable in recent years. The area is most widely known as the residence of quite a few of the exiled kings and princes of Europe, among them the former kings of Rumania and Italy and the pretenders to the thrones of France and Spain.

The presence of so many former and would-be crowned heads on Portuguese soil is symbolic of another aspect of Portugal, its importance as a place of refuge. During World War II, Portugal remained neutral. Thus it became a haven for many of those fleeing the Nazis. The country's location was another attraction, as a jumping-off place from the Continent. For the most fortunate of these refugees, American airplanes provided regular service to the United States, and British aircraft to Great Britain. Also this influx of foreigners and the presence of Axis diplomats made Portugal a vital listening post in the cause of the United Nations. Today, Portugal is a member of the North Atlantic Treaty Organization and an ally of the United States as well as of Great Britain.

Portugal falls to Spain

Alcobaça, Batalha and the Abbey of St. Jerome are milestones in the rise of a tiny nation, in three centuries, to a pinnacle of power. But the price paid by Portugal for its glory was heavy. There were less than two million people living in the country during the time of the great discoveries. The fragile wooden ships that took soldiers, settlers, merchants and priests to the colonies often did not return from their dangerous voyages, and many of the most gifted Portuguese gave their lives to further their country's ambitions. Spain, much larger than Portugal and greater in resources and population, was able to make good its claim to Portugal in 1580 after the last Portuguese king of the House of Aviz died. For sixty years thereafter Spain ruled the country, thus ending Portugal's golden age.

Nevertheless Camões' poems, celebrating the grandeur that was Portugal at the zenith of its history, were not quite the swan song. In 1640 the Portuguese revolted against Spanish rule. Then the third of Portugal's royal houses, the Braganza, came to the throne of a newly independent Portugal. Late in the 1600's and during the 1700's a silver age flowered in Portugal, based not on the wealth of the Indies but on that of Brazil.

Acquisition of Brazil

No one knows how often violent storms may have driven Portuguese vessels clear across the Atlantic to the shores of the Americas long before Columbus. In any event, the claiming of Brazil in 1500 by a Portuguese sea captain brought that part of America firmly into Portugal's empire.

At first Brazil was insignificant to the Portuguese, for their wealth and power then came from control of the main sea route to the Indies. But after 1640, when much of that eastern empire was lost, the gold and diamonds of Brazil came pouring into the coffers of Portuguese royalty,

LOADING BARGES beside the two-storied Dom Luis I Bridge at Oporto. The bridge spans the Douro River and links the city with Vila Nova de Gaia. This suburb is widely known for its store-houses where port wine is aged.

CHARLES MAY

LOADING CORK BARK. First stripped at 20 years old, trees are stripped thereafter every 8 or 10 years. Good trees yield for 150 years.

DRIED CODFISH is a popular food. From early times, Portuguese fishermen have sailed far across the Atlantic for cod.

Products for international trade

WINE CELLAR IN OPORTO. There the famous port wine matures in huge casks. Vintage port, however, is bottled quite early and ages in the bottle.

HARNESS ON THE DOURO RIVER near Oporto. In Portugal the river plunges through gorges. Further hydroelectric development could help meet the need for power for industry.

GAY POTTERY BOWLS for sale in the open-air market at Vila Nova de Famalicão.

and for domestic consumption

SALT BASINS AT TAVIRA, a southern port on an inlet of the Atlantic Ocean.

The salt is obtained by a natural process of evaporation in the heat of the sun.

ALL PHOTOS ON THESE TWO PAGES, CASA DE PORTUGAL

Portuguese merchants and the Church. In the early eighteenth century, Lisbon was one of the most elegant of European capitals, and Portugal, if only a pale reflection of its former splendor, was once more a nation to be reckoned with. But not for long.

As we have already mentioned, in 1755 a great earthquake followed by a tidal wave and fire destroyed much of Lisbon. Half a century later, Portugal was occupied for several years by the French troops of Napoleon. Seven years after the Napoleonic Wars, Brazil declared its independence. In the nineteenth and twentieth centuries, Portugal shrank in importance. Yet its colonies in Africa— mainly Mozambique and Angola; its outposts in Asia—mainly Goa (on the coast of India) Macao (in China) and Portuguese Timor (in Indonesia)—have thus far remained little changed in our age of dissolving colonial empires.

Roman and medieval architecture

Portugal's present-day charm resides in the reminders of its great past, in its unique works of art, in the simplicity and delightful courtesy of its people. Alcobaça, Batalha and the Abbey of St. Jerome are the best-known examples of Portuguese architecture but not the only ones. Small towns and villages throughout the country treasure humble yet lovely churches, for Portugal is a country where the Roman Catholic faith is strong. The use of strong color, in churches as well as in homes, is a characteristic of Portuguese architecture. The clear hues harmonize with the beauty of Portugal's native stone, mellowed by age to a warm brown-yellow.

Evora, the trade center of Upper Alentejo, is frequently called the "museum city." Seen from afar, across wide, open plains, Evora's great cathedral soars above both city and countryside, an inspiring monument to the Christian faith. The city traces its history to the Romans and to the Moors. The latter ruled Evora for centuries before crusading knights made it a Christian city and offered it in homage to Portugal's first

king, Alfonso I, in the twelfth century.

Of Roman times there remains a stone platform with a group of slender and elegant pillars. They once supported the roof of a Roman temple possibly dedicated to Diana. Evora cathedral is adorned with some of the most extraordinary statues of any Portuguese church, wonderfully realistic figures of saints and apostles. Wandering about the narrow streets, some still bearing their ancient names, such as the Street of the Kitchen of His Highness, one is reminded of the days when Evora was a residence of kings, the seat of a university (suppressed about 1750), and, in 1637, started a rebellion against Spanish rule.

Nowadays Evora is a quiet, sleepy country town, which comes to life only one day a week. Then the market brings merchants from afar and farmers from the neighborhood, who bargain over the price of an ox for the spring plowing or

BLACK AND WHITE "LACE"—fishing nets spread out to dry just above the reach of the surf breaking on the beach at Nazare, a town largely dependent on the sea's bounty.

CHARLES MAY

of a new copper pot for a country kitchen.

Although there are many notable paintings in Portuguese museums and churches, the greatest single work is the altarpiece of St. Vincent. It was painted by Nuno Gonçalves in the mid-fifteenth century and is today in Lisbon's national gallery. It is a magnificent panorama of the great and the humble of Portugal, then on the threshold of its golden age. The splendid figures of kings, princes and bishops, in rich robes, stand side by side with fishermen and merchants, all brought together in adoration of St. Vincent, one of Portugal's patron saints.

Our Lady of Fatima shrine

Pilgrimages are among the highlights of the year in the lives of many Portuguese. Some of these pilgrimages have as their goal ancient shrines, such as Braga, in northern Portugal, where the faithful end their long journey by climbing a long flight of steps to the Church of the Good Jesus of the Mountain. Others seek out small country churches on high holidays—at Christmas, Easter, Ascension Day. But the most famous of all Portuguese shrines today is that of Our Lady of Fatima, north of Lisbon.

Near the site of the present church, three children, all less than ten years old at the time, are supposed to have seen an angel, who spoke to them of God's desire to see peace in the world. The year was 1916, when the first World War was raging over much of Europe. Some months later, in 1917, a second vision appeared to the children. This time it was the Blessed Virgin, who told them of her desire to see a shrine built on the spot. According to the children, she made the sun stop in the sky and turn around, much to their amazement. The shrine now standing there attracts pilgrims not only from Portugal but from all over the world, and the shrine's statue of the Virgin of Fatima is credited with many miracles during the years since.

The mood of "saudade"

Were you to speak to a Portuguese about his country, its arts and especially its music, you would soon hear the Portuguese word *saudade*. It is a hard word to translate, for it does not express a specific idea but, rather, a state of mind— of sadness, of resignation. *Saudade* is the underlying mood of Portugal's famous folk songs, the *fado*. In a tiny restaurant on one of Lisbon's seven hills, two men will sit in their shirt sleeves, plucking guitars and sing of a pair of lovers or of a hero in Portugal's past who lost his life fighting the Moors or of a renowned bullfighter killed in the arena. The melancholy of the *fado* also pervades other kinds of Portuguese music.

Bullfighting is as popular in Portugal as it is in Spain, but the performance is quite different in the two countries. In Portugal the bull is brought into the ring, tormented and pursued, and finally confronted by a toreador. However, his aim is not to kill the bull but to demonstrate his mastery over the beast. East of Lisbon, in the wide plains of the Tagus River, are the great ranches where fighting bulls are raised. The cowboys, wearing chaps, ride small, swift horses and round up the herds much as cowboys do in the West of North America.

As in neighboring Spain, *futbol,* soccer, today rivals bullfighting as a spectator sport in Portugal. Games attract vast audiences every week end of the season.

Schools and universities

Portuguese children are supposed to attend school for at least six years, yet illiteracy is one of the country's most serious problems. Many children, especially in the villages, never complete the elementary grades. The middle schools on the other hand are well attended, and the quality of their teaching is high. English and French are the principal foreign languages taught. In Lisbon and Oporto especially, where shipping and the export trade employ many people, many Portuguese are fluent in one or both of these foreign languages.

There are three universities in Portugal, at Coimbra, Lisbon and Oporto. Coimbra is one of the oldest universities in the world. Founded in Lisbon in 1290,

SHUCKING CORN in Algarve. At harvesttime, in October, every farm has an *esfolhada,* a merry gathering with much singing.

Where toil
does not hinder life's simple joys

BREAKERS AND RUGGED CLIFFS frame fishermen of Nazare. Almost every day the men brave the sea to wrest a slim living from it. When the day's catch is sold the whole community shares in the proceeds.

AT THE YEARLY FAIR in Vila Franca de Xira, fighting bulls are driven through the streets. The most daring youths tease the beasts.

FRESH-CAUGHT EELS mean a delicious meal to Nazare women. Their head pads serve to balance burdens.

A GAITADEFOLLES, or Portuguese bagpipe. From ancient times the instrument has been used by shepherds in northern Portugal.

COIMBRA UNIVERSITY STUDENTS.
The more ragged the gown the more popular
the student. A piece is a token of friendship.

Student life at Coimbra

Traditions still rule student life at Coimbra. First-year students are supposed to return to their quarters when the bells of the university chapel sound curfew. When a student first enters the university he must pass through its most ancient gate and thence between the rows of an honor guard of older students. Students still live and eat in groups called "republics," each named for the district of Portugal from which the particular students have come. Black academic gowns are the required dress for students, as they are at Oxford and Cambridge in England. Many of Portugal's best-known men have been Coimbra graduates.

In the varied settings of the Portuguese countryside a modern highway may lead you to a small, sleepy town still renowned for its colored tile or pottery or embroidery; or to a huge modern church, such as the one at Fatima; or to a lovely seaside resort, such as Estoril near Lisbon, or Figueira da Foz farther north on the coast. A visit to a Portuguese farmer's house is also a memorable experience. The heart of such a house is the kitchen where gleaming copper pots stand above a huge oven. Your host is likely to offer you highly seasoned chicken and a pleasant, light local wine.

Living conditions

For all their glorious past, the present offers only hard work to most Portuguese. They have few of the amenities more fortunate countries have long taken for granted. Between the wealth of a very few and the poverty of the great majority there is an enormous gap. There is good reason for the sadness that permeates so much of Portuguese music and poetry.

As one might expect in so deeply religious a country the great Church holidays, Christmas and Easter, are widely celebrated. The Christmas manger, or *presepio,* with its many carved-wood or pottery figures, is among the most treasured symbols of the Christmas season in churches and homes.

the university changed its residence several times between the capital and its present location. Since 1537 it has occupied a former royal palace perched on a hill overlooking the Mondego River in the charming town of Coimbra. Coimbra justly deserves its fame. Prince Henry the Navigator endowed several chairs there, among them, mathematics and astronomy, and some of the navigation instruments developed at Coimbra during the fifteenth century were of great importance in the age of discovery.

Watching the fishermen in their gay checked shirts pulling in nets at Nazare, listening to a shepherd's flute high in the mountains of the northeast, waiting for a heavily loaded wine barge to dock at Oporto, seeing a great airliner land at Lisbon—these extreme contrasts bring home to the observer how far Portugal must go before it relinquishes the cherished past and becomes a truly twentieth-century nation.

By George Kish

PORTUGAL: FACTS AND FIGURES

THE COUNTRY

Bounded on the north and east by Spain, on the west and south by the Atlantic Ocean. Area, including the Azores and Madeira Islands, 35,598 sq. mi.; population, 9,000,000.

THE GOVERNMENT

In 1933 a new constitution was adopted, establishing a dictatorship on a corporative basis. It provides for a president, a cabinet (whose chief minister is the premier), a National Assembly of 120 members elected for four years, and a Corporative Chamber of appointed representatives of the corporative associations.

COMMERCE AND INDUSTRY

Agricultural and forest products are the most important. Wheat, corn, oats, barley, rye, rice, French beans, and potatoes are the country's principal crops. Vineyards abound and the making of wine is important. Forest area, comprising 19% of the total, includes oak, pine, cork oak, and chestnut. Cork is one of the most valuable exports. Much olive oil is produced, as well as resin and turpentine. Sardine fishing is important and great quantities of the canned fish are exported yearly. Mineral deposits include coal, pyrites, lead, copper, tin, wolfram, titanium and other ores but production is slight. Manufactures: textiles, building materials, chemicals, glass, wood and paper products, tobacco products and household goods.

Principal imports: machinery, raw cotton and cotton goods, iron and steel products, wheat, motor vehicles, coal and coke, sugar, dried codfish, ammonium sulfate, coffee, hides, gasoline, dyes. Exports: cork and cork products, wine, wolfram, canned sardines, olive oil, resin, pyrites, turpentine and pit props. The escudo is the monetary unit.

COMMUNICATIONS

Railway mileage, 2,229, about half state-owned; 18,330 miles of roads; 167,562 motor vehicles; 304,937 telephones; 593,514 radio and 8,000 TV sets; merchant marine, 537,000 gross tons; domestic and international air service.

RELIGION AND EDUCATION

Roman Catholicism is dominant but all faiths have freedom of worship. Primary education is compulsory but illiteracy is about 40%. In a recent year there were in public and private elementary schools, 846,757 pupils; secondary, 83,071; professional, technical and vocational, 61,320. The universities are Lisbon, Coimbra and Oporto. Lisbon also has a Technical University.

CHIEF TOWNS

Population, Lisbon, capital, about 835,000; Oporto, 297,000; Setubal, 44,000; Coimbra, 43,000; Funchal (Madeira), 55,000; Braga, 33,000; Evora, 25,500; Covilhã, 20,500.

CONICAL TOWERS grace the fifteenth-century St. Bras Hermitage at Evora, where one steps into the Middle Ages. Both Romans and Moors left their mark on the city. It changed hands several times in the struggle with the Moors.

CHARLES MAY

STRIPES OF MANY COLORS mark cultivated fields near Lousã. The town's famous chapel, Nossa Senhora da Piedade, draws many pilgrims.

COIMBRA, celebrated for its ancient university, sits amid a lowland watered by the Mondego River.

The look of city and countryside

POINTED ARCHES against the sky. The structure is an aqueduct, which brings water to Lisbon. There are thirty-five such arches.

DELICATE BALCONIES and laundered linen are familiar sights in the colorful byways of Lisbon.

» A CRENELATED WALL still surrounds Obidos (near Lisbon). The town is an unspoiled example of medieval architecture, its highest summit crowned with a castle —a hotel today.

THE ALFAMA, Lisbon's old quarter, is a maze of narrow streets and leaning houses. In the Alfama, among the poor, *fado,* the sad, haunting Portuguese folk songs, may be heard in their authentic setting.

Mediterranean
Islands

... Balearics to Cyprus

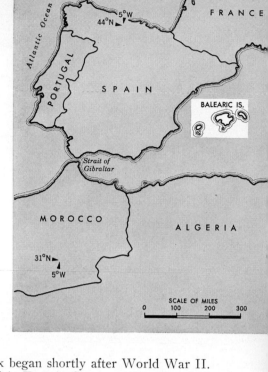

SCALE OF MILES
0   100   200   300

T HE Mediterranean was the cradle of Western civilization and was once the center of world commerce. Nearly all of the islands discussed in this chapter—the Balearics, Corsica, Sardinia, Malta, Corfu, Crete and Cyprus—have at some time enjoyed a certain importance. As world power shifted westward, however, they were largely cast off from the mainstream of events. Most of them sank into a sleepy, pastoral existence, peaceful havens of white sand and blue sky for occasional visitors seeking escape from the pressures of life elsewhere. The lyrical description of Majorca written in 1838 by Frédéric Chopin, the Polish composer, could well be applied to all: "The sky is turquoise blue, the sea is azure, the mountains are emerald green; the air is as pure as that of Paradise."

Since World War II the picture has been changing rapidly. Twentieth-century innovations in transportation and communications, the political turmoil of our time, the demand for improved standards of living—all are having an impact on the islands and their people. The four Balearic Islands, off the coast of Spain, are fast becoming one of the most popular tourist spots in the Mediterranean, particularly Majorca, the largest. The great

influx began shortly after World War II. English, French, Germans, Scandinavians were attracted there by the irresistible combination of perfect weather and low prices. Around 1952, Americans too began flocking to Majorca. Income from tourism has thus become one of the main-stays of the Balearics.

Corsica, the French island northeast of the Balearics, appeared on the world stage in the late 1950's for another reason. In 1958, when French army officers revolted and seized control of Algeria (which led to the downfall of the Fourth French Republic and the return of Charles de Gaulle to power), Corsica joined the revolt. Committees of public safety were formed in Ajaccio, the capital, and other main towns. They seized government buildings and other property, and turned Corsica into a Gaullist stronghold. Many observers are inclined to credit the Corsica revolt with being the decisive factor in the fall of the Fourth Republic. "It proved," said one, "that the existing Government was powerless to keep order only 570 miles from Paris." Whatever its merit, the revolt put Corsica in the spotlight of world attention, from which it had been absent since the days of Napoleon. After De Gaulle was safely in-

stalled in Paris the Corsicans returned to their main concerns: agriculture and tourists.

Just below Corsica lies the Italian island of Sardinia, which is slowly gaining a new lease on life. The Italian Government has begun an ambitious program to develop the lagging economies of Sardinia as well as Sicily and southern Italy. In southeastern Sardinia a series of dams on the Flumendosa River and elsewhere will irrigate 250,000 acres and generate 90,-000,000 kilowatt hours of electricity per year.

Affecting the personal lives of the Sardinians even more closely was the Rockefeller Foundation's energetic campaign against malaria. Beginning in 1946 the island was sprayed with tons of DDT to wipe out the malaria-carrying mosquitoes. So successful was the foundation's work that by 1952 the island had not a single case of the weakening disease. Today the island's once atrocious death rate is lower than the European average.

Both Malta and Cyprus have been centers of political unrest. Malta, which lies south of Sicily, is a British colony. From time to time, Maltese political leaders have been demanding varying degrees of independence from British rule. In 1955

the Legislative Assembly proposed a merger between Malta and Britain. Malta was then to become a county with representation in London and certain local powers, like the six counties of Northern Ireland. By 1958 it became clear that Britain wouldn't agree to all features of the proposal, and a series of upheavals followed. Malta's Prime Minister resigned, the Assembly was dissolved and riots spread across the island. Whatever the final settlement may be, Malta is unlikely to sever all ties with Britain. Most of the island's income is derived from British military and economic interests there.

Cyprus, the easternmost of the islands covered in this chapter, did sever all ties with Britain after a long struggle for independence that is discussed later. Though the new Republic was not proclaimed officially until 1960, its people elected a president and vice-president late in 1959. The new officials were faced at once with difficult economic problems. Like Malta, Cyprus has been bolstered for many years by British military expenditures. There was some fear that with independence these expenditures would decrease. They still might do so although by the agreement for independence Britain retains the bases there on the promise

ENJOYING THE SUN on the wall at Oliena, a village that clings to a slope in the mountainous heart of Sardinia. Such villages are still little touched by the bustle of the twentieth century. In the vicinity are many nuraghi—odd towerlike structures of stone, erected by an unknown people in prehistoric times.

370

SORTING WOOL YARN at a weaving school in Dorgali, Sardinia. The vividly colored strands will be used to make rugs in various bold patterns.

THE SKIRT of the Sardinian woman's traditional dress is tightly crimped. It is beautiful in motion as the bands of bright scarlet or green flare out.

COSTUMED CAVALRY assemble for a procession in Cagliari, Sardinia's capital. Phoenicians, Carthaginians, Romans—all dropped anchor in the city's safe harbor.

371

that they will never be used for other than military purposes.

Corfu and Crete, Greek islands in the eastern Mediterranean, have shared closely in the postwar fortunes of the mainland. As in Greece itself, the advent of electric power and improved farming methods is slowly stepping up agricultural output. Then, too, an increasing number of tourists are being lured by the charms of the "isles of Greece," both to bask in the sun and gaze upon the remains of the ancient world that dot these islands—especially Corfu and Crete. Nor are the archaeologists through digging up such treasures. Not long ago they excavated the remains of the ancient Roman city of Tarrha, on Crete's southwestern coast.

History Graced with Beauty

The four Balearic islands—Majorca, Minorca, Iviza and Formentera—have been ruled in turn by Carthaginians, Romans, Vandals, Moors and Spaniards. In the eighteenth century, France and England each gained temporary footholds. The British left their mark upon Mahon, which they made the capital of Minorca, but the Balearics are essentially Spanish.

The Majorcan climate is almost perfect, never too hot nor too cold. The only thing lacking is a good water supply; rains are infrequent and the islanders have had to terrace their fields and build reservoirs. Not a drop that falls is wasted. Olive trees abound in the islands, with their delicate gray-green leaves and thick gnarled trunks. Fine big melons, oranges, lemons, figs, almonds, peppers and other vegetables, and carob beans—which grow on trees—are luscious products of the islands. Besides the ancient industries of farming and fishing, Minorca manufactures shoes.

Corsica is less idyllic than the Balearics. It is a part of France but lies nearer to Italy, and its people speak an Italian dialect. Imagine an island with mountains rising steeply from the blue waters of the Mediterranean—an island possessing great forests of pine and chestnut, hills covered with vineyards, olive orchards and lemon groves and, above, wild stretches of uncultivated rocky ground where sweet-flowering scrub, the maqui, makes the air fragrant. This is Corsica, a land of troubled, bloody history and terrible vendettas, and famous as the birthplace of Napoleon I. Its story is confused and distressing, especially after the end of Roman rule in the year 469, when northern barbarians and eastern Muslims alike began to attack it, and rival Corsican barons fought each other. The Italian city of Genoa claimed the land, and France supported now Genoa and now the Corsicans, who might more than once have made good their independence had they been able to stop quarreling. Finally, in 1768, Genoa ceded the island to France. Since 1815, it has been a French department (state).

The appalling misgovernment and confusion of centuries encouraged the vendetta, or blood feud. When a man could not hope for justice from the authorities—and often there were no authorities—he took matters into his own hands and killed his enemy. Since the island became French the vendetta has been eliminated.

Ajaccio, the capital, is a delightful seaport cupped in mountains. The streets are lined with palms and orange trees and the houses painted in gay colors. The house where Napoleon was born is still to be seen there.

Like Corsica, Sardinia is a mountainous land, still wild and desolate in places. There are many fascinating ruins of strange dwelling houses and temples built long ago, in the Bronze Age. The Sardinian farmers are a simple people, short of stature, with dark hair and eyes. They speak various dialects, as their ancient speech has been influenced by both Italian and Spanish. In Roman days, Sardinia was chiefly a source of food. Galleys carried load after load of golden grain from Sardinian harbors to the Roman markets. After Rome fell the Vandals conquered Sardinia and then it became part of the Byzantine Empire. The Saracens attacked it constantly until they were finally defeated by the Pisans, who in turn were driven out by the Spanish king of Aragon. In 1720 Savoy and some other parts of

A CORSICAN IN HIS FRENCH BERET SMOOTHS A BLOCK OF MARBLE

The rock under the workman's chisel and hammer may be fashioned into a statue or used in a building. Marble with delicate veining and granite are quarried in the mountains of Corsica.

LONG AGO, Genoese merchants made Bastia, on the northeast coast of Corsica, a fortified port. An old citadel still remains. Today Bastia is the largest city on the island.

WALL PAINTINGS at Cnossus (Knossos), Crete, remnants of the Minoan civilization. Though they are some four thousand years old, they are still vibrant with a love of life.

OIL JARS from the Minoan age at Cnossus. Here it was that the legendary King Minos had a great palace. It was so complex that it may have been the labyrinth of Greek myth.

374

A VILLAGE CHURCH caps a rise of land along the rocky northern coast of Corsica between L'Ile-Rousse and Calvi. From 1312 to 1755 the Genoese held Corsica, and Calvi was their chief stronghold. It was also at Calvi, during a bombardment in 1794, that the English Admiral Nelson lost his right eye.

head kerchiefs are delightfully various. The men wear a peculiar stocking-cap called a "berretta," the end of which falls to the shoulder and serves as a pouch. These beautiful, valuable old costumes are nowadays worn only on Sundays and special occasions. On the Campidano (or plain), in the mining district of the south and in the cities, Cagliari and Sassari, ordinary modern European clothes are the rule, and as communications become better and better, the medieval styles are sure to disappear.

From Sardinia we shall voyage to the British island of Malta, that lies south of Sicily in a most strategic position. Valletta, the capital, is built upon one of the finest harbors in the Mediterranean, and is an important naval base. But Malta has not always been a British possession. Like Sardinia, it has many very ancient ruins, in this case built by men of the Stone Age. Before the sixth century B.C., it was a Phœnician colony, and the Maltese of to-day are descended from those settlers of long ago, whose language they still speak. Carthaginians,

SUNNY DAY IN OLIENA, SARDINIAN HILL TOWN
From the bridge, the street winds on up past tile-roofed houses that have almost no windows. Oliena is in central Sardinia, in a region of vineyards. Nearby there are strange, prehistoric towers of stone, called nuraghi.

Italy were combined with the island and called the Kingdom of Sardinia, which in 1861 became the core of united Italy.

The Sardinians have escaped to some extent the standardization of costume and custom that is so noticeable among more sophisticated peoples. A kilted shepherd from the southern Sulcis might have stepped out of the Middle Ages, and in the Barbagia, or eastern interior of the island, we find people whose scarlet and white costumes also remind us of the pageantry of past ages. Each peasant community has its distinctive patterns, colors and embroidery, and the styles in

Romans, Arabs, Normans and Aragonese all governed Malta without vitally changing the character of the people. The Knights of St. John of Jerusalem were an ancient military and monastic order which fought against the Mohammedans during the Crusades and for years afterward. They were driven from the Holy Land to Cyprus and Rhodes and eventually, in 1530, to Malta. There they made a stand against the Turks and were victorious in the great siege of 1565. The Grand Master of the Order, Jean de la Vallette, built and fortified Valletta and the Knights ruled Malta until Na-

LABOR IN VAIN—THE LOOSENED SOIL WILL SOON WASH DOWN

Farmers on Sardinia work long hours to eke a living out of land that is mountainous and denuded of the forests that once held the topsoil in place. Digging the hillsides means barren gulleys next year. Only about a fourth of the island is actually suitable for planting, chiefly in the lowlands. About half can be used as grazing land for sheep, goats and cows.

Courtesy, British Information Service

REBUILDING RAID-DAMAGED STRUCTURES IN MALTA

Although Malta suffered more than 2,500 air raids in World War II, the repairing and rebuilding of the island never stopped. There are many natural bomb shelters cut deep in the solid rock foundations and after each raid, civilians would climb out to clean up the damage. The people of Malta received the George Cross for their heroism.

poleon drove them out. Malta later became a British possession. The island won imperishable renown in World War II, when it withstood over 2,500 Axis air raids. In 1942, the George Cross was conferred on the island fortress by King George VI.

The city of Valletta, laid out on a rocky promontory, is fascinating. The beautiful old palaces of the Order of St. John remind us of feudal days; we can almost imagine that a proud red or black-robed Knight with an eight-pointed white Maltese cross upon his breast will presently step from one of the massive door-ways, though such medieval figures disappeared from Malta well over a century ago. Malta owes its importance to its location on the trade route between eastern and western Mediterranean lands.

Corfu long ago was a great commercial city because it lay just off the Greek coast, yet not far from the heel of Italy, and Greek ships on the way to Italy and Sicily always put in there. It was settled before 700 B.C. by men from the Greek city of Corinth, and was called Corcyra in those days. It was an independent city-state until the Mediterranean world became Roman, and belonged to the Byzantine Emperors after the Roman Empire split apart. In the Middle Ages the Venetians governed it longer than did any other power, and during much of the nineteenth century it was a British protectorate. Now, along with the other Ionian islands, it is part of Greece.

It has been called the most beautiful of the isles of Greece, and indeed it is an enchanting spot. The mountains of the

PIX

A PLEASANT TASK IN A VINEYARD ON CRETE'S GENTLE HILLS

The vineyard worker is washing grapes in a sievelike pail by dipping it into a tub of water. The grapes will then be spread out and allowed to dry into raisins. Crete is an island of vineyards and olive groves. Its chief exports are olive oil, wine and raisins. Most of the people are of Greek origin and are skillful at tending grove and vine.

LOUTEROS, TINY HILLSIDE VILLAGE ON THE ISLAND OF CYPRUS

This sleepy little settlement is on Morphou Bay on the north coast of the "copper island" as Cyprus has been called. The tile-roofed cottages seem to cling precariously to the steep slopes.

northern part are bare and rugged, but the fertile valleys are covered with the gray-green of countless olive trees, the brighter green of vineyards and the very dark green of tall conical cypress trees. White-walled houses stand out sharply against the foliage, and over all is the intensely blue sky which seems to belong to Greece. Close at hand the Mediterranean sparkles in the sun. Olive oil, fragrant honey and many fruits are the products which the farms of Corfu send to other countries.

Crete, which also belongs to Greece, is another beautiful and pleasant land, extremely fertile, picturesque and interesting. It is a long narrow island, and

serves to divide the Ægean Sea from the Mediterranean. As we read in the chapter Relics of Ancient Man, it contains many remains of long-vanished civilizations, which are among the oldest and most extraordinary known to us. In later years the island was a Roman province, and eventually the Saracens conquered it. Venice ruled it during four centuries, then the Turks seized it and in spite of many revolts maintained at least nominal power until 1909. In 1913 the island was incorporated with Greece, but in 1941, it fell to the Germans. After the war it was restored to Greece.

Most Cretans are of Greek origin and

belong to the Greek Orthodox Church, and the towns resemble those of Greece. But at Candia, the old capital, there are massive fortifications, old breakwaters, warehouses and fountains bearing the winged lion of St. Mark, the symbol of Venice. The long Turkish occupation has also left its impress; mosques with their white minarets gleam above the blue harbor at Canea, which is the capital today.

The beauty of Crete is more stern than soft and its pleasant valleys are shut in by rocky, inaccessible, snow-covered mountains. One of the highest was called Mount Ida by the ancient Greeks, and a deep gorge on its slopes was venerated as the birthplace of Zeus. In some places the mountains suddenly open out as though by magic, and there before us lies a wide flat plain walled in by hills, with olive orchards on all sides and the fruit of the vineyards golden in the autumn sunlight. Crete sends many basketsful of fresh grapes to Greece and Egypt, and crate after crate of fine raisins to more distant parts of the world. Along the harborfronts of the north shore, raisins by the yard are spread to dry in the sun. Citrons, too, are to be seen along the docks, cut in half and soaking in brine before being shipped. With citrus fruits, olives and grapes, Crete is typically Mediterranean.

Both the Greeks and the Phœnicians colonized Cyprus, the most eastern island in the great sea, and it was conquered by Egyptians, Assyrians, Persians and Romans, for everyone coveted its copper mines. Some say that the island was named for the copper found there—others, that copper takes its Latin name, *cyprium,* from the name of the island.

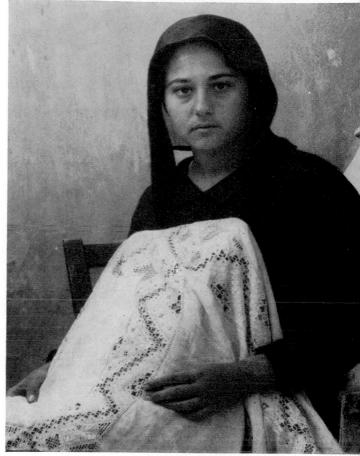

CYPRUS EMBROIDERER AND HER WORK

A needlewoman of Lefkara exhibits the embroidery for which her town is noted. Work and hands are both beautiful.

Be that as it may, Cyprus is a famous spot and has seen stirring history in ancient, medieval and modern times. The Byzantine emperors and the Saracens were its rulers after the Romans, and in 1191 Richard the Lion-hearted, on his way to the Holy Land to fight the Third Crusade, took Cyprus from the Byzantines and sold it to Guy de Lusignan. This knight was theoretically king of Jerusalem, but the Saracens held Jerusalem, so Guy sailed to Cyprus. His successors ruled it for three hundred years, and under them it was brilliantly prosperous. Churches, abbeys and castles were built, the ruins of which bear mute witness to

THE SUN SHINES BRIGHT ON A SPANISH ISLAND

Majorca, the largest of the Balearic Islands, in the Mediterranean, is about 120 miles from Spain. The climate is pleasant and mild, and in many parts of the island the vegetation grows luxuriantly. Grapes for Majorca's light wines are cultivated in sunny vineyards on terraced slopes above the sea. Large orchards of figs, oranges and olives are also carefully tended.

A JEWEL-LIKE CITY OF THE MEDITERRANEAN

Palma, the capital of Majorca, is located on the Bay of Palma on the island's south coast. The city, built around its excellent harbor, is beautiful and picturesque with its Moorish architecture and colorful tiled roofs. The Gothic cathedral (at right of picture) was under construction from 1322 to 1601; it contains the tomb of King Jayme II of Aragon.

their former splendor. Then the Venetians occupied it, but the Turks took it from them, and the British took it from the Turks and made it a colony.

During the 1950's a three-way conflict developed. The Greek Cypriotes (almost 80 per cent of the island population) had long dreamed of union with Greece—*enosis*. Violence began to erupt in 1955, which was further inflamed when the British exiled Archbishop Makarios, the leader of the Greek Cypriotes, in 1956. At the same time the Turkish Cypriotes (about 18 per cent of the population),

backed by the Turkish Government, strongly opposed *enosis* and advocated dividing the island between Greece and Turkey. Great Britain was reluctant to give up the island because of its possible military value.

In 1959, however, the governments of Britain, Greece and Turkey and the leaders of the Greek and Turkish Cypriotes reached agreement. By the terms of the final pact, Cyprus became an independent republic in August 1960. Britain retained sovereignty over only two military bases.

ISLES OF THE MEDITERRANEAN: FACTS AND FIGURES

BALEARIC ISLANDS (Baleáres)

Group of 15 islands off Gulf of Valencia: Majorca, Minorca, Iviza, Formentera and 11 islets. Total area, 1,936 square miles; population, 424,710. Governed as a province of Spain; capital, Palma (on Majorca) has a population of 138,100. Religion, Roman Catholic; language, Spanish. Products: olives, olive oil, grapes, almonds, oranges, figs, carob beans, green vegetables, shoes, filigree work.

CORSICA (Corse)

Lies due south of Genoa and 51 miles west of Italian coast. Area, 3,367 square miles; population, 247,000. Governed as a department of France. Chief towns: Ajaccio, the capital, population, 33,000; and Bastia, 52,000. Religion, Roman Catholic; language, Italian dialect. Chief products: olive oil, wine, honey, gallic acid, chestnuts, citrus fruits, cereals and mulberries.

SARDINIA (Sardegna)

Lies 7 miles south of Corsica. Area, 9,196 square miles; population, 1,273,850. Governed as a department of Italy. Chief towns: Cagliari, the capital, 141,600; Sassari, 55,400. Religion, Roman Catholic; language, Spanish and Italian dialects. Products: lead, zinc, salt, timber, cork, tanning bark, charcoal, olive oil, wine, almonds, wheat, oranges, lemons, cattle, cheese and tuna fish.

MALTA (Colony of Great Britain)

Three islands (Malta, Gozo and Comino) lying 60 miles south of Sicily. Total area, 122 square miles; civilian population, 320,650. Administration by a governor, Council of Government and National Assembly for local affairs. Capital, Valletta (on Malta), 19,145. Religion, Roman Catholic; languages, English, Italian and Maltese. There are 118 primary, secondary and technical schools with about 48,000 pupils;

1 university and adult education classes. Imports: wheat, flour, sugar, coal, textiles, petroleum products, metal goods. Products: wheat, barley, potatoes, green vegetables, grapes and other fruits, hides and skins, cotton and cotton goods, lace, filigree work and cigarettes.

CORFU (Corcyra)

Lies 2 miles off the Greek coast, at the Albanian border. Area: 229 square miles; population, 105,226. Governed as a department of Greece; capital, Corfu, 30,706. Religion: Greek Orthodox and Roman Catholic; language, Greek. Products: olive oil, honey, grapes and other fruits.

CRETE (Candia)

Lies about 60 miles southeast of the Greek mainland and 110 miles southwest of Asia Minor. Area: 3,235 square miles; population, 463,458. Governed as a part of Greece. Chief towns: Canea, the capital, 35,237; and Candia, 54,541. Religion: Greek Orthodox and others are tolerated. Products: olive oil, soap, cheese, citrus fruits, raisins and grapes. For a time during World War II, Crete was occupied by the Germans, but it was returned to Greece when peace was made in 1945.

CYPRUS, REPUBLIC OF

Lies 40 mi. south of Turkey and 60 mi. west of Syria. Area: 3,572 sq. mi.; population, 544,000. A republic, its president is elected from and by the Greek Cypriotes; its vice-president, from and by the Turkish Cypriotes. The legislature is 70% Greek and 30% Turkish, a 7-to-3 ratio that prevails in most other government bodies. Products: copper, citrus fruits, wine. Education is free; each group has its own schools and follows its own religion, Greek Orthodox or Islam. Chief cities: Nicosia, capital, 81,700; Limassol, 36,500; Famagusta, 26,800; Larnaca, 17,900.